OCR GCSE

Religious Studies B
Philosophy & Applied Ethics

Philosophy

Vicky Bunting · Gavin Collins · Janet Dyson
Opinderjit Kaur Takhar · Jon Mayled
Debbie Newton · Neera Vyas

Series Editor: Janet Dyson
Series Consultant: Jon Mayled

www.heinemann.co.uk

✓ Free online support
✓ Useful weblinks
✓ 24 hour online ordering

01865 888080

OCR AND HEINEMANN ARE WORKING TOGETHER TO PROVIDE BETTER SUPPORT FOR YOU

Official Publisher Partnership

Heinemann is an imprint of Pearson Education Limited, a company incorporated in England and Wales, having its registered office at Edinburgh Gate, Harlow, Essex, CM20 2JE. Registered company number: 872828

www.heinemann.co.uk

Heinemann is a registered trademark of Pearson Education Limited

First published 2009

13 12 11 10 09
10 9 8 7 6 5 4 3 2 1

British Library Cataloguing in Publication Data
A catalogue record for this book is available from the British Library

ISBN 978 0 435 50150 1

Edited by Linda Free and Sarah Christopher
Reviewed by Richard Gray and Imran Mogra (Birmingham City University)
Proofread by Tracey Smith
Designed by Pearson Education Limited
Project managed and typeset by Wearset Ltd, Boldon, Tyne and Wear
Original illustrations © Pearson Education 2009
Illustrated by Chris Coady, Alasdair Bright and Wearset Ltd
Picture research by Q2AMedia
Printed by Rotolito, Italy

Acknowledgements
The author and publisher would like to thank the following individuals and organisations for permission to reproduce photographs:

Page 2 Alessandro Bianchi. Page 6 Henry William Fu/Shutterstock. Page 7 Robert Harding Picture Library Ltd/Alamy. Page 9 ClassicStock/Alamy. Page 11 Ace Stock Limited/Alamy. Page 13 ArkReligion.com/Alamy. Page 14TL Igor Grochev/Shutterstock. Page 15 Chantal Boulanger/www.worldreligions.com. Page 17BL Robert Nickelsberg/Getty Images. Page 17BR Ann Eriksson/Nordic Photos/Photolibrary. Page 17TL Peter Adams/zefa/Corbis. Page 17TR Michael Winokur/Jupiter Images. Page 18 Adek Berry/AFP/Getty Images. Page 19 Photodisc/StockTrek. Page 24 Christine Osborne/Photographersdirect. Page 28 Firehouse/iStockPhoto. Page 29BL Cathy Yeulet/123RF. Page 29BR Ed Kashi/Corbis. Page 29TL Christof Koepsel/Staff/Bongarts/Getty Images. Page 29TR Sascha Burkard/Shutterstock. Page 33ML Sinibaldi/Corbis. Page 34 Philippe Lissac/Godong/Corbis. Page 38 Ange/Alamy. Page 45 Chris Niedenthal/Contributor/Time & Life Pictures/Getty Images. Page 47B Fred de Noyelle/Godong/Corbis. Page 47T Javarman/Shutterstock. Page 48 Daniel Jones/Alamy. Page 49 Leonard de Selva/Corbis. Page 51 DMA/Alamy. Page 52 Shangara Singh/Alamy. Page 53 Robert Harding World Imagery/Corbis. Page 54 ArkReligion.com/Alamy. Page 58 Daniel Leppens/Shutterstock. Page 60 Arts & Authors/Alamy. Page 62 Nathan Benn/Alamy. Page 64 Robert Harding Picture Library Ltd/Alamy. Page 66 Stringer/Reuters. Page 68 Michelangelo (1475–1564)/Vatican Museums and Galleries, Vatican City, Italy/The Bridgeman Art Library. Page 70BL Zsolt Nyulaszi/Shutterstock. Page 70BR iStockPhoto. Page 70TL Eg004713/Dreamstime. Page 70TR Angelo Cavalli/zefa/Corbis. Page 74 Ustin/Shutterstock. Page 75 Fancy/Veer/Corbis. Page 76 Bernard Bisson/Sygma/Corbis. Page 78 Helene Rogers/Art Directors & Trip Photo Library. Page 79 Ed Spiegel/Corbis. Page 80 Kevin Frayer/Associated Press. Page 81 Israel images/Alamy. Page 82 Phil Noble/Reuters. Page 84 Helene Rogers/Art Directors & Trip Photo Library. Page 85 Helene Rogers/Art Directors & Trip Photo Library. Page 88 Dr Alfizar, University of Syiah Kuala, Banda Aceh, Indonesia. Page 90 Yad Vashem Museum. Page 92 Dpa/Corbis. Page 94 Fredrik Renander/Alamy. Page 96 Titian (Tiziano Vecellio) (c.1488–1576)/Prado, Madrid, Spain/Index/The Bridgeman Art Library. Page 100BR Associated Press. Page 100L Ronald Grant Archive. Page 100M Capital Pictures. Page 100TR The Illustrated London News Picture Library. Page 101L Helene Rogers/Art Directors & Trip Photo Library. Page 101M Helene Rogers/Art Directors & Trip Photo Library. Page 101R Helene Rogers/Art Directors & Trip Photo Library. Page 103BL Swaminarayan Aksharpith. Page 103R Interfoto Pressebildagentur/Alamy. Page 103TL Helene Rogers/Art Directors & Trip Photo Library. Page 105BL Stringer Peru/Reuters. Page 105BR Susan Schulman/Rex Features. Page 105TL National Geophysical Data Center/Dennis J. Sigrist/International Tsunami Information Center, Honolulu, Hawaii. Page 105TR David Hartley/Rex Features. Page 106 Caro/Alamy. Page 108 Associated Press. Page 111 Dynamic Graphics, Inc. Page 114 Helene Rogers/Art Directors & Trip Photo Library. Page 118 Raj Patidar/Reuters. Page 120 Caro Photo Agency. Page 122 Christophe Boisvieux/Corbis. Page 126 Galyna Andrushko/Shutterstock. Page 131 Southern Stock Corp/Corbis. Page 132 Demonoid/iStockPhoto. Page 133 Maa-illustrations/Dreamstime. Page 134 Josef F. Stuefer/Shutterstock. Page 135B Damir Cudic/iStockPhoto. Page 135T ArkReligion.com/Alamy. Page 136C. Lyttle/zefa/Corbis. Page 137 Ami Vitale/Getty Images. Page 138 Comstock Select/Corbis. Page 139 Israel Images/Alamy. Page 141 Eugen/zefa/Corbis. Page 144 Christine Osborne/Photographersdirect. Page 148 Rafael Ramirez Lee/Dreamstime. Page 149B Pearson Education Ltd/Tudor Photography. Page 149TR Lepas/Shutterstock. Page 150 The Illustrated London News Picture Library. Page 152 Photodisc/StockTrek. Page 154 D. Vo Trung/Eurelios/Science Photo Library. Page 156 Giovanni Benintende/Shutterstock. Page 160 Giovanni Benintende/Shutterstock. Page 162 Tim Pannell/Corbis. Page 163 Stapleton Collection/Corbis. Page 164 Werner H.Mueller/zefa/Corbis. Page 168 Associated Press. Page 169B Photodisc/StockTrek. Page 169T Photodisc/StockTrek. Page 170 Stringer Peru/Reuters. Page 171 Luedke & Sparrow/Photolibrary. Page 172 NASA/JPL. Page 173 CERN. Page 174 Terry Brown.

Contents

Introduction

A note for teachers

This student book has been written especially to support the OCR Religious Studies Specification B Units B601: *Philosophy 1 (Deity, Religious and Spiritual Experience, End of Life),* and B602: *Philosophy 2 (Good and Evil, Revelation, Science).* The book covers all six religions within the specification: Buddhism, Christianity, Hinduism, Islam, Judaism and Sikhism. It is part of an overall series covering the OCR Specification B, which comprises:

- three Student Books: this book, a companion book on Applied Ethics, which also covers all six religions, and a book covering Christian Philosophy and Applied Ethics – further details on pages viii and ix.
- a Teacher Guide: covering Buddhism, Christianity, Hinduism, Islam, Judaism and Sikhism – further details on page pages viii and ix.

Who are we?

The people who have planned and contributed to this series of books include teachers, advisers, inspectors, teacher trainers and GCSE examiners, all of whom have specialist knowledge of Religious Studies. For all of us the subject has a real fascination and we believe that good Religious Studies can make a major contribution to developing the skills, insights and understanding people need in today's world. In the initial development of this series, Pamela Draycott lent us her expertise, which we gratefully acknowledge.

Why is Religious Studies an important subject?

We believe that Religious Studies is an important subject because every area of life is touched by issues to do with religion and belief. Following a Religious Studies GCSE course will enable students to study and explore what people believe about God, authority, worship, beliefs, values and truth. Students will have opportunities to engage with questions about why people believe in God and how beliefs can influence many aspects of their lives.

Students will also explore why members of a particular religion may believe different things. In lessons students will be expected to think, talk, discuss, question and challenge, reflect on and assess a wide range of questions. As young people growing up in a diverse society studying religion will help them to understand and relate to people whose beliefs, values and viewpoints differ from their own, and help them to deal with issues arising, not only in school, but in the community and workplace.

The study of religion will also help students to make connections with a whole range of other important areas, such as music, literature, art, politics, economics and social issues.

The specification for OCR B Philosophy and/or Applied Ethics

The specification outlines the aims and purposes of GCSE. The content to be covered is divided into six different Topics. The book's structure follows these Topic divisions precisely:

Unit B601: Philosophy 1

Topic 1: Belief about deity

Topic 2: Religious and spiritual experience

Topic 3: The end of life

Unit B602: Philosophy 2

Topic 1: Good and evil

Topic 2: Religion, reason and revelation

Topic 3: Religion and science

The Topics focus on developing skills such as analysis, empathy and evaluation, which will enable students to gain knowledge and understanding of the specified content.

In following this specification students will have the opportunity to study Philosophy and/or Applied Ethics in depth and will learn about the diversity of religion and the way in which people who believe in a religion follow its teachings in their everyday lives.

This book covers everything students will need to know for the examination and shows them how to use their knowledge and understanding to answer the questions they will be asked.

Changes to the specification

The specification has changed dramatically according to the developing nature of education and the need to meet the demands of the world for students. The new specification will be taught from September 2009 onwards. The main changes that teachers and students should be aware of include the following:

- The Assessment Objectives (AOs) have changed, with a 50% focus now given to AO1 (Describe, explain and analyse, using knowledge and understanding) and a 50% focus to AO2 (Use evidence and reasoned argument to express and evaluate personal responses, informed insights and differing viewpoints). Previously, the balance was 75% to 25% respectively. There is more information on this on pages x and xi.

- There is an increased focus on learning *from* religion rather than simply learning *about* religion, and explicit reference to religious beliefs is now required in answers marked by Levels of Response.

- Levels of Response grids have been changed to a new range of 0 to 6 marks for AO1 questions and 0–12 marks for AO2 questions. The complete grids are reproduced on pages x and xi.

- Quality of Written Communication (QWC) is now only assessed on parts (d) and (e) of each question.

- There is now a greater choice of Topics within the specification including Religion, reason and revelation and Religion and the media.

Why did we want to write these resources?

We feel strongly that there is a need for good classroom resources that take advantage of the changed Assessment Objectives which:

- make the subject lively, interactive and relevant to today's world

- encourage students to talk to each other and work together

- challenge students and encourage them to think in depth in order to reach a high level of critical thinking

- train students to organise their thoughts in writing in a persuasive and structured way, and so prepare them for examination

The book has many features which contribute towards these goals. **Grade Studio** provides stimulating and realistic exercises to train students in what examiners are looking for and how to meet those expectations. **Exam Café** provides an exciting environment in which students can plan and carry out their revision.

Of course learning is about more than just exams. Throughout the book you will find **Research Notes**, which encourage students to explore beyond the book and beyond the curriculum. All of these features are explained in more detail on the next two pages.

What is in this book?

This student book has the following sections;

- the **Introduction**, which you are reading now
- the six **Topics** covered in the specification
- **Exam Café** – an invaluable resource for students studying their GCSE in Religious Studies
- **Glossary** – a reference tool for key terms and words used throughout the book.

Each of the above is covered in more detail in the text below.

The six Topics

Each Topic in this book contains:

- a Topic scene-setter including a look at the key questions raised by the Topic, and the key words associated with those questions (**The Big Picture**)
- two-page spreads covering the **main Topic content**
- exam-style questions with level indicators, examiner's comments and model answers (**Grade Studio**).

These features, which are explained more fully in the following pages, have been carefully planned and designed to draw together the OCR specification in an exciting but manageable way.

The Big Picture

This provides an overview of the Topic. It explains to students **what** they will be studying (the content), **how** they will study it (the approaches, activities and tasks) and **why** they are studying it (the rationale). It also includes a **Get started** activity, often linked to a picture or visual stimulus, which presents a task designed to engage students in the issues of the Topic and give them some idea of the content to be studied.

Develop your knowledge

This lists the **key information**, **key questions** and **key words** of the Topic. At a glance, it allows students to grasp the basic elements of knowledge they will gain in the study of the Topic. It is also a useful reference point for reflection and checking information as it is studied.

Main Topic content

The main content of each Topic is covered in a number of two-page spreads. Each spread equates to roughly one lesson of work – although teachers will need to judge for themselves if some of these need more time.

Each spread begins with the learning outcomes, highlighted in a box at the top of the page, so that students are aware of the focus and aims of the lesson. The text then attempts to answer, through a balanced viewpoint, one or two of the key questions raised in **Did you know?** The text carefully covers the views of both religious believers and non-believers. It is also punctuated with activities that range from simple tasks that can take place in the classroom to more complex tasks that can be tackled away from school.

A range of margin features adds extra depth and support to the main text both for students and the teacher.

- **For debate** invites students to examine two sides of a controversial issue.
- **Must think about!** directs students towards a key idea that they should consider.
- **Sacred text** provides an extract from the sacred texts of the religion to help students understand religious ideas and teachings.
- **Research notes** provide stimulating ideas for further research beyond the material covered in the book and in the OCR specification.

Activities

Every Topic has a range of interesting activities which will help students to achieve the learning outcomes. Every two-page spread has a short starter activity to grab students' attention and to get them thinking. This is followed by a development section where the main content is introduced, and a plenary activity, which may ask students to reflect on what they have learnt, or may start them thinking about the next steps.

All activities are labelled AO1 or AO2 so you can tell at a glance which skills will be developed.

What is Grade Studio?

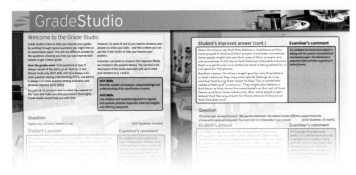

Everyone has different learning needs and this section of the book gives clear focus on how, with guidance from the teacher, students can develop the skills that will help them to achieve the higher levels in their exam responses.

Grade Studio appears as boxes within each Topic, as well as a two-page spread at the end of every Topic. It includes tips from the examiner, guidance on the steps to completing a well structured answer, and sample answers with examiner comments.

What is the Exam Café?

This is the revision section of the book. Here students will find useful revision tools and tips on how to get started on their revision and exam preparation. Students will also find assessment advice, including examples of different types of questions and samples of frequently asked questions. A useful **revision check list** allows students to review each Topic's content and explains where to find material in the book that relates to the exam questions.

Exam Café also has:

- sample student answers with examiner's comments
- help on understanding exam language, so students can achieve higher grades
- examiner tips, including common mistakes to be avoided.

For the Student: ActiveBook CD-ROM

In the back of this book is an ActiveBook CD-ROM. This contains an electronic version of the book, with easy-to-use and intuitive navigation controls. Pages are displayed in double-page spreads and users can flick to whichever page they choose. The CD also contains an Exam Café, with fresh revision content that complements and extends the Exam Café in the printed book.

For the Teacher: ActiveTeach CD-ROM

An accompanying ActiveTeach CD-ROM can also be purchased by schools and teachers. As well as containing an electronic version of the book, it provides a host of other features and interactives for classroom teaching. An icon on the electronic book page indicates where an ActiveTeach activity can be accessed. More detail on the ActiveTeach CD-ROM is given on the next page.

Heinemann's OCR Religious Studies B Series

Below is a snapshot of the complete OCR Religious Studies B series. Further detail can be found at www.heinemann.co.uk/gcse

OCR B Philosophy and Applied Ethics Teacher Guide with Resource Browser CD-ROM
ISBN 978-0-435-50152-5

Philosophy ActiveTeach CD-ROM
ISBN 978-0-435-50155-6

The **Teacher Guide** has been designed to correspond closely to the Student Book. For every Topic, the Teacher Guide offers four sample lesson plans and worksheets on Christianity, as well as a two page **Grade Studio**. There is careful cross-referencing throughout to help Teachers make the most out of these resources.

In addition, the Teacher Guide contains one sample lesson plan per Topic for Buddhism, Hinduism, Islam, Judaism and Sikhism. Any Teacher covering more than one religion in their course will find this a uniquely valuable resource.

Finally, the Teacher Guide comes with a CD-ROM, which contains the lesson plans along with a fully customisable version of all the worksheets.

The **ActiveTeach CD-ROM** contains an electronic version of the **Philosophy Student Book**, along with interactive **Grade Studio** and interactive whiteboard activities for front-of-class teaching. These activities are invaluable in engaging students with the specification content and bringing religious debates and issues to life. Equally valuable are the video and audio clips offered throughout the content. **ActiveTeach** has a special zoom feature, so any part of the book's content can be expanded on the whiteboard, as well as a special **My Resources** feature, where favourite activities, pages or clips can be stored. Finally, **ActiveTeach** includes an electronic **Exam Café**, which offers fresh revision content, complementing and extending the **Exam Café** in the printed book. A VLE version of **ActiveTeach** is available at no extra cost.

Applied Ethics Student Book with ActiveBook CD-ROM

ISBN 978-0-435-50151-8

This book provides complete coverage of both units of Applied Ethics (B603 and B604) and covers all six religions: Buddhism, Christianity, Hinduism, Islam, Judaism and Sikhism. It provides information, activities, and **Grade Studio** examples for all aspects of the course, as well as an 8-page Exam Café for revision. This book comes with a free **ActiveBook CD-ROM. ActiveBook** contains an electronic version of the **Student Book**, as well as an exciting, electronic **Exam Café**, which offers fresh revision content, complementing and extending the **Exam Café** in the book itself.

For the Teacher, the book is fully supported by the **OCR B Teacher Guide** (see above) and by the **Applied Ethics ActiveTeach CD-ROM** (see below).

Christian Philosophy & Applied Ethics Student Book

ISBN 978-0-435-50158-7

This book provides complete coverage of both units of Philosophy (B601 and B602) and Applied Ethics (B603 and B604) from the perspective of Christianity. It provides information, activities, and **Grade Studio** examples for all aspects of the course, as well as an 8-page **Exam Café** for revision. Comprehensive support for the Teacher is provided through the corresponding **OCR B Teacher Guide** (see above).

Applied Ethics ActiveTeach CD-ROM

ISBN 978-0-435-50156-3

The **ActiveTeach CD-ROM** contains an electronic version of the **Applied Ethics Student Book**, along with interactive **Grade Studio** and interactive whiteboard activities for front-of-class teaching. These activities are invaluable in engaging students with the specification content and bringing religious debates and issues to life. Equally valuable are the video and audio clips offered throughout the content. **ActiveTeach** has a special zoom feature, so any part of the book's content can be expanded on the whiteboard, as well as a special **My Resources** feature, where favourite activities, pages or clips can be stored. Finally, **ActiveTeach** includes an electronic **Exam Café**, which offers fresh revision content, complementing and extending the **Exam Café** in the printed book. A VLE version of **ActiveTeach** is available at no extra cost.

Assessment Objectives and Levels of Response

Assessment Objectives, AO1 and AO2

In the new specification, the questions in the examination are designed to test students against two Assessment Objectives: AO1 and AO2. In the specification 50% of the marks will be awarded for AO1 questions and 50% will be awarded for AO2 questions.

AO1 Questions require candidates to 'describe, explain and analyse, using knowledge and understanding'.

AO2 Questions require candidates to 'use evidence and reasoned argument to express and evaluate personal responses, informed insights, and differing viewpoints'.

Each question in the examination is composed of 5 parts, a–e. In more detail:

- Parts **a–c** are worth one, two and three marks respectively and test a candidate's knowledge (AO1 skills).
- Part **d** is worth six marks and tests a candidate's understanding (AO1 skills).
- Part **e** is worth twelve marks and tests a candidate's AO2 skills.

LEVELS OF RESPONSE FOR MARKING AO1 PART (D) QUESTIONS

LEVEL 1
(1–2 marks)

A **weak** attempt to answer the question.

Candidates will demonstrate little understanding of the question.

- A small amount of relevant information may be included.
- Answers may be in the form of a list with little or no description/explanation/analysis.
- There will be little or no use of specialist terms.
- Answers may be ambiguous or disorganised.
- Errors of grammar, punctuation and spelling may be intrusive.

LEVEL 2
(3–4 marks)

A **satisfactory** answer to the question.

Candidates will demonstrate some understanding of the question.

- Information will be relevant but may lack specific detail.
- There will be some description/explanation/analysis although this may not be fully developed.
- The information will be presented for the most part in a structured format.
- Some use of specialist terms, although these may not always be used appropriately.
- There may be errors in spelling, grammar and punctuation.

LEVEL 3
(5–6 marks)

A **good** answer to the question.

Candidates will demonstrate a clear understanding of the question.

- A fairly complete and full description/explanation/analysis.
- A comprehensive account of the range and depth of relevant material.
- The information will be presented in a structured format.
- There will be significant, appropriate and correct use of specialist terms.
- There will be few, if any, errors in spelling, grammar and punctuation.

LEVELS OF RESPONSE FOR MARKING AO2 PART (E) QUESTIONS

LEVEL 0
(0 marks)

No evidence submitted or response does not address the question.

LEVEL 1
(1–3 marks)

A **weak** attempt to answer the question.

Candidates will demonstrate little understanding of the question.

- Answers may be simplistic with little or no relevant information.
- Viewpoints may not be supported or appropriate.
- Answers may be ambiguous or disorganised.
- There will be little or no use of specialist terms.
- Errors of grammar, punctuation and spelling may be intrusive.

LEVEL 2
(4–6 marks)

A **limited** answer to the question.

Candidates will demonstrate some understanding of the question.

- Some information will be relevant, although may lack specific detail.
- Only one view might be offered and developed.
- Viewpoints might be stated and supported with limited argument/discussion.
- The information will show some organisation.
- Reference to the religion studied may be vague.
- Some use of specialist terms, although these may not always be used appropriately.
- There may be errors in spelling, grammar and punctuation.

LEVEL 3
(7–9 marks)

A **competent** answer to the question.

Candidates will demonstrate a sound understanding of the question.

- Selection of relevant material with appropriate development.
- Evidence of appropriate personal response.
- Justified arguments/different points of view supported by some discussion.
- The information will be presented in a structured format.
- Some appropriate reference to the religion studied.
- Specialist terms will be used appropriately and for the most part correctly.
- There may be occasional errors in spelling, grammar and punctuation.

LEVEL 4
(10–12 marks)

A **good** answer to the question.

Candidates will demonstrate a clear understanding of the question.

- Answers will reflect the significance of the issue(s) raised.
- Clear evidence of an appropriate personal response, fully supported.
- A range of points of view supported by justified arguments/discussion.
- The information will be presented in a clear and organised way.
- Clear reference to the religion studied.
- Specialist terms will be used appropriately and correctly.
- Few, if any, errors in spelling, grammar and punctuation.

Topic 1: Belief about deity

The Big Picture

In this Topic, you will be addressing religious beliefs and teachings about:

- the nature of God
- reasons for belief in God
- the concept of miracles.

You will also think about ways in which these beliefs affect the life and outlook of religious people in the world today.

What?

You will:

- develop your knowledge and understanding of key religious beliefs and ideas
- explain what these beliefs and ideas mean to believers and think about how they might affect the way believers live
- make links between these beliefs and ideas and what you think/believe.

Why?

Because:

- these beliefs and ideas underpin and are reflected in the ways many people live their lives
- understanding people's beliefs can help you understand why they think and act in the way they do
- understanding these beliefs helps you compare and contrast what others believe, including thinking about your own beliefs and ideas.

How?

By:

- recalling and selecting information about religious beliefs and ideas about deity, explaining their importance for people today
- reflecting on the relevance of these beliefs in 21st-century Britain
- evaluating your own views about these beliefs.

DAILY NEWS

BABY ONLY SURVIVOR OF HORRENDOUS PLANE CRASH

"It's a miracle," say relatives

"What he did was wrong — that's the absolute truth."

"I have faith that the England Team will do an excellent job," says England Manager

Explain what is meant in each of these headlines by the terms: miracle, faith and truth.

Write your own definition of each of these words and compare your ideas with a partner.

Mass at St Peter's Basilica in the Vatican City, Italy.

Belief about deity

KEY INFORMATION

What do people believe about the nature of God and why?

- The Buddha refused to discuss whether there was a creator God, because such knowledge did not help Buddhists seek the path to enlightenment or **nibbana**. However, many Buddhists do believe in gods or deities. These gods are trapped within the cycle of **samsara**, much as humans are.

- Christians believe there is only one God (monotheism) who is **omnipotent** and **omniscient**. Their God is a loving God and cares how people behave and treat each other. They believe in the doctrine of the **Trinity**, which shows that God can be understood in three different ways – as Father, Son and Holy Spirit. Christians believe God designed and created the universe and that God has a purpose for humanity. They experience God in many different ways and communicate with him through prayer.

- In Hinduism there are many different gods and goddesses, called deities. Many Hindus believe there is only one God, called **Brahman**, and that all the deities are different ways of understanding the many characteristics of the one God. Hindus experience God in a personal way through prayer and meditation. They believe the way the universe is made shows everything is part of God.

- Muslims believe there is only one God – Allah. Allah cannot be described, but is omnipotent and omniscient. Allah created the world and everything in it and has a purpose for humanity. The **Shahadah** states: 'There is no god but Allah and Muhammad ﷺ is his prophet.' Muslims believe they can see evidence for Allah's goodness in the world.

- Jews believe there is only one G-d. G-d is holy, omnipotent and omniscient. Jews believe G-d created the world and everything in it and has a purpose for humanity. The **Torah** and **Talmud** are sources of authority for Jewish belief in G-d.

GET STARTED

Is there something you believe in although you cannot prove it exists?

- Sikhs believe in one God whom they call **Waheguru**. God is timeless and without form or gender. Sikh beliefs are summarised in the **Mool Mantar**. They believe that God is within everyone, good and bad. Creation is the visible evidence that God exists and it reflects God's nature.

Beliefs about the nature of miracles and divine intervention in the world

- Buddhists disagree over how much Buddhas are able to influence the world. Some believe **bodhisattvas** who have achieved **nibbana** intervene to help others along the path. Such interventions are seen as miraculous.

- Christians believe the most important example of God's intervention in the world was in God taking human form as his son, Jesus, known as the incarnation. They believe God is active in the world and performs miracles such as healing the sick.

KEY QUESTIONS

KNOWLEDGE AND UNDERSTANDING
Many people believe in God because they say they can see evidence for God's existence in the world. What sort of examples might members of a religion you have studied give to support their belief?

ANALYSIS AND EVALUATION
'There is no evidence that God exists.' Do you agree? Give reasons to support your answer from your own experience and the religion(s) you have studied.

Avatar the form of a person or animal taken by some Hindu gods when they come to earth

Bodhisattva in Buddhism, a being destined for Enlightenment

Brahman the universal spirit, the source of life in all living things in the universe

Dukkha suffering – the nature of existence according to the first Noble Truth in Buddhism

Gurdwara Sikh place of worship, literally 'the doorway to the Guru'

Guru teacher; a title reserved for the ten human Gurus and the Guru Granth Sahib Ji

Kamma in Buddhism, intentional actions that affect your circumstances in this and future lives

Mool Mantar a sacred text summarising Sikh beliefs

Nibbana in Buddhism, achieving freedom from greed, hatred and delusion resulting in freedom from rebirth

Omnipotent in religion, when God is all powerful

Omniscient in religion, when God is all knowing

Polytheism belief in many gods

Samsara in Buddhism and Hinduism; a continuing cycle of birth, ageing, death and rebirth

Shahadah declaration of faith in Islam

Shema important Jewish prayer that states belief in one G-d

Talmud collection of teachings and explanations of rabbis, which helps Jews understand the Torah

Torah Jewish law, or teaching, made up of the Five Books of Moses

Trimurti in Hinduism, the three faces of Brahman: Brahma the Creator, Vishnu the Sustainer and Shiva the Destroyer

Trinity Christian belief that there are three persons within one God – Father, Son and Holy Spirit

Waheguru a Sikh name for God

- Hindus believe Brahman is beyond human understanding and chooses to be revealed by three faces known as the **Trimurti**: Brahma the Creator, Vishnu the Sustainer and Shiva the Destroyer. They believe that sometimes the gods take the form of a person or animal when they come to earth, particularly at times of crisis.

- Muslims do not consider miracles to be very important. As Muhammad ﷺ was a prophet, not a god, there is no reason for him to have performed miracles. Allah can perform miracles and there are many examples of Allah's interventions in Muhammad's ﷺ life.

- Jews believe G-d has intervened in the world through miracles and through the words of prophets who warned people of the consequences of not following G-d's will.

- Sikhs believe that the will of God was revealed through the ten **Gurus** and that their sacred book, the Guru Granth Sahib Ji, contains God's message. Everyone has direct access to God. A Sikh's duty is to learn about God.

FOR INTEREST

What is a miracle? Can your class agree a definition?

Take a class vote on the question 'Do miracles happen?'

Something to think about

A young boy strays onto a railway line into the path of a train. At the same time, the train driver has a heart attack, the dead man's handle (emergency brake) is activated, and the train stops less than a metre from the boy. A miracle or coincidence?

Buddhism:
Belief about deity

Do Buddhists believe in God?

People often say that Buddhists do not believe in God. In some ways this is true: the Buddha refused to discuss whether there was a creator God, because such knowledge did not help Buddhists to seek the path to enlightenment or **nibbana**.

However, many Buddhists do believe in gods or deities. These gods are trapped within the cycle of **samsara**, much as humans are: only those who have achieved nibbana are free of the cycle of death and rebirth. These gods are often seen as beings who have built up positive **kamma** by carrying out positive actions, resulting in rebirth in the godly realm when they die. Eventually, the positive consequences of these actions wear off, and the gods are reborn into another realm within the wheel of samsara.

In fact, many Buddhists do not see the godly realm as the best realm to be reborn into, but think a human rebirth is more desirable. For most, the godly realm is so pleasant that the gods are lulled into a false sense of security, with no desire to seek a cure for suffering or **dukkha**, so make no progress towards achieving enlightenment. In the human realm there is a mix of pleasure and pain, so beings can see that life could be better, and thus seek a solution for suffering.

The action of gods, Buddhas and bodhisattvas in the world

Gods

In Buddhism, gods can only intervene in the world in a limited way. A Buddhist might worship a local deity to ensure good crops, but the worship of gods is not universal or expected. Whether a Buddhist worships the god is likely to be determined by the cultural background of the individual, rather than the fact they are a Buddhist.

The next two pages will help you to:

- explain why gods only have a limited importance in Buddhist beliefs
- evaluate the importance of believing that others can intervene in the world to help humans
- understand Buddhist beliefs about miracles.

Theravada and Mahayana Buddhists disagree over how much Buddhas can still influence the world.

AO2 skills ACTIVITIES

'The Mahayana view that Buddhas and bodhisattvas can intervene in the world is more comforting than the Theravada view that they cannot.'

How do you think Buddhists of these two traditions might respond to this statement?

RESEARCH NOTE

The life of the Buddha might have more impact on the life of a Buddhist than the gods. Find out the key events in the Buddha's life, and how these might affect the way a Buddhist lives their life.

Buddhas

In the Theravada Buddhist tradition, the Buddha achieved enlightenment, provided teachings for his followers, and then died – so he cannot intervene in the world to help people now. People must seek their own path to enlightenment using the example and teachings he left behind.

In the Mahayana Buddhist tradition, the Buddha did not die, but appeared to do so, to spur people on to achieve their own path. Mahayana Buddhists also believe that other Buddhas are also alive and can be called on for help.

Bodhisattvas

In the Mahayana tradition **bodhisattvas** – or 'Buddhas-to-be' – are able to intervene in the world to help others.

Are miracles important in Buddhism?

If you understand miracles as God's intervention in the world, you might query whether miracles can take place in Buddhism at all. However, if you consider a miracle to be an event beyond natural explanation, miracles do occur in Buddhism.

In Theravada Buddhism, Buddhists who have reached the stage of nibbana (arhats) are considered to be able to perform miracles, such as flying through the air. However, they are discouraged from demonstrating these abilities unless to do so would help another to progress along the path to enlightenment.

In the Mahayana tradition, Buddhas or bodhisattvas are said to perform miracles, again to help people on the path to enlightenment.

It might be argued that miracles are of limited importance because they are limited in purpose and the Buddha discouraged their use. However, you might argue that they are extremely important for those who experience them.

The Wheel of Life.

ACTIVITIES

Using images from the Wheel of Life, explain in words and pictures the status of the gods in Buddhism.

GradeStudio

AO1

QUESTION

Explain Buddhist beliefs about the gods. **[6 marks]**

You could build an answer like this:

Level 1

The examiner will expect you to know how the gods are viewed within Buddhism. A typical response might mention that the gods are trapped in the world of samsara along with humans.

Level 2

To develop this answer further, you might discuss whether the gods are able to help humans at all, and if so, how important they might be considered.

Level 3

To gain the highest levels, you should explicitly show that the gods have limited status, since they have not achieved nibbana, and will eventually be reborn again. They do not therefore understand the cure for dukkha, as Buddhists see it, which is the highest aim within Buddhism.

Christianity: Belief about deity 1

What do Christians believe about God?

The next two pages will help you to:

- explore what Christians believe about the nature of God
- identify and analyse the reasons given to support this belief.

Christians believe that there is only one God – this is called monotheism. They also believe that God is not like any other living being and this makes it difficult to describe God. One word they do use is holy and this means special, pure and set apart.

Here are some of the qualities that Christians attribute to God.

AO1 skills ACTIVITIES

Think about the superheroes you have seen on television or film. Make a spider diagram to show their qualities and skills. Add any other things you think a supreme being should be able to do. Compare your results with someone else.

Omnibenevolent (all loving and good)
Judge
Perfect
Omnipotent (all powerful)
Eternal (existing without beginning or end)
Omniscient (all knowing)
Creator
God
Immanent (within the world and supporting it)
Loving
Father
Has a plan for the world
Son
Holy spirit
Transcendent (outside time and space)

The Trinity

Christians suggest that God can be understood in three different ways, rather like the way water can take three different forms.

This does not mean that Christians believe there is more than one God, but that there are three different aspects of God:

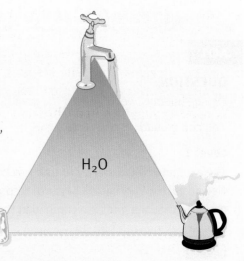

H_2O

- **God the Father – God in heaven**
  For Christians, the image of the father suggests that God loves human beings – God is the Creator and cares for them. God also acts as a judge and will punish humans if they do wrong. However, God will forgive people if they show they are sorry. Some Christians may refer to God as a mother to show that God is beyond gender.

- **God the Son – God in the form of Jesus**
  Christians believe that Jesus was the Son of God. Jesus showed people how to live in the right way so that they could enter the kingdom of heaven. Jesus was crucified so that humans could be forgiven for their wrongdoing. Christians believe that God showed power over death when Jesus rose from the dead – the resurrection.

- **God the Holy Spirit – God at work in the world**
  After the resurrection, Jesus stayed on earth for a short time and he worked with his disciples (followers). He then went to heaven – the ascension – and God sent the Holy Spirit to guide and support Christians.

Why do Christians believe in God?

The following are some of the reasons why a Christian might believe in God.

- Many Christians would say that the universe could not simply have started by itself. They see God as the Creator, who made it according to a plan.

- The world seems to be carefully designed – nothing happens by accident. In the 18th century, a Christian philosopher, William Paley, suggested that it is like the workings of a watch, created by a skilled artisan. This is known as the teleological argument. Einstein suggested that the design of the world must have had a 'helping hand' – God.

- For some people, a personal experience of God may have convinced them that God exists: for example, New York ex-gang member Nicky Cruz, who experienced a religious conversion.

- Humans have a sense that tells them what is right or wrong, often called conscience. Others suggest that the feeling of guilt if we do wrong is God, who knows our actions even if no one else does.

- People brought up in a Christian family may accept that God exists because they have always been taught this.

- The teaching and authority of the Bible may convince people of God's existence.

- People may find the life and work of Jesus evidence of the existence of God.

ACTIVITIES

Make a fact file to show the nature of the Christian God. Include as many examples as you can of what this God does in the world.

ACTIVITIES

Go to the Nicky Cruz website to help you write a diary showing how Nicky Cruz felt his life was changed by his religious experience.

The Holy Spirit is often pictured as a dove.

Christianity:
Belief about deity 2

Miracles in Christianity

A miracle is a marvellous event that cannot be explained by any human activity. It is said, by Christians, to be evidence of God intervening in the world. Christians say this happens because God is **omnipotent**. In the New Testament, two terms are used to describe miraculous events – 'mighty works' and 'signs'. Christians believe that the miracle stories in the New Testament show the presence and love of God at work in the world through the actions of Jesus.

The miracles of Jesus

There are a number of accounts of miracles performed by Jesus in the four Gospels (Matthew, Mark, Luke and John). Miracles in the New Testament can be divided into four main groups, as follows:

- natural miracles (Mark 4:35–41)
- casting out demons (Mark 7:24–30)
- healing the sick (Mark 10:46–52)
- raising the dead (Mark 5:22–42).

Christians would also say that the final miracle was the resurrection of Jesus and the appearances he made to his followers after his death. The first miracle Jesus performed was a natural miracle, at a wedding in Cana. Christians have different views about the miracles of Jesus: some take them literally, others look for rational explanations, and some do not think they are as important as other aspects of Jesus' ministry.

Water into wine

The next two pages will help you to:

- identify and understand Christian ideas about miracles
- explore what Christians believe about God's intervention in the world.

 **ACTIVITIES**

Over a week, look at news reports in papers, on the Internet and on television. Collect three examples of modern miraculous events. Make a group collage to show the variety of events in the world that are not easily explained by rational and scientific explanations.

John 2:1–11

On the third day, a wedding took place at Cana in Galilee. Jesus' mother was there, and Jesus and his disciples had also been invited to the wedding. When the wine was gone, Jesus' mother said to him, 'They have no more wine.'

'Dear woman, why do you involve me?' Jesus replied. 'My time has not yet come.'

His mother said to the servants, 'Do whatever he tells you.'

Nearby stood six stone water jars, the kind used by the Jews for ceremonial washing, each holding from twenty to thirty gallons. Jesus said to the servants, 'Fill the jars with water,' so they filled them to the brim.

Then he told them, 'Now draw some out and take it to the master of the banquet.'

They did so, and the master of the banquet tasted the water that had been turned into wine. He did not realise where it had come from, though the servants who had drawn the water knew.

Then he called the bridegroom aside and said, 'Everyone brings out the choice wine first and then the cheaper wine after the guests have had too much to drink; but you have saved the best till now.'

The Holy Spirit

According to Acts 1, Jesus promised that his followers would receive the power of the Holy Spirit to guide them. When this happened, on the Day of Pentecost (see Acts 2), it was such an amazing experience that their lives were totally changed.

Christians believe that the Holy Spirit still works in the world today. Some churches have charismatic services. Pentecostal worship is an example of this. Services are lively and some members of the congregation may feel overtaken by the Holy Spirit, faint, fall into a trance or speak in tongues. Sometimes healing takes place. Some worshippers may feel moved to make a prophecy and say that they can hear the voice of God.

Roman Catholics believe that, when they celebrate Mass, they can be certain that they are in the presence of Jesus, shown by the bread and wine that become his body and blood.

Christian belief in the Holy Spirit is written in the Apostles' Creed. This statement reminds Christians of their key beliefs. It was probably based on statements from the early Church and goes back to the fourth century CE: 'I believe in the Holy Spirit, the holy Catholic Church, the communion of the saints...' This Holy Spirit has been in the world since the Creation and can be seen in the Old Testament.

Miracles in the world today

Christians believe that they can experience the power of God through prayer and meditation, and may ask God for a miracle to help them in a crisis: for example, when a loved one is suffering an illness. They may also thank God when a miraculous event has occurred.

 **ACTIVITIES**

Go to the rejesus website and visit Story/The miracles of Jesus/Read the miracles to find out more about the miracles of Jesus. Describe one miracle in each of the four groups. Use words or pictures to help you remember the accounts. Explain why Christians believe that the resurrection of Jesus is the greatest miracle of all.

 **ACTIVITIES**

Write a speech for a class debate for or against a belief in miracles.

 CASE STUDY

Knock, Northern Ireland

In August 1879, an image of the Virgin Mary, St Joseph and St John appeared on the wall of the Catholic Church in the village of Knock. More than a dozen people saw it, and agreed that it reached almost to the ground and was very bright. When they tried to touch it, they could only feel the wall. There was no logical explanation for the image. To this day, Knock is a special site of pilgrimage.

Lourdes, France

Bernadette Soubirous was a poor shepherdess when, in 1858, at fourteen years old, she saw an apparition in a grotto – a vision of a beautiful lady. When she told her family, they did not believe her, but she returned to the grotto and, over the next five months, the Lady appeared eighteen times. Bernadette was told to 'drink from the fountain' and although she could see no water, she did as she was told and dug in the earth until a bubbling pool of water appeared. This water is said to have miraculous healing powers. Lourdes has become a site of healing and many believers go there on pilgrimage hoping for a cure.

The Rosary Basilica at Lourdes.

Hinduism:
Belief about deity 1

One person may represent many different things to different people at the same time.

What is God?

Many Hindus refer to God as Brahman, which means 'blessed'. Most Hindus also believe that God is present all around us in nature and in every life form.

Although there is some debate about the words used, some Hindus use the term pantheism to describe their faith. Others may emphasise they believe in one God, not many – the deities represent aspects of the Supreme Spirit, and help to make God personal, but they are not separate gods and goddesses in the way the Ancient Greeks and Romans would have thought of them.

It may help to think about it like this: although for you, it is likely that your teacher is just your teacher, he or she is actually many other things at the same time as being your teacher. Who your teacher really is, is the sum total of all the roles he or she has, not just one or two of them. In the same way, you may be at once a son or daughter, sibling, friend, pupil, musician, athlete and many more things. They all make up who you are.

Similarly, for most Hindus the different deities symbolise the different roles God serves – each is a different aspect of what, together, is the one Supreme Spirit.

One reason the Supreme Spirit is divided into deities is to help explain how the universe works.

 REMEMBER THIS

Pantheism – believing in many deities who are all really one because they are all aspects of a single creative life source.

For Hindus, there are three key aspects to all that exists. These are:

- creation
- preservation
- destruction.

These have been deified (made godly) as the **Trimurti**:

- Brahma (the creator god)
- Vishnu (the preserver god, who takes care of creation)
- Shiva (the destroyer god and re-creation god).

Many Hindus believe that *this* universe is just one of many in an infinite cycle, and that humans are not the main or only purpose of creation, but simply one aspect of it (see Topic 6).

Lord Shiva is depicted with weapons and animal skins, showing how powerful he is. However, at the same time, the moon sits in his hair, from which, also, a river flows. These signs of creation symbolise the fact that what destroys can also create, and that one is necessary for the other to happen (see Topic 3).

The Vishvarupa, meaning 'all creation in one form/body', depicts one version of Hindus' central beliefs of one God in many forms and as the universe itself.

Svetasvatara Upanishad, part 6

'The Supreme Being is the source of all being, the seed of all things, that in this life have their life. Beyond time and space, and yet the God of forms infinite, who dwells in our innermost thoughts, and who is seen by those who love him.'

This quote helps to explain the concept of God being at once the universe beyond human understanding (**Brahman**) and personal to individuals.

Hindu beliefs in God come from the sacred texts (see Topic 5) and also from tradition and the teachings of the Hindu community..

EVERYTHING I EXPERIENCE SUGGESTS THERE IS MORE THAN JUST WHAT WE SEE. I FEEL SUCH AWE AT NATURE'S MAGNIFICENCE AND CRUELTY; MY INNATE SENSE OF MORALITY; THE INTENSE PEACE I FEEL WHEN I MEDITATE; THE SENSE SPOKEN IN MANY OF THE SACRED TEXTS; FOR ME IT ALL POINTS TO THE EXISTENCE OF THE SUPREME SPIRIT.

Why believe in Brahman (God)?

ACTIVITIES

How close is this quote to your own definition of what God is? Do you think God, to be worthwhile, needs to be both within human consciousness *and* outside of time? Explain your responses.

Hinduism:
Belief about deity 2

The next two pages will help you to:

- evaluate Hindu beliefs about miracles
- analyse the impact of God being represented as female.

Avatars

God as Vishnu (the preserver) is believed by many Hindus to have **avatars** on earth at times of chaos or danger. These include popular incarnations, such as Lord Krishna and Prince Rama, as well as figures at the centre of other faiths, such as the Buddha and Jesus (see Topic 5).

Many Hindus believe God interacts with the earth in this way to teach people the right way to live, and as part of the ongoing battle between good and evil. Hinduism does not have a concept of a devil as such, but many believe that souls that keep on living in a selfish and ignorant way can eventually become demonic (see Topic 4).

The purpose of avatars is to destroy ignorance and show the right way to live.

> **Bhagavad Gita 4:7**
> *Whenever there is decline of righteousness and rise of unrighteousness, then I manifest Myself.*

You may use or have seen avatars on emails or chat rooms, where the avatar is a form the site-user wishes to take on or be seen as. This is basically a slight corruption of the word, but there is a link in the meaning.

Many Hindus believe avatars reflect part of God's nature and show humans the right way to live. Sometimes the Gods can give their power to a human for a special reason. These are called Shaktyavesha (or living) Avatars.

The example of Lord Krishna

Lord Krishna, believed by many to be the eighth avatar of Lord Vishnu:

- demonstrates how God can be both human and divine
- is a fun-loving and cheeky character as well as a wise, powerful and brave person
- shows that God can be at once human and super-human.

As a teenager, he and his friends hid the clothes of the young ladies bathing at the river so they had to come out naked. However, the tales also say that, as a child, he fought off a seven-headed serpent. He lifted up an entire mountain on one finger to protect the people of a village from severe storms, and successfully battled his wicked uncle to restore peace and security to the kingdom.

 REMEMBER THIS

The original meaning of **avatar** is God on earth in a human (or animal) form.

 **ACTIVITIES**

Create a spider diagram that shows some of the ways in which avatars represent aspects of God.

 **ACTIVITIES**

Demonstrate your understanding of pluralism within Hinduism – how one may also be many – by creating a piece of art. For example, one rainbow is also seven colours; one orchestra is also scores of instruments; one flower is also many petals. Use language, diagrams, artwork, models, music, dance or any combination of these.

 FOR DEBATE

'For every birth there is a death, and for every joy there is a sorrow. What may seem like a miracle is simply a balancing act on behalf of the universe and has nothing to do with a Divine Power.' Do you agree or disagree? Explain your view, giving examples to justify it.

The example of Prince Rama

Prince Rama, believed by many to be the seventh avatar of Lord Vishnu:

- is held up as an ideal son, brother and husband
- shows obedience and loyalty to his parents
- shows no jealousy, only respect to his brothers
- is devoted to his wife, whom he rescues from a demon with immense bravery.

You may know one of the stories of Divali, which features Prince Rama.

Miracles in Hinduism

Lifting mountains? Surely this is fantasy?

Many Hindus believe in a time called the satya yuga – the age of truth – when the divine could easily interact with humans because people were more tuned in to the Spirit and less earthbound. This means the miracles described in scripture and stories could happen, because God can do anything. The current age is called the kali yuga – the age of darkness – because many people are only interested in material things rather than spiritual ones.

Some Hindus believe that, having had nine previous major incarnations, Lord Vishnu will finally incarnate at the end of the kali yuga to save human kind again. Others believe there are miracles occurring around us all the time, which prove God is all around us – for example, every birth and the amazing power of love; we just need to notice them.

Why may a Hindu believe Jesus is divine?

The pluralist idea of one God in many forms means that some Hindus believe that exceptional world-changing human beings may be incarnations of God. Jesus falls into this category; some Hindus may have an image of Christ in their family shrine alongside other deities. Be aware, however, that believing Jesus may be an incarnation of God is not the same as believing he is the only begotten son of God, which is the Christian belief.

Goddess

Although many texts refer to God as 'he', it is clear in most Hindu thought that the Supreme Spirit, which has no form, can appear as male or female and as human or animal. The divine is thought of and worshipped in the female, as well as male, form. Goddesses not only demonstrate the need for feminine qualities in life, but also show that the female can be as strong as the male.

The **Trimurti** all have female counterparts:

- Saraswati – goddess of learning, music and poetry
- Lakshmi – goddess of wealth and good fortune
- Parvati – goddess of plenty.

Powerful individual goddesses have huge followings:

- Durga (aka Amba) – goddess of strength
- Kali – female equivalent of Lord Shiva (see above).

The picture of Shiva and Parvati as one deity shows that male and female are both aspects of the divine.

AO1+AO2 skills **ACTIVITIES**

- Explain how expressing the divine as both male and female may help to create a gender-balanced society.

- Do you think Hindu culture reflects the religious teachings about the female? Give examples to support your views.

Islam:
Belief about deity 1

What do Muslims believe about the nature of Allah?

The next two pages will help you to:

- understand and describe the characteristics of Allah
- explore the story of Muhammad ﷺ and his role in Muslim beliefs.

Muslims believe there is only one God, Allah. Tawhid – belief in one God – is the core belief that underpins the religion. The **Shahadah**, one of the five pillars of Islam – the foundations of belief on which Islam stands – states: 'There is no God but Allah and Muhammad ﷺ is the Messenger of Allah.'

Muslims are expected to express this 'oneness' of God in their daily lives and through their lifelong duty to Allah. This can be through accepting Allah's authority, divinity and characteristics; it may be put into practice by regular worship, offering daily prayers or by respecting other people and the world.

Muhammad ﷺ was clear that a belief in **polytheism** was wrong. In Makkah, where he was a merchant, people would make offerings to idols at the Ka'bah. The Qur'an says:

'Not an apostle did We send before thee without this inspiration sent by Us to him' (from Surah 21:25) and 'He is Allah, the One and Only' (Surah 112:1).

Muslims believe that Allah is eternal; Allah has always existed and is beyond the ideas of time and space. Allah is **omniscient** and **omnipotent**. Allah created the world for all humans and sustains it for the benefit of humans. In return, humans are expected to care for Allah's creation and take, with respect, what it gives. Muslims believe in Allah because of the teachings of the Qu'ran, the life and example of Muhammad ﷺ and because of the evidence of Allah which they see in the world around them.

The names of Allah

Although Muslims do not try to describe or picture Allah, the Qur'an contains ninety-nine names for Allah and they are often called 'beautiful names'. These may be used during prayer or meditation. These names offer a good insight into how Muslims understand the nature of Allah.

ACTIVITIES (AO1 skills)

Check your understanding of the names of Allah in the diagram, using a dictionary if you need to. Create your own mind map or thought shower bringing out the meanings. Extend and explain each description, drawing images to help you.

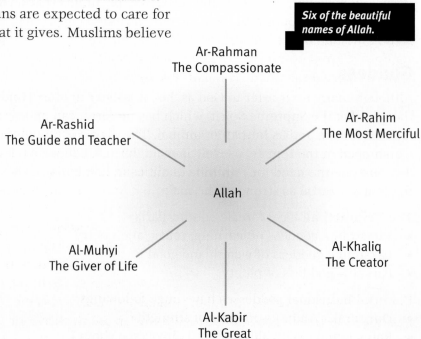

Six of the beautiful names of Allah.

Ar-Rahman
The Compassionate

Ar-Rahim
The Most Merciful

Ar-Rashid
The Guide and Teacher

Allah

Al-Khaliq
The Creator

Al-Muhyi
The Giver of Life

Al-Kabir
The Great

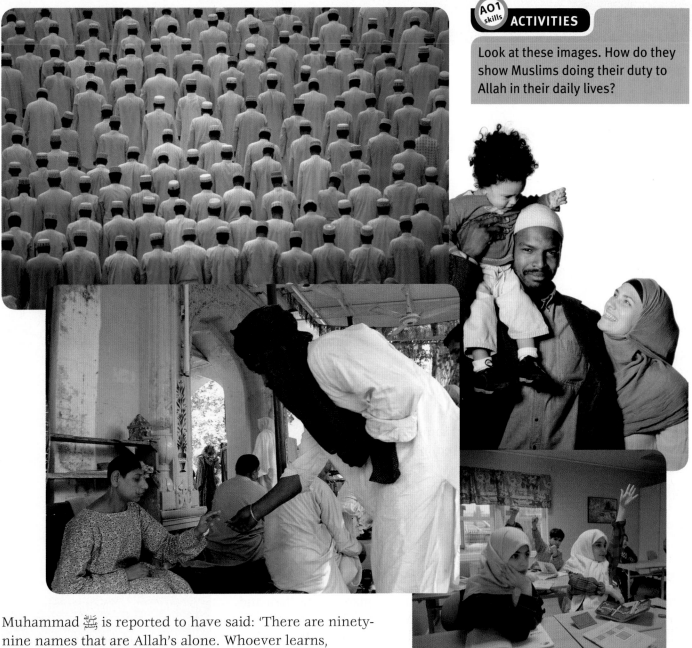

AO1 skills **ACTIVITIES**

Look at these images. How do they show Muslims doing their duty to Allah in their daily lives?

Muhammad ﷺ is reported to have said: 'There are ninety-nine names that are Allah's alone. Whoever learns, understands and enumerates them enters Paradise and achieves eternal salvation.' (Bukhari 8:418)

Muhammad ﷺ

Muslims believe their holy book, the Qur'an, was gradually revealed to Muhammad ﷺ starting in 610 CE on Mount Nur, Saudi Arabia. It is regarded as the direct words of Allah, and is unchangeable. After these revelations, and after speaking to his family, Muhammad ﷺ preached about his revelations and his belief in Allah, the one true God. He was a well-known and respected man, but at first his message was not always readily accepted by the people of Makkah, who worshipped idols at the Ka'bah – especially by the merchants who profited from the people who worshipped there. However, his message began to have an impact, and belief in Allah gradually spread across the region. The events of these revelations and the Qur'an are the basis for Muslim belief in Allah and the way Allah is revealed today.

FOR DEBATE

- Why do you think the merchants of Makkah were not happy with Muhammad's ﷺ message?
- Why might Muhammad's ﷺ message have been appealing to the people of Makkah?
- What would you think if someone came with a similar message for the world today, claiming we should stop worshipping money?

Islam:
Belief about deity 2

The next two pages will help you to:

- evaluate the importance of miracles in Islam
- describe how Muslims believe Allah created the world
- explain how Muslims believe Allah intervenes in the world
- evaluate and express the importance of the teaching of Muhammad ﷺ in Islam.

What do Muslims believe about miracles?

Miracles are very important in Islam. Examples include events which happened to previous prophets such as the miracle of Musa (Moses) dividing the Red Sea, found in the Old Testament, and the Virgin Birth of 'Isa (Jesus), found in the New Testament – both of which are included in the Qur'an. In the Qur'an, miracles are referred to as **ayah** or signs given by God.

Muhammad ﷺ was a prophet and is not considered divine, so there is no reason to expect that he would have performed miracles. However, miracles took place during his life. One example is a story told about his birth. It is said that on the night he was born a great star appeared in the sky. His grandfather, Abd al-Muttalib, prayed for six days for guidance on deciding a name for the child. On the seventh day, he and Muhammad's ﷺ mother both dreamed that he should be called Muhammad, which means 'the Praised One.'

Relief camps surround a mosque in the Aceh province of Lamno, Indonesia after an earthquake on 29 January 2005. Muslims believe Allah may appear to the world today in many ways, seen and unseen.

The Ascent, or Night Journey

The most important miracle in the life of Muhammad ﷺ was 'Isra and Mi'raj – the Night Journey and the Ascent. Muslims believe that Muhammad ﷺ was woken from his sleep by the Angel Jibril and was taken from Makkah to Jerusalem (al-Aqsa) on the back of a winged animal called Buraq, which means lightning. The Hadith describes Buraq as 'an animal white and long, larger than a donkey but smaller than a mule, who would place its hoof at a distance equal to the range of vision.' Muhammad ﷺ prayed in Jerusalem and then ascended to the heavens where he met the prophets Adam, Ibrahim, Musa, 'Isa and Harun. He then travelled until he came before Allah. He returned from this miraculous journey in a single night.

The Qur'an describes 'Isra, Surah 17:1
Glory to (Allah) Who did take His servant for a Journey by night from the Sacred Mosque to the farthest Mosque, whose precincts We did bless – in order that We might show him some of Our Signs: for He is the One Who heareth and seeth (all things).

 **REMEMBER THIS**

ayah – signs given by God.

Allah as creator of the world

Allah began, created and sustains the world that humans live in today, which is a miracle in itself. The first chapter of the Qur'an, al-Fatihah says: 'In the name of Allah, Most Gracious, Most Merciful. Praise be to Allah, the Cherisher and Sustainer of the worlds.'

Muslims believe that Allah created the world and everything in it. For this reason, Allah is often regarded as the first cause of creation: beginning its creation with intention and will for the benefit of humans. Muslims see evidence for the existence of Allah in their daily lives and in the world around them.

Allah is regarded as being the creator who began and is responsible for human life. All life must be respected and not taken advantage of. The world and its resources belong to Allah and are a gift to humans. Human life, in this respect, is one of these gifts.

> **Surah 3:6**
>
> *He it is Who shapes you in the wombs as He pleases. There is no god but He, the Exalted in Might, the Wise.*

Allah intervening in the world

Muslims believe Allah may appear in the world today in many ways, seen and unseen. Allah is omnipotent and is capable of performing miracles for the benefit of humans if deemed appropriate.

> **Surah 2.117**
>
> *'To Him is due the primal origin of the heavens and the earth. When He decreeth a matter he saith to it: "Be" and it is.'*

What did Muhammad ﷺ teach about the nature of Allah?

While Muhammad ﷺ was teaching, he was once asked to perform a miracle by making a spring come out of the ground. He responded:

> **Surah 17:93**
>
> *Glory to my Lord! Am I aught but a man – an apostle?*

It was clear to the people that, if Muhammad ﷺ was claiming to have a message from God, he should perform a miracle to show that God had chosen him for this purpose. His response is clear: he is human and cannot perform miracles. He often repeated that he was just a man and miracles should not be expected of him. In Islam, it is clear that Allah is omnipotent, and miracles can be seen through creation itself and Allah's revelation of the Qur'an to Muhammad ﷺ.

ACTIVITIES

How do Muslims believe Allah intervenes in the world?

ACTIVITIES

For what reasons might miracles not be regarded as central and important in Islam?

ACTIVITIES

Muhammad ﷺ did not perform miracles but his message was believed. What other strengths did he have that convinced people to believe in his message?

Judaism: Belief about deity

The next two pages will help you to:

- explain Jewish beliefs about G-d
- evaluate the importance of believing that G-d can intervene in the world to help humans, i.e. miracles.

What do Jews believe about G-d?

Jews are monotheists. They believe there is only one G-d who is unlike anything else that exists. This key belief that there is only one G-d is stated in one of the central Jewish prayers – **the Shema**.

> **Deuteronomy 6:4–9**
>
> *Hear, O Israel! The Lord is our G-d, the Lord alone. You shall love the Lord your G-d with all your heart and with all your soul and with all your might. Take to heart these instructions with which I charge you this day. Impress them upon your children. Recite them when you stay at home and when you are away, when you lie down and when you get up. Bind them as a sign on your hand and let them serve as a symbol on your forehead; inscribe them on the doorposts of your house and on your gates.*

The Shema.

Jews also believe that:

- G-d is eternal. G-d has no physical body and is everywhere at all times.
- G-d is the creator of the world and has a purpose for the world.
- G-d is completely good and completely loving.
- G-d has given commandments as to how people should treat each other.
- G-d is **omnipotent** and **omniscient**.
- G-d will judge everyone.
- G-d is the creator of everything in existence.

> **Genesis 22:17–18**
>
> *I will bestow My blessing upon you and make your descendants as numerous as the stars of heaven and the sands on the seashore; and your descendants shall seize the gates of their foes. All the nations of the earth shall bless themselves by your descendants, because you have obeyed My command.*

Why Jews believe in G-d

The ultimate truth about the G-d of the Jews is found in the Jewish Scriptures, in particular in the **Torah**.

The Jews believe that they have a special relationship with G-d because of the agreements or 'covenants' G-d made with the Patriarchs: Adam, Noah, Abraham and Moses. According to the Torah, Abraham made a covenant with G-d that he and his whole family would worship G-d and no other god. In return, G-d would look after Abraham's family and descendants forever.

Although there are many occasions in the Bible where the Jews break this agreement, G-d always forgives them and this special relationship continues.

 RESEARCH NOTE

The text above is about just one of the covenants G-d made with Abraham. Find out about two more of the covenants G-d made with the Patriarchs Adam, Noah and Moses, and two more covenants that G-d made with Abraham.

The actions of G-d in the world

There are two ways in which Jews believe G-d intervenes in the world:

- through the words of the prophets
- by performing miracles.

The words of the prophets

The Jewish scriptures are in three parts: Torah (Law), Nevi'im (Prophets) and Ketuvim (Writings) (see p. 138).

The prophets were people chosen by G-d to warn the Israelites what would happen if they did not follow G-d's teachings and laws. In the Nevi'im there are books by the prophets:

Amos	Hosea	Joel	Nahum
Ezekiel	Isaiah	Jonah	Obadiah
Habbakuk	Jeremiah	Micah	Zephaniah

Some of these prophets told the people that they would be punished for breaking G-d's laws; others talked about the eventual coming of a time of peace when everyone will live according to G-d's laws.

Micah's prophecy

> **Micah 4:1–4**
>
> *In the days to come,*
> *The Mount of the Lord's House shall stand*
> *Firm above the mountains;*
> *And it shall tower above the hills.*
> *The peoples shall gaze on it with joy,*
> *And the many nations shall go and shall say:*
> *'Come,*
> *Let us go up to the Mount of the Lord,*
> *To the House of the G-d of Jacob;*
> *That He may instruct us in His ways,*
>
> *And that we may walk in His paths.'*
> *For instruction shall come forth from Zion,*
> *The word of the Lord from Jerusalem.*
> *Thus He will judge among the many peoples,*
> *And arbitrate for the multitude of nations,*
> *However distant;*
> *And they shall beat their swords into ploughshares*
> *And their spears into pruning hooks.*
> *Nation shall not take up*
> *Sword against nation;*
> *They shall never again know war.*

G-d performing miracles

Many people understand miracles as G-d's intervention in the world. For Jews there are many miracles in the Torah, particularly when G-d intervenes to save the Israelites. In the book of the Exodus (the second book of the Torah), there are stories of Moses and a stick which turned into a snake, of a bush which was on fire but did not burn, of the ten plagues of Egypt, of the parting of the Red Sea so that the Israelites could cross safely and of food and water which G-d produced for the believers while they were living in the desert for 40 years.

Many Jews believe that the accounts of these miracles must be true because they are in the Torah, which is the word of G-d. However, some people say that G-d would not create something as complex as the universe, set up the physical laws by which it operates and then just break those laws. This does not mean that G-d *could* not break the laws but that G-d *would* not. But why do there not appear to be any miracles today? And why does G-d not perform miracles to help everyone who needs them? If G-d does perform miracles then why does G-d pick and choose – this seems unfair? These questions are often asked today.

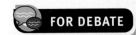

FOR DEBATE

What would you consider to be a miracle? How could you know if it was a real miracle? If you thought a real miracle had happened to one person who needed it but not to someone else in the same position, what would that make you think about G-d?

ACTIVITIES

'If G-d loved people so much, G-d would not make so many rules for them.'

Give reasons to support this view and reasons against it, as well as giving your own view.

Sikhism:
Belief about deity 1

The next two pages will help you to:

- express understanding of what Sikhs believe about God
- explain what this belief about God means for Sikhs.

> *But ask forgiveness of your Lord, and turn into Him (in repentance): for my Lord is indeed full of mercy and loving-kindness.*

Surah 11.90 (Islam)

> *Hear, O Israel! The Lord is our G-d, the Lord alone! You shall love the Lord your G-d with all your heart and with all your soul and with all your might.*

The Shema (Judaism)

AO1+AO2 skills ACTIVITIES

- Write down two reasons why some people believe in God.
- Write down two reasons why some people do not believe in God.
- Can we prove whether God exists? Write down your thoughts.
- Compare your answers with three pupils in your class.

> **Sikhs believe that God has no form. Importantly, the Sikh Gurus are the messengers who impart knowledge of the divine to Sikhs.**

AO1 skills ACTIVITIES

Many religious books agree on many characteristics about God such as a Creator. Read what these extracts from the Qur'an and the Shema say about God and also think of your own ideas about God. Make a list of all the characteristics and conceptions of God or deities and then write down why you think they are important for theists (people who believe in the existence of a God). For example, God as a creator which could mean that God has a purpose for human life.

God is immanent within our hearts

Belief in a personal God is central to the beliefs of a Sikh and is found in the Guru Granth Sahib Ji and the teachings of the human Gurus. One of the most popular terms to refer to God in Sikh religious literature is **Waheguru** – Wonderful Lord.

Essentially, Waheguru is without gender, so there are no pictures or statues of God in Sikhism. This enables God to be **nirguna** – without form and gender. However, God becomes **saguna** – appears through creation, especially within the hearts of human beings.

Sikhs believe in the supremacy and **omnipotent** nature of God. The nirguna and saguna aspects of Waheguru make God both **transcendent** (beyond human comprehension) and **immanent** (in the hearts of humans) for Sikhs. The attributes and qualities of God are found in the important Sikh prayer, the **Mool Mantar**, which also forms the opening words of the Guru Granth Sahib Ji.

Mool Mantar

> **Guru Granth Sahib Ji, page 1**
>
> *There is only One God,*
> *Truth is His Name,*
> *He is the Creator,*
> *He is Without Fear,*
> *He is Without Hate,*
> *He is Timeless and Without Form,*
> *He is Beyond Death, the Enlightened One,*
> *He can be known By the Guru's Grace.*

A personal loving relationship with God, also known as **bhakti**, is essential in Sikh philosophy. The immanence of God for Sikhs means that there are very few rituals as these are not needed. The believer's love for God is often depicted in Sikh teachings as the bride's love for her groom. In Sikh teachings, the whole of humanity (male and female) is described as the 'bride' of God, emphasising once again that Waheguru is beyond gender.

Many scholars believe the concept of God in Sikhism to have been influenced by the Northern Sant Tradition. This tradition emphasised the immanence of God in all beings and placed importance on experiencing God through mystical experiences and music.

> **Guru Granth Sahib Ji, page 663**
> *Thousands are thine forms, yet Thou hast not even one.*

RESEARCH NOTE

Find out more about the similarities between Sikhism and the Northern Sant Tradition of India.

AO1 skills **ACTIVITIES**

The Mool Mantar, composed by Guru Nanak Dev Ji, describes the basic belief in God for all Sikhs.

In your own words, summarise the Sikh concept of God as described in the Mool Mantar.

AO2 skills **ACTIVITIES**

Think/pair/share

- In pairs, discuss your answers to the above exercise. What points do you agree and disagree on?
- 'Surely there must be a difference in different religions' perception of God, otherwise we would all have one shared universal religion?' Discuss this idea with a partner and then share your answers with the class.

Sikhism: Belief about deity 2

The next two pages will help you to:

- explain how Sikhs support their belief in God
- explore how their beliefs affect attitudes towards miracles
- express and evaluate your own ideas and make links between these beliefs and attitudes to miracles and what you think/ believe.

Guru Gobind Singh Ji instructed that after his death the Guru Granth Sahib Ji would become the eternal Guru of the Sikhs.

How do Sikhs support their belief in God?

Sikhs justify their belief in God by referring to the teachings contained in the Guru Granth Sahib Ji. The Guru Granth Sahib Ji repeatedly reminds Sikhs to love God through bhakti. Sikhs believe that the saguna nature of God enables a believer to enter into a loving relationship with God. The ultimate goal in Sikhism is to achieve union with God and escape the illusion of **maya**, which causes the individual to wrongly believe that people are not dependent on God.

Since there are no images of God in Sikhism, Sikhs are encouraged to meditate on the name of God through the practice of nam japna, also referred to as **nam simran**. Through this practice Sikhs meditate on either Waheguru (The Wonderful One) or Satnam (The True Name) as the two most frequently used names for God in Sikhism. The name of God is constantly repeated and occasionally beads can be used.

The Sikh view of miracles

Sikhs differ widely in their attitudes towards miracles, but are generally discouraged from believing in them.

Here is one well-known story of a miracle in Sikhism.

ACTIVITIES

- Imagine you have been commissioned by the Sikh Missionary Society to enable young children to understand the concept of God in Sikhism. How would you go about producing a pamphlet in which your task is to explain and ensure that young children can appreciate the idea that God has no form and yet is immanent?

- The children have also been learning about miracles in school. How are you now going to teach them about the Sikh attitude towards miracles?

A poor man, named Lalo, invited Guru Nanak Dev Ji to a meal. A rich man, Malik Bhago, also invited Guru Nanak Dev Ji to dinner the same evening. Bhago was annoyed that Guru Nanak Dev Ji had accepted the poor man's invitation over his own. Guru Nanak Dev Ji took bread – roti – from the home of each man. He squeezed the roti in each hand. From Lalo's bread came forth milk, to show his food had been earned by honest means; from Bhago's bread came forth blood, to show his meal had been earned by the exploitation of his servants.

This story highlights important notions about ritual purity and pollution attached to food during the time in which Guru Nanak lived. People at that time would not take cooked food from lower castes due to fear of becoming 'polluted'. Guru Nanak taught that one's caste is irrelevant when eating together. He taught that all human beings are equal. The practice of langar in a Sikh **gurdwara** carries this message on to the present day (see Topic 2).

Does Waheguru intervene in the world through miracles?

Sikhs believe that the creation of the universe is a miracle from Waheguru. They also believe that God will intervene in the lives of devotees in times of need and in response to prayer.

Sikhs believe that everything happens in accordance with the Will (hukam) of Waheguru and Waheguru's Grace (nadar) will be offered in response to unconditional love from the believer. You cannot be a true Sikh without having belief in the supremacy of God in all matters. To this effect, a Sikh will wear a kara (steel bracelet) to affirm belief in the one eternal Waheguru.

ACTIVITIES

Collect a number of articles from newspapers or from the Internet that show the possible working of miracles in our day-to-day lives. Working in pairs, produce a poster to show how both theists and atheists would respond to the idea that miracles may be a possible explanation for extraordinary events. What are your own opinions about the events you have described?

FOR DEBATE

- Do you think Guru Nanak Dev Ji wanted people to believe he was a miracle-maker, or is this just a story with an important underlying message? Explain your answer in detail.
- Generally Sikhs are discouraged from believing in miracles. Why do you think this is so? Share your thoughts with a partner.

GradeStudio

AO1

QUESTION

Explain Sikh beliefs about God.　　　[6 marks]

You could build an answer like this:

Level 1

First, let the examiner know that you are aware what the question is about. For example, 'Fundamental to Sikh belief is the existence of a Supreme God as contained in the Mool Mantar'.

Level 2

Next go on to explain in detail the importance of both the impersonal (nirguna) and personal (saguna) aspects of God. You might include here a discussion of the importance of the immanence of God within the hearts of human beings. A detailed analysis could be undertaken of the meaning of the words of the Mool Mantar.

Level 3

Finally, explain how God intervenes in the lives of devotees who love God unconditionally. You could also develop here the underlying importance of God's will (hukam) and God's grace (nadar) as supporting a Sikh's belief in God.

GradeStudio

Welcome to the Grade Studio

Grade Studio is here to help you improve your grades by working through typical questions you might find on an examination paper. You will see different answers to the questions, showing you how you can improve each answer to get a better grade.

How the grades work: OCR questions in Spec B always consist of five parts, a)–e). Parts a)–c) test factual recall only (AO1 skill). Part d) is always a six-mark question testing understanding (AO1), and part e) is always a 12-mark question testing evaluation and personal response (AO2 skills).

For parts a)–c), you just need to revise the material for the Topic and make sure that you know it thoroughly – Grade Studio cannot help you with this!

However, for parts d) and e) you need to structure your answers to show your skills – and this is where you can use the Grade Studio to help you improve your answers.

Examiners use levels to measure the responses (these are marked in the answers below). You can find a full description of the levels examiners will use to mark your answers on p. x and xi.

> **AO1 Skills**
> Describe, explain and analyse, using knowledge and understanding of the specification content.
>
> **AO2 Skills**
> Use evidence and reasoned argument to express and evaluate personal responses, informed insights and differing viewpoints.

AO1

Question

Explain why Christians believe in God.

[6 marks]

Student's answer

Christians believe in God because this is the teaching they find in the Bible, which is the main source of belief and teachings for Christians. Some Christians might also believe in God because they believe that miracles happened in the past in the Bible and continue to happen in the present. This includes miracles at places like Lourdes, where sick people go to be healed. Some Christians say that they believe in God because they have prayed to God and their prayers have been answered.

Examiner's comment

The candidate has given a satisfactory answer to the question. There are several relevant points but only one of them, the miracles at Lourdes, is explained in any detail. The answer needs to give more information and examples in order to reach Level 3. The candidate could also use more technical terms from the specification to show the breadth of their knowledge and understanding.

Student's improved answer

Christians believe in God because this is the teaching they find in the Bible, which is the main source of belief and teachings for Christians. Some Christians might also believe in God because they believe that miracles happened in the past in the Bible and continue to happen in the present. This includes miracles at places like Lourdes, where sick people go to be healed.

Examiner's comment

This is now a competent answer to the question. The candidate has shown a clear understanding of the question. There is good description and explanation of a variety of different reasons why Christians might believe in God.

Student's improved answer (cont.)

Some Christians say that they believe in God because they have prayed to God and their prayers have been answered. Some people might also say that, even if their prayers are not answered, it still shows that God has listened but knows that in a particular circumstance what is being asked for is not good for the person.

Another reason Christians might give for why they believe in God is because they may have special feelings during worship that bring them closer to God. This is sometimes called a feeling of 'numinous'. They might also believe in God because they share the same beliefs as the rest of their family and their local community. Also, some people might believe that the arguments for the existence of God prove that God does exist.

Examiner's comment

The candidate has shown some analysis in dealing with the question of answered and unanswered prayers. The information is presented clearly and there is good use of technical terms.

AO2

Question

'If God existed, we would know it.' Discuss this statement. You should include different, supported points of view and a personal viewpoint. You must refer to Christianity in your answer. **[12 marks]**

Student's answer

Christians might say that they do know that God exists because they can see God's work all around them in the world. Some Christians might also say that they know God exists because God sometimes answers their prayers and they know people who have been made better after people have prayed for them.

Some people, on the other hand, might think that because of the amount of suffering, disease and poverty in the world, there cannot be a God and if there is one then God is not a good God.

My personal opinion is that there is not enough evidence either way to decide whether God exists or not. There are some events, such as miracles, that suggest that God does exist while other things like the Boxing Day Tsunami seem to suggest that there is no God.

So God may exist, but I do not believe that we can 'know' this – it is a matter of faith.

Examiner's comment

This is a competent answer to the question. The candidate has shown a clear understanding of the question and has presented a range of views supported by evidence and argument. The answer explains Christian views, among others, and includes a personal viewpoint, which is also supported.

These specimen answers provide an outline of how you could construct your response. Space does not allow us to give a full response. The examiner will be looking for more detail in your actual exam responses.

These examples only use Christianity but you could use the Grade Studio to apply to any of the religions you are studying and the structure of the answers would work in the same way.

Topic 2: Religious and spiritual experience

The Big Picture

In this Topic, you will be addressing religious beliefs and teachings about:

- the place and nature of private and public worship
- the concepts of prayer and meditation
- the place of fasting and food.

You will also think about ways in which these beliefs affect the life and outlook of believers in the world today.

What?

You will:

- develop your knowledge and understanding of key beliefs and ideas about religious experience
- explain what these beliefs and ideas mean to people of different faiths, and think about how they might affect how they live
- make links between these beliefs and ideas and what you think/believe.

Why?

Because:

- these beliefs and ideas underpin and are reflected in the ways many people live their lives: for example, in helping them to make moral choices
- understanding people's beliefs can help you understand why they think and act in the way they do
- understanding these beliefs helps you compare and contrast what others believe, including thinking about your own beliefs and ideas.

How?

By:

- recalling and selecting information about religious beliefs and ideas about worship, meditation, food and fasting, explaining their importance for people today
- thinking about the relevance of these beliefs in 21st-century Britain
- evaluating your own views about these beliefs.

Many secular (non-religious) activities have things in common with religious practices. Think of a hobby, a sport or other leisure activity you enjoy. What activities do you do on your own or with others? What special things do you have to show that you support that interest?

Odd one out
Which is the odd one out and why?

Many believers see God in the beauty of the world.

Religious and spiritual experience

What is meant by worship? Is there any point to worship if there is no one to pray to?

KEY INFORMATION

The concept of worship

Worship is a feature of all religions. It is the expression of reverence shown to a deity. Members of all the major religions worship both privately in their homes and communally in specially designed buildings. Worship in the different religions has many features in common. It usually includes prayer or meditation and may feature music and singing, readings from a sacred text and a talk or sermon from a religious leader.

The use and significance of symbolism in worship

- Although Buddhists do not believe in a creator God, and do not worship the Buddha they do take part in worship. Buddhists may bow three times, with their forehead touching the floor, before the image in a temple or shrine representing the Buddha, **dhamma** and the sangha (community). Candles symbolise the light of the Buddha's teachings. Incense reminds them of the sweetness of the Buddha's teachings.

- Many Christians kneel to pray, symbolising humility and respect to God. Symbols used in worship vary between Christian groups. Most Christians share bread and wine to recall the body and blood of Jesus when they celebrate the **Eucharist** (also known as Mass or Holy Communion).

- Many Hindus believe that worshipping God is a route to **moksha**, an escape from the cycle of birth and rebirth that means becoming absorbed into the Universal Spirit. The form worship takes may vary.

- The Five Pillars are central to the life of a Muslim and are **ibadah**, acts of worship. The prayer positions symbolise submission to the will of Allah.

- For Jews, the **Torah** is at the centre of worship in the synagogue. It is carried round the synagogue and people touch it as a sign of their love and respect for G-d's Law.

- For Sikhs, the Guru Granth Sahib Ji is at the centre of their worship and represents the physical embodiment of the **Guru**.

The use and significance of art, music and drama in worship

Art is a feature in many religious buildings. Paintings, sculptures and stained glass help to remind people that they are in a special building. In Christianity, Buddhism and Hinduism there may be statues or images to remind people of God. Jews and Muslims do not have any images of people or animals. While art and architecture are very important in Islam, music is not. However Buddhists chant, Christians and Jews sing hymns and Psalms, and the Sikh scriptures are sung to the accompaniment of musical instruments, kirtan. Evangelical churches may include a lot of singing and dancing.

The concepts of prayer and meditation

- Christians talk to God through prayer privately and when they worship together. The most famous prayer is the Lord's Prayer, taught by Jesus. Church services often have a time of silence for people to have their own thoughts and prayers.

KEY QUESTIONS

KNOWLEDGE AND UNDERSTANDING
Describe the key features of worship in two religions you have studied. What are the similarities and what are the differences?

ANALYSIS AND EVALUATION
'God can be worshipped anywhere so there's no need for religious buildings.' Do you agree? Explain the reasons for your views.

- Buddhists practise some form of meditation to attain calm and insight, to accept the world as it is and to stop craving.

- For Hindus, prayer is an important means of escape from the cycle of rebirth. Some Hindus meditate by repeating the name of God. Meditation helps them feel close to God.

- Muslims pray five times a day – **salah** – as the Qur'an requires. They may pray anywhere that is clean and must be clean themselves. Washing before prayer is called **wudu**.

- Jews have set prayers for different times of day. The **Shema** is said when they get up and when they go to bed.

- For Sikhs, prayer is part of group and private worship. Meditation on the name of God – **nam simram** – is important even in the middle of busy lives.

The place of food and fasting in different religions

In some religions, special foods are used in worship to represent a religious idea. Sharing food brings people together and special food is eaten at festivals and celebrations. Some people think fasting helps them to think about God and less about their own needs.

- Some Buddhists are vegetarians; others may give up meat or fast for short periods to make their minds clearer for meditation. Lay people gain good **kamma** by donating food to the **bhikkhus**.

- Many Christians share bread and wine when they celebrate the Eucharist, Mass or Holy Communion, as the body and blood of Jesus. Many Christians give up special treats during Lent to remind them of the suffering of Jesus.

- For Muslims, sawm is one of the Five Pillars. Muslims fast from just before dawn to sunset during the month of Ramadan.

- Many Hindus do not eat meat because they believe in **ahimsa** – doing no harm. The cow is sacred to Hindus. Many Hindus fast on holy days.

- Jewish food laws are very important. Food is sometimes used to remind them of important events in their history: for example, the symbolic foods on the Seder plate. Jews fast several times during the year. The most important day of fasting is Yom Kippur when Jews fast for 25 hours.

- Sikhs share a sweet mixture – **karah parshad** – at the end of worship as a sign that all are equal before God. Volunteers serve a free vegetarian meal – the langar – after worship.

FOR INTEREST Stained glass is often used in churches and synagogues to make the buildings beautiful and help create an atmosphere for worship. Go to the education > schools part of the CUBE (Centre for the Urban Built Environment) website to find out about the Signs and Symbols project where a group of Manchester primary school children worked with artists to design their own stained-glass windows.

Buddhism:
Religious and spiritual experience 1

The next two pages will help you to:

- explain the role of worship for Buddhists
- understand how Buddhists worship.

Buddhists do not believe in a creator God, so what is the point of worship?

 ACTIVITIES

Think/Pair/Share
Think about what the purpose of worship is. Share your ideas with a partner and then as a class. Think about how the ideas you have explored might apply to Buddhism.

MUST THINK ABOUT!

You must think about explaining why Buddhists worship, since this can be very different from other religious traditions.

 ACTIVITIES

Create a mind map or chart showing which elements of Buddhist worship might be connected to the different reasons Buddhists give for worship.

Worship for Buddhists

Most people hearing the word worship would assume this referred to an act designed to praise a God. Since in Buddhism there is no creator God, there must be another purpose to worship.

On the surface, Buddhist worship might appear similar to many other acts of worship and particularly to those in Hinduism. However, the meaning given to these acts is different. Not all Buddhists see the importance of worship in the same way, but here are some of the most common reasons Buddhists give for worshipping:

- to develop generosity
- to remind me that **nibbana** can be achieved
- to show respect for the Buddha
- to try and develop the qualities the Buddha had
- to help remember Buddhist teachings.

 RESEARCH NOTE

You could research the differences between worship in different Buddhist traditions, to give you examples to use in the exam.

How do Buddhists worship?

Buddhists do not have a set day, time or place for worship, nor are there set practices. Buddhist worship in a Zen monastery in Japan might look very different to that taking place in a Tibetan monastery, or at a shrine in Thailand. Some Buddhists may meditate without any aids to help them; others use elaborately decorated shrines to help them focus. Also, although some Buddhists may worship at a vihara (a Buddhist monastery) on festival days or other special occasions, it is not usual for the laity (unordained members of the Buddhist religion) to go to a set building to worship regularly. Most lay Buddhists will worship at home, often using a shrine.

The pattern of worship using a shrine is similar in a vihara or at home, though in a vihara the monks or **bhikkhus** will usually perform the main actions while the laity watch. Before entering the shrine room, shoes will be removed as a sign of respect. The worshipper may greet the Buddharupa or image of the Buddha by prostrating themselves, bowing or kneeling, or placing their hands together in front of their chest and bowing slightly. These are all ways to show respect to the Buddha.

Gifts may be offered to the Buddha, which may include light in the form of candles, food, flowers, and incense. In some Mahayana Buddhist traditions, seven offerings are made in small bowls to represent the seven things that would be provided for an honoured guest (drinking water, washing water for the feet, perfumed bath water, flowers, food, incense and light). These offerings help develop generosity and compassion.

Chants or readings from the scriptures may be said to remind worshippers of the Buddha's teachings. In a vihara, a bhikkhu might give a talk explaining the Buddha's teachings. The worshippers will meditate, often using the Buddharupa, or other symbolic elements of the shrine, to help them focus on specific ideas or qualities.

A Buddhist shrine has many symbolic items.

FOR DEBATE

- Do you think there is any point to worship if there is no one to pray to?
- Could Buddhist worship lead to Buddhists worshipping the Buddha, instead of following his example and teachings?

Item	Symbolism
Buddharupa	May remind Buddhists that nibbana can be achieved. Could help Buddhists remember the Buddha's teachings. Might aid Buddhists in trying to follow the Buddha's example.
Candles	A symbol of the light and truth contained in the Buddha's teachings. A reminder of anicca and the ever-changing nature of life.
Flowers	A reminder of samsara: life is born, lives a short while, dies and is reborn.
Incense	To involve all the senses in worship. The sweet smell symbolises the sweetness of the Buddha's teachings.
Offerings	Way of showing respect to the Buddha. The action of giving helps develop compassion and generosity.

Buddhism:
Religious and spiritual experience 2

The next two pages will help you to:

- analyse the importance of meditation in Buddhism
- explore the importance of food and fasting in Buddhism.

Why is meditation so important in Buddhism?

Meditation is perhaps the defining feature of Buddhism. Although there are many different meditation practices across different Buddhist schools, every tradition practises some form of meditation.

This is because the main focus in Buddhism is trying to change the way in which people see and think about the world. The Buddha believed that people suffered because they were constantly craving for more. They might crave material goods, like televisions, or more time with someone who died, or less time with someone they did not like – but they were never satisfied. The Buddha taught that, in order to prevent **dukkha**, people needed to accept the world as it was, and stop craving.

These ideas are explained in the Buddha's teaching of the Four Noble Truths.

RESEARCH NOTE

Find out more about the eightfold path, especially the aspects which relate to meditation.

AO2 skills **ACTIVITIES**

With a partner, create a list of the benefits that meditation brings to Buddhists. With your partner, rank these in order of importance. Be prepared to explain to someone else why you chose this order.

First Noble Truth	Second Noble Truth	Third Noble Truth	Fourth Noble Truth
There is dukkha	Dukkha is caused by craving	Dukkha can be stopped	The way to stop dukkha is by following the middle path, or the eightfold path

AO1 skills **ACTIVITIES**

Close your eyes for a few minutes and listen to all the sounds being made around you. When you concentrated, did you notice sounds that you do not normally notice?

Mandalas are often used as a focus for meditation in Buddhism, different colours and images helping Buddhists focus on different meditative themes.

In Buddhism, meditation is used to help change attitudes to ensure that craving is reduced or eliminated. Buddhists who find it hard to be compassionate might practise the metta meditation, projecting compassion towards others. Those who find themselves too attached to food might meditate on the bodily processes involved in digesting food. Chants or coloured discs can be used as a focus, as can a Buddharupa. Whatever practices are used, all aim to change the attitude of the mind, so enlightenment can be achieved.

Food and fasting in Buddhism

Unlike many other religious traditions, there are no set festivals celebrated by all Buddhists across the world. Most Buddhists may celebrate Wesak, which remembers the Buddha's birth, death and enlightenment. However, other festivals are unique to the country of origin – for example, the Festival of the Tooth in Sri Lanka. There are therefore no set food rules in relation to Buddhist festivals. Each festival will reflect the foods and expectations of the culture in which it originated, rather than anything distinctively Buddhist.

There are however other areas of Buddhism in which food does play a role.

The alms round

In most Theravadan Buddhist countries, the bhikkhus will go on an alms round to collect food early in the morning. They will walk round the village or town with a bowl, and the laity will place food in the bowl. For the bhikkhus, accepting whatever food is offered shows that they are seeing food as sustenance, and not craving particular tastes. For the laity, offering food to the bhikkhus allows them to practise generosity, and to gain good kamma.

In most Mahayana countries the monasteries are too large for the alms round to be practical, so the laity might donate food to the monastery, or work for the monastery producing food for the bhikkhus.

Fasting

In some Buddhist traditions, fasting is used as a spiritual discipline. The Buddha taught that Buddhists should follow a middle path and eat enough to stay healthy: having found for himself that extreme fasting did not stop dukkha. However, Buddhists sometimes fast for short periods. This may be because they feel too attached to food and wish to lose this greed. In some cases, it is believed that fasting for short periods can cleanse the mind and body of attachments, and allow deeper levels of meditation.

Are all Buddhists vegetarian?

It is a common misconception that all Buddhists are vegetarian. The Buddhist teaching of **ahimsa** or non-harming encourages Buddhists to avoid harm to all living creatures. However, this is simply not practical in all Buddhist countries due to the economic or farming climate. Since the Buddha taught the middle path, most Buddhists feel that it is acceptable to eat meat or fish when there is no practical alternative.

AO2

QUESTION

'Everyone should thank the gods for their food.' Discuss this statement. You should include different, supported points of view and a personal viewpoint. You must refer to Buddhism in your answer. **[12 marks]**

In an AO2 question like this you must make sure you include Buddhist views in your answer, as well as your own viewpoint. You could build an answer like this:

Level 1

At a basic level, you might refer to the limited status of the gods, say that Buddhists do not worship the gods in the same ways as other religions, and therefore they may not thank the gods at all.

Level 4

A good response might show awareness of the difference between Buddhist groups. It might explain that some Buddhists might have asked the gods for help with their crops and might therefore thank them for their food. On the other hand, some Buddhists may not believe in the gods and therefore will not ask them for help. In this case they would feel no need to thank them. A personal opinion might be that anyone who believes in a god ought to give thanks for food at every meal.

ACTIVITIES

- Design a poster showing the importance of food and fasting for Buddhists.
- Explain why there are no clear rules about food and fasting in Buddhism.

Christianity: Religious and spiritual experience 1

The next two pages will help you to:

- examine the importance of worship for a Christian, and how they worship
- evaluate the significance of religious symbols in worship.

What is worship?

When a believer honours or respects God with extreme love or devotion, they can be said to be carrying out an act of worship.

Public worship

Most Christians worship in a holy building, usually called a church. Some have different names: for example, Quakers (the Religious Society of Friends) worship in a Meeting House. All Christian places of worship are designed to help a believer to praise God communally or corporately.

The most common form of worship is the **Eucharist** (meaning 'giving thanks'), also known as Holy Communion, Mass or the Lord's Supper. It takes the form of sharing bread and wine as Jesus did with his disciples at the Last Supper the day before his death.

> **1 Corinthians 11:23b–26**
>
> *The Lord Jesus, on the night he was betrayed, took bread, and when he had given thanks, he broke it and said, 'This is my body, which is for you; do this in remembrance of me.' In the same way, after supper he took the cup, saying, 'This cup is the new covenant in my blood; do this, whenever you drink it, in remembrance of me.' For whenever you eat this bread and drink this cup, you proclaim the Lord's death until he comes.*

Other forms of public worship include: hymns (prayers set to music); Bible readings, a sermon (a talk given by the vicar or priest); and prayers (when a believer talks to God).

Some Christian denominations worship without formal songs or readings; others may worship together in silence, or speak, as they feel moved to. Evangelical churches may include a lot of singing, dancing and interactive participation.

Private worship

Some Christians put aside a daily 'quiet time' to study a Bible passage, either individually, in the family or in study groups. Prayer is another form of private worship. Individual prayer might focus on more personal issues than prayer said during public services.

 **AO1+AO2** skills **ACTIVITIES**

In pairs
Make a list of the different ways respect can be shown to another person.

Compare your list with a partner and between you make a list of your 'top ten' ways.

AO1 skills **ACTIVITIES**

Visit the Places of Worship section on the Know Britain website and choose three popular hymns that you feel show how Christians worship God. Make a note of key ideas and important lines.

Religious symbols in Christianity

Religious symbols were originally used as a code in the early Church as believers were often persecuted (punished for their beliefs). Today, these symbols are used to help Christians focus on key beliefs and worship God. However, some denominations, such as Quakers, feel that symbols are distracting and prefer to worship in plain surroundings.

REMEMBER THIS

Check back on the features and shape of a traditional church from your work in KS3.

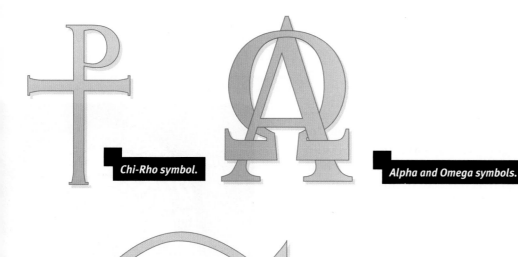

Chi-Rho symbol.

Alpha and Omega symbols.

Icthus symbol.

The most important symbols for Christians are the crucifix (a cross with Jesus hanging on it) and cross, seen on places of worship or worn by a believer. Crucifixes remind Christians of the death of Jesus and his sacrifice, while the empty cross is a celebration of the fact that Jesus defeated sin by rising from the dead.

Another common symbol is the Chi-Rho, made of the first two letters of the Greek word 'Christ'.

The Alpha and Omega is also taken from the Greek alphabet, using the first and last letters. This reminds Christians that God was first in the world (as the Creator) and will be the last in the world (as judge).

Early Christians, afraid of persecution by the Romans, used the fish symbol – ICTHUS – as a secret symbol. The letters show that Christians believe in 'Jesus Christ God's Son Saviour'. The three points also remind Christians of the **Trinity**.

Other symbols may be seen in different places of worship:

- images of Mary with the baby Jesus
- Mary as an intercessor (go-between) on behalf of humans
- Jesus as a caring Good Shepherd
- the dove is sometimes used to represent peace
- icons – pictures of Jesus, Mary and the saints – used as an aid to worship.

NEXT STEP

Look at an aerial photograph of a traditional church. Describe the shape and explain its importance.

Christianity: Religious and spiritual experience 2

The next two pages will help you to:

- analyse how art and music can be used to express belief about God
- investigate the use and power of prayer in worship
- evaluate the use of food and fasting as an aid to worship.

Art and music in Christian worship

Some churches use a lot of art. Probably the most common form is stained-glass windows, originally designed to tell stories from the Bible at a time when many people could not read. Today they remind a believer of the light given by God. In the Middle Ages, paintings might also be found on the walls of a church and these were based on subjects such as the Day of Judgement.

Icons of Christian figures are also common in some traditions, such as Orthodox and Roman Catholic, but some groups feel they might encourage idolatry (worshipping the images or idols themselves, instead of God) and do not use them.

Some Christians believe that music is a way of praising and thanking God. Prayers can be sung, and in some Orthodox churches the whole service can be chanted. Organ music often accompanies hymns. Evangelical church services may include spontaneous music, but some traditions prefer silent or spoken worship.

What is prayer?

Prayer is a solemn appeal to God, said privately or publicly. A prayer can be offered for many reasons: to ask for something; to give thanks; as a form of meditation; or as a formal set response to God, as in the Lord's Prayer. This prayer was taught by Jesus to his followers and can be used in a service, or as a basis for private prayer.

What does the Lord's Prayer mean to Christians?

Our Father, who art in heaven, hallowed be thy name.
Praises God and gives thanks ('hallowed' means made holy)
Thy kingdom come, thy will be done on earth as it is in heaven.
Asks for God's will to be done in the world
Give us this day our daily bread,
asks for help, or for God to provide in particular circumstances
And forgive us our trespasses, as we forgive those who trespass against us,
Requests forgiveness of sins (trespasses) or wrongdoings, agreeing that a Christian should be prepared to forgive the faults of others
And lead us not into temptation, but deliver us from evil.
Christians understand that they can only have their faith tested so much – and they ask God to protect them from more than they can bear
For thine is the kingdom, the power and the glory forever and ever, Amen.
Ends with praise and thanks, and an acknowledgement that God's power is everlasting.

Stained-glass windows were originally used to remind people of Bible stories and the lives of the Saints.

AO1+AO2 skills ACTIVITIES

Pair/share

- In pairs, discuss the pros and cons of praying as a part of a group, or as an individual.
- Share your ideas with another pair and build up some points on both sides of the argument.
- Have a group debate on the most effective way to pray to God.

Some Christians, especially Roman Catholics, may use a rosary (a string of beads with a crucifix hanging from them) as an aid to concentration and prayer. The beads are divided into five sets of ten by a larger bead, each set being a 'decade'.

Other Christians may prefer to pray silently and do not use a formal set of words. They prefer their prayers to be spontaneous and personal.

How do Christians use food in worship?

There are no religious laws to tell Christians what they may or may not eat. Some are vegetarian as they feel that they have a responsibility to look after the animals in the world, but many are not – they might quote from the vision of Peter, which suggests that God wants them to eat all sorts of food.

Acts 10:9–16

About noon the following day as they were on their journey and approaching the city, Peter went up on the roof to pray. He became hungry and wanted something to eat, and while the meal was being prepared, he fell into a trance. He saw heaven opened and something like a large sheet being let down to earth by its four corners. It contained all kinds of four-footed animals as well as reptiles of the earth and birds of the air. Then a voice told him, 'Get up, Peter. Kill and eat.' 'Surely not Lord!' Peter replied. 'I have never eaten anything impure or unclean.' The voice spoke to him a second time, 'Do not call anything impure that God has made clean.' This happened three times, and immediately the sheet was taken back to heaven.

Many Christians are concerned that the food they eat is not exploiting (taking advantage of) poor farmers in the developing world. They might try to buy Fairtrade products to make sure that the producers get paid fairly.

The best-known use of food in Christian worship is the bread and wine in the Eucharist (see p. 36).

The most common time for fasting is during Lent (the 40 days of preparation for Easter). Christians will often give up a particular food during this time as a way of sharing the time when Jesus was tempted in the wilderness by the Devil.

RESEARCH NOTE

Find out more about Fairtrade at the Fairtrade website.

AO1 skills ACTIVITIES

Write a letter explaining the importance of fasting for a Christian during Lent. Look at Matthew 4:1–11 to see what happened to Jesus.

AO1 skills ACTIVITIES

Using symbols, design a stained glass window for a church. Explain the meaning of the symbols and show how they might help a Christian worship God.

GradeStudio

AO2

QUESTION

'There are no advantages to fasting.' Discuss this statement. You should include different, supported points of view and a personal viewpoint. You must refer to Christianity in your answer. **[12 marks]**

You could build an answer like this:

Level 1
First, show the examiner that you understand what the question is about, and then state an opinion. For example, some Christians believe that fasting brings you closer to God.

Level 2
Next, go on to justify this point of view by referring to a religious teaching, such as 'Blessed are the poor'.

Level 3
Next, talk about the importance of Lent, when some Christians fast, and others feel it is a time when people should do something extra to help the less fortunate, not just give up treats. Give a personal view.

Level 4
Finally, go on to offer a deeper explanation of the second viewpoint, explaining more about the different Christian views about fasting. Finish by giving your own opinion and supporting it.

Hinduism: Religious and spiritual experience 1

The next two pages will help you to:

- explain the purpose and symbolism of worship for many Hindus
- look at how images, music and dance are used as part of worship.

Incense
To perfume the air and atmosphere, suitable for worship.

Water pot
To wash the deity as a symbol of washing away one's own ignorance.

Diva lamp
Fire is a symbol of eternity – used to worship by circling clockwise around the plates chosen as a focus for worship.

Fruit (or other food)
As an offering to show thanks for the food God provides for us and symbolic of the worshipper offering all they do to God.

Rice or betel nuts
A symbol of fertility, recognising the creative aspect of God, but also the need for humans to rise above sensual pleasure.

Flowers
Placed around the statue or picture as a mark of love and adoration.

Mala
Used to help a person concentrate their mind during prayer or meditation.

Bells
Rung during hymn singing and as a symbol of worship. The ringing focuses minds and worship, and absorbs distractings sounds.

Pot containing kumkum or sandalwood paste
Used to adorn the statue or picture with a tilak mark symbolising love and unity with God.

The objects used for worship at home and in the mandir represent aspects of the divine and are symbolic of the heartfelt devotion worshippers may feel.

The avatar Lord Krishna in the Bhagavad Gita 9:13–14

…the great souls, partaking of My divine nature, worship me with a single mind, knowing Me as the imperishable source of beings. Always glorifying Me, striving, firm in vows, prostrating (bowing low) before Me, they worship Me with devotion…

AO1 skill ACTIVITIES

Create a table that describes and explains the symbolism of the items detailed on the puja tray above.

Many Hindus believe that worshipping God is a route to **moksha**, an escape from the cycle of birth and rebirth that means becoming absorbed into the Supreme Spirit. The form worship takes may vary. The Bhagavad Gita states that worship may take place through four channels:

- bhakti – devotion
- **karma** – action
- jnana – academic learning
- raja – spiritual insight.

These are all types of yoga, which is sometimes misunderstood as just exercise and relaxation. Most Hindus understand yoga to be a means of becoming one with the Universal Spirit by mastering eight principles: restraint; discipline; posture; breathing; detachment; concentration, meditation and trance.

Many Hindus believe that the use of meditation helps to increase jnana and raja and therefore moksha can be achieved sooner. If the mind is focused and in tune with the divine, knowledge gained from learning will be clearer and intuition better understood.

Whether at home or in a mandir (temple), many of the main aspects of formal Hindu worship are quite similar. The most popular ritual showing bhakti is called puja, which usually involves adoration of images of the divine. A key part of puja for many Hindus is arti, an ancient and popular means of connecting with the divine, which many Hindus perform as duty and pleasure. Arti shows the belief that God is reflected in the elements. The flame also symbolises cleansing and purification of the place and the worshippers' souls.

Images, music and dance in Hindu worship

Many Hindus use murti or painted images of deities as the focus for worship. Some mandir are dedicated to particular gods or goddesses, and most families and individuals have their own preferred image(s) of God.

Formal worship usually includes singing bhajan (hymns), followed by communal and personal prayer. Most Hindus accept music and dance as forms of worship. Traditional Indian dance styles, particularly kathakali and bharat natyam, developed as a means of retelling stories from sacred texts to a largely illiterate audience; folk dances were usually set to songs in praise of the divine or particular deities. Stories from scripture may also be retold as plays or musicals.

Every autumn, many Hindus participate in the festival of Navaratri – 'Nine nights' – which is dedicated to praise of the divine as female. Dancers circle a central shrine containing images of favourite goddesses.

Most Hindus are comfortable with people depicting deities because of the key belief that the Universal Spirit is part of everything – there is a spark of the divine in all living things. Depicting a god or goddess is simply interaction with the divine, and even a sign of the regard in which the deities are held.

NEXT STEP

Choose one (or more) from the following first three principles of yoga and try to develop it over time.

- Restraint – stop yourself from doing or saying anything negative: for example, overeating, swearing
- Discipline – stay committed and purposeful: for example, be punctual and fully equipped for every lesson
- Posture – be aware of how you stand and sit: try to keep your back straight, head upright

ACTIVITIES

Create a mind map or poster that:

- describes different types of worship
- explains how each different type of worship suits different personalities, and benefits society or individual people in different ways.

Hinduism: Religious and spiritual experience 2

Prayer, meditation and other forms of worship

Not all Hindus choose to worship using imagery or ritual. Some choose to simply light a diva in recognition of the divine in the elements and nature. Others prefer to communicate with the divine just through prayer or meditation. Others show their love for God by studying the sacred texts or undertaking pilgrimage and others do so by performing acts of charity, self-sacrifice and benevolence. Most often, people who choose to follow sanatan dharma (the term many Hindus prefer for their faith) do so by incorporating some aspects from all of the above as a means of worship.

ACTIVITIES

- Which of the views in the speech balloons is closest to your own regarding what prayer actually is? Explain your view with detailed reasons and examples from your experience or from the media. Explain, using reasons and examples as above, why others may disagree with you.

The psychological need to appeal to a higher force at times of great joy or great anxiety – we just need to say 'thank you' or ask for help, even if we know there is no one actually listening

A means of communicating with the divine

A private conversation I have with God

A list of pleas and thanks that we are forced to say or listen to at school/place of worship

What is prayer?

ACTIVITIES

Choose one of the statements below and answer the following question.

- 'Meat is Murder!'
- 'Fasting is only of value if you give up everything except water – you can hardly empathise with starving people if you can eat everything except meat, fish and grains!'

Do you agree with this statement? Give reasons and evidence for your answer and try to show both sides of the argument.

You are what you eat?

Bhagavad Gita 17:8–10

The foods that increase life, purity, strength, health, joy and good appetite … are dear to sattwic (pure) people. The foods that are bitter, sour, saline, very hot or pungent are liked by rajasic (passionate) people; they produce pain, grief and disease. That which is stale, tasteless, putrid, rotten and impure, is the food liked by tamasic (ignorant) people.

Fasting

Many Hindus fast on a regular basis and the scriptural reasons for this are: to cleanse the mind, body and soul; and to show self-sacrifice. Many Hindus also believe that fasting shows solidarity with those who are starving or hungry. Some Hindus believe that the good **karma** of fasting will be paid back in the form of them finding an ideal life partner, or having healthy and long-living children.

The exact form of the fast depends upon the person fasting. Some people go to the extreme of only taking water, or just fruit and water. When this is done often or for a long period, the person fasting may be described as an ascetic. Most give up meat and fish (if eaten) and grain, and eat only fruit, vegetables, nuts, seeds and dairy products.

Vegetarianism and Hinduism

Whether a Hindu eats meat and/or fish is largely a matter of conscience and upbringing.

- Many Hindus are vegetarian because they believe that all living things have a soul. To kill without dire need or for the greater good could create bad karma.

- Some Hindus are strict followers of the principle of **ahimsa**, which means causing harm to any living thing is also an act of violence towards God.

- Traditionally, only those who needed extra energy and nutrients ate meat: for example, warriors, manual workers and labourers.

- Meat and fish are classed as rajasic foods, so some Hindus avoid them in order to attain moksha sooner.

Offering food

Many Hindus include offering sattwic (pure) food before murti or pictures of deities as part of puja (see above), then sharing it out as prashad (sacred food) among family and friends. Prashad is also distributed to worshippers and visitors after puja or aarti services at the mandir, on feast days and during festivals. Many Hindus believe that such food is blessed by God and this is what makes it prashad (as opposed to just 'food').

Offering food back to God before consuming it shows that people are grateful for it and also demonstrates love for God. Some families have the tradition of placing a portion from the main meal of the day before the family deity. Feast foods, that are especially enjoyed and therefore to be 'shared' with the divine and entail more thanks, may also be placed before the family deity.

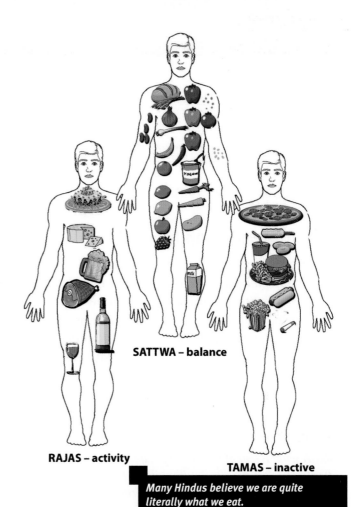

SATTWA – balance

RAJAS – activity

TAMAS – inactive

Many Hindus believe we are quite literally what we eat.

AO1 skills ACTIVITIES

Using the pictures as a guide, list at least five foods under each of these titles: sattwa (balanced); rajas (active); tamas (inactive).

Add at least three effects the different types of food may have on health and wellbeing: for example, fruit helps the immune system; alcohol causes dehydration; processed meat may have a high salt content and raise blood pressure.

Islam: Religious and spiritual experience 1

The next two pages will help you to:

- explore the concept of worship in Islam
- explain and assess the importance of Jumu'ah prayer
- evaluate and express how worship benefits the life of a Muslim.

What is worship in Islam?

The concept of worship in Islam is embedded in the term **ibadah**, which means all acts of worship that are performed with the intention to obey Allah. For Muslims, worship shows humble submission to the one true God, a total dedication to Allah, his nature and beliefs. Daily prayer and worship, in all its forms – at home, at work or in a mosque – shows a Muslim's obedience to Allah. Muslims try their utmost to remain committed to praying regularly and often. According to the Qur'an, prayer is the greatest form of worship.

> **Surah 29:45**
>
> *Recite what is sent of the Book by inspirtion to thee, and establish regular Prayer: for Prayer restrains from shameful and unjust deeds; and remembrance of Allah is the greatest (thing in life) without doubt. And Allah knows the (deeds) that ye do.*

How do Muslims worship in the mosque and at home?

There are particular requirements that must be observed before a Muslim can take part in daily prayer.

- **Wudu**, a ritual washing of hands, mouth, nose, face, arms, ears and feet must take place before prayer. A person must be mentally prepared for the prayer to come and have the correct intention or niyyah.

- Clothes must be clean and well maintained, with particular attention to modesty.

- There must be a clean place to pray, with no dust or dirt. A prayer mat is often used to ensure this.

- Worshippers must face the Ka'bah in the city of Makkah in Saudi Arabia. This direction is called the Qiblah and a special Qiblah compass can be used to determine the correct direction.

Prayer involves special movements or prostrations. These movements consist of standing (qiyam), bowing (ruku') or prostrating (sujud), with the forehead touching the clean ground or prayer mat. Special hand movements are made and words are repeated: for example, 'Allah is great' and 'Glory belongs to Allah.' A rak'ah is a unit of **salah**, made up

Muslims may use a Qiblah compass to show them the direction of the Ka'bah.

AO1+AO2 skills **ACTIVITIES**

In what way do you show your commitment to a club or organisation? Write a list of objects or items that you have which show your participation.

of recitation, standing, bowing and two prostrations. Each of the daily prayers has a certain number of rak'ahs to be completed, ranging from two to four.

Many Muslims say the daily prayers at home however, the Qur'an encourages Muslims to pray at the mosque when possible:

> **Surah 9:18**
>
> *The mosques of Allah shall be visited and maintained by such as believe in Allah and the Last Day, establish regular prayers, and practise regular charity, and fear none (at all) except Allah. It is they who are expected to be on true guidance.*

The start of prayers is signalled, from a mosque, by a mu'adhin's recitation of the call to prayer, the Adhan. On entry to the mosque, shoes are removed and wudu takes places in a dedicated washroom.

A muezzin gives the call to prayer.

Adhan

Allah is the greatest
I bear witness that there is no god but Allah
I bear witness that Muhammad ﷺ is Allah's messenger
Rush to prayer
Rush to welfare
Prayer is better than sleep [used only at salat-ul-fajr]
Allah is the greatest
There is no god but Allah

Jumu'ah prayer, or congregational prayers, on a Friday, just after the zenith, are of particular importance. During Jumu'ah prayer, a special sermon or khutbah is preached by the Imam. This is then followed by Du'a, personal prayer. The congregation may then socialise with other members of their community and give sadaqah (charity).

> **Surah 62:9**
>
> *'O ye who believe! When the call is proclaimed to prayer on Friday (the Day of Assembly), hasten earnestly to the Remembrance of Allah, and leave off business (and traffic): That is best for you if ye but knew!'*

Tawhid

Tawhid is the belief that there is only one God, Allah. Allah created the universe and Allah rules and controls everything, so all creation is connected to Allah. Some Muslims believe that this connection with Allah means that humans and the natural world reflect the nature of Allah, and that Allah unites everything. This sense of unity with Allah may be expressed through art, worship and everyday living.

REMEMBER THIS

The information about prayer in Topic 1: Belief about deity will be useful in helping you understand more about religious experience.

AO1+AO2 skills **ACTIVITIES**

Read the Adhan. In what ways would regular prayer benefit the life of a Muslim and remind them of Allah?

Islam:
Religious and spiritual experience 2

Expressing belief

Shirk

In Muslim worship, the use of pictures or images of living things, and of the prophets, is seen as idolatry. Idolatry is prohibited according to the Qur'an and Hadith. To make something of equal importance to Allah is called shirk. It is regarded as one of the most terrible sins, and it is unforgivable if the person who is committing shirk dies while still doing it.

The use of calligraphy

As an alternative to the use of idols as a way of expressing belief, mosques are often decorated with calligraphy – a way of writing words to show the beauty and meaning of the words themselves. The art of writing has great significance in Islam. In the 14th century, Muhammad ibn Mahmud-al-Amuli declared: 'Fine utterances in elegant handwriting are a pleasure to the eye, a joy to the heart and fragrance to the soul' (from *Approaches to Islam*, Richard Thames). Important mosques are often decorated with gold and brightly coloured tiles.

The role of prayer

Salah, one of the Five Pillars of Islam, is compulsory for Muslims. It consists of five daily prayers:

- Fajr – normally between dawn and sunrise
- Zuhr – normally from the zenith until mid-afternoon
- Asr – normally from mid-afternoon to before sunset
- Maghrib – normally between sunset and darkness
- Isha – night until midnight or dawn.

Why do Muslims fast?

The month of Ramadan constitutes another Pillar of Islam, sawm. As Islam follows the lunar calendar, the month for the observation of Ramadan changes each year. Muslims must fast for this month, not allowing any liquid or food to pass their mouths, and not engaging in any sexual activity, from the time of Fajr prayer at dawn until sunset.

The next two pages will help you to:

- describe how Muslims express their beliefs through the use of calligraphy
- explain and analyse how fasting in the month of Ramadan shows dedication and commitment to Allah
- evaluate and assess Muslim food laws and regulations.

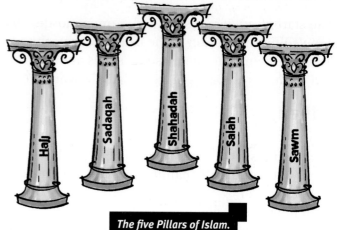

The five Pillars of Islam.

RESEARCH NOTE

Do some research in your class to find out how many people will not eat certain foods because they believe it is wrong in some way: for example, battery-reared chickens. Analyse your findings and discuss them as a class.

It is also a time of deep dedication and reflection. Muslims are expected to be the best Muslims they can be, abstaining from foul language or immoral behaviour. A special Ramadan Du'a is recited during the day, and as much time as possible is spent at the mosque. If the fast is broken on purpose, it must be made up at a different time and a specific penalty or fidyah must be made.

> **Surah 2:183**
>
> *O you who believe! Fasting is prescribed to you as it was prescribed to those before you that ye may (learn) self-restraint.*

When sunset approaches, Muslims prepare themselves for the end of the fast, called 'fast breaking' or iftar. Muslims try to end the fast among friends or family or at the mosque, ending the day by first eating a date, according to a tradition started by Muhammad ﷺ. A light meal will then follow.

Fasting is obligatory for every Muslim, except for:
- the insane
- children, although teenagers must fast from the start of puberty
- the elderly
- pregnant women
- those who are ill
- people who are travelling
- women during menstruation.

What special foods are eaten at festivals?

Preparing food for festivals is always a joyful family experience, in particular for the feasts held at Id-ul-Fitr and Id-ul-Adha. The food often follows cultural traditions: for example, a Muslim family preparing a meal in the UK may eat food of Bangladeshi or Pakistani origin.

Haram and halal

The term haram means unlawful. According to the Qur'an, a Muslim must not consume certain foods. Food that can be eaten is called halal, meaning allowed. The Qur'an's teaching means that the eating of animals such as pigs, almost all reptiles and insects, and the bodies of animals that have died, is forbidden. Alcohol is not allowed. Meat must be slaughtered according to specific Islamic rules, so that blood is not consumed.

The Qur'an's teaching on food

> **Surah 5:3**
>
> *Forbidden to you (for food) are: dead meat, blood, the flesh of swine, and that on which hath been invoked the name of other than Allah; that which hath been killed by strangling, or by a violent blow, or by a headlong fall, or by being gored to death; that which hath been (partly) eaten by a wild animal; unless ye are able to slaughter it (in due form); that which is sacrificed on stone (altars).*

ACTIVITIES

Look carefully at this example of tawhid expressed in Islamic art.

- What shapes can you see?
- Which shapes seem to be the most important?
- What do you notice about the way the shapes are formed?
- How might this image help to explain the tawhid and the idea that Allah is connected to and unites everything?

A Halal butcher selling meat which has been prepared according to Muslim law.

AO1 skills **ACTIVITIES**

Construct a mind map exploring fasting and its benefits. Why might it please Allah?

Judaism:
Religious and spiritual experience 1

The next two pages will help you to:

- explain why Jews worship
- explain how and where Jews worship
- evaluate the importance of prayer and worship in Judaism.

Jews and worship

Jews may worship G-d for several reasons:

- to show respect and love for G-d
- to thank G-d for creating the world
- to thank G-d for protecting them for many thousands of years
- to remind themselves of how they should live according to G-d's wishes
- to ask for help or strength
- to ask G-d to continue to look after them and protect them and everyone.

Screaming fans at a music festival.

How do Jews worship?

In Judaism, unlike in many other religions, people follow the faith of their mother, and so a person is born Jewish if their mother is a Jew. Jews believe that they should follow G-d's will. These beliefs are stated in **the Shema** (see p. 20).

Jews are required to follow 613 mitzvot (commandments) found in the Torah. These include the Ten Commandments (Exodus 20:1–14) and cover many aspects of life including food, prayer, worship, clothing and sexual relationships.

The Ten Commandments

G-d spoke all these words, saying:

> *I the Lord am your G-d who brought you out of the land of Egypt, the house of bondage: You shall have no other gods besides Me.*
>
> *You shall not make for yourself a sculptured image, or any likeness of what is in the heavens above, or on the earth below, or in the waters under the earth. You shall not bow down to them or serve them. For I the Lord your G-d am an impassioned G-d, visiting the guilt of the parents upon the children, upon the third and upon the fourth generations of those who reject Me, but showing kindness to the thousandth generation of those who love Me and keep My commandments.*
>
> *You shall not swear falsely by the name of the Lord your G-d; for the Lord will not clear one who swears falsely by His name.*

AO1 skills **ACTIVITIES**

What is the difference between worshipping a god, hero-worshipping or perhaps worshipping a new pair of trainers you desperately want? Make a list of the many differences and similarities between these forms of worship.

 RESEARCH NOTE

On p. 20, you will find the first paragraph of the Shema. Look up the other two paragraphs in Deuteronomy 11:13–21 and Numbers 15:37–41. List the teachings and beliefs you find.

Remember the Sabbath day and keep it holy. Six days you shall labour and do all your work, but the seventh day is a Sabbath of the Lord your G-d: you shall not do any work – you, your son or daughter, your male or female slave, or your cattle, or the stranger who is within your settlements. For in six days the Lord made heaven and earth and sea, and all that is in them, and He rested on the seventh day; therefore the Lord blessed the Sabbath day and hallowed it.

Honour your father and your mother, that you may long endure on the land that the Lord your G-d is assigning to you.

You shall not murder.

You shall not commit adultery.

You shall not steal.

You shall not bear false witness against your neighbour.

You shall not covet your neighbour's house: you shall not covet your neighbour's wife, or his male or female slave, or his ox or his ass, or anything that is your neighbour's.

Solomon's Temple.

Where do Jews worship?

Jews worshipped in the first Temple in Jerusalem, built by King Solomon in the 10th century BCE, or the second built later by Herod, until this was destroyed by the Romans in 70 CE.

After this, Jews worshipped in their homes and in synagogues (buildings designed for Jewish public prayer, study and meetings). Animal sacrifices could only take place in the Temple, so Jews now concentrated on the reading of the Sefer Torah: the five books of Moses handwritten on parchment and rolled to form a scroll.

Synagogues are often plain buildings from the outside. The main feature inside is the Aron Hakodesh – the ark where the Sefer Torah are kept, usually on a wall facing Jerusalem, with the scrolls behind a decorated door or curtain.

It is important that there are no statues or pictures in a synagogue – see the second of the Ten Commandments. There is often a seven-branched candlestick (menorah) to represent the one that stood in the Temple. The Torah is read from a platform called a bimah.

In an orthodox synagogue, there will be a gallery for the women or a screen for them to sit behind. The reason for this is said to be to prevent the women from distracting the men during worship. Most of the service takes place in Hebrew.

Although services may be held every day in the synagogue, most Jews will worship there on the Sabbath – Friday evening until Saturday evening.

 REMEMBER THIS

The sixth commandment is 'You shall not commit murder', not 'You shall not kill'.

AO1+AO2 skills ACTIVITIES

- Write out the Ten Commandments in your own words.
- With a partner, put them into two groups: those that apply only to Jews and those you think should apply to everyone.

The interior of a synagogue.

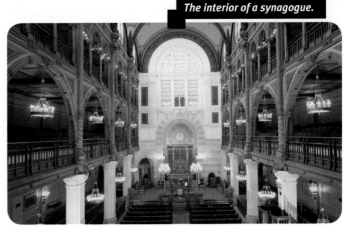

Judaism: Religious and spiritual experience 2

The next two pages will help you to:

- investigate the importance of the Sabbath to Jews
- analyse the importance of prayer in Judaism
- explore the importance of food and fasting in Judaism.

The Sabbath

The Sabbath is an occasion when Jews will worship at home as well as at the synagogue, particularly at a special family meal on Friday evening. The woman welcomes in the Sabbath by lighting two candles. The Sabbath ends with the Havdalah service on Saturday evening. Daily prayers usually take place at home too and so worship there is often seen as more important than at the synagogue.

The fourth commandment says what Jews cannot do on the Sabbath. This was expanded into 39 categories of forbidden work, including:

- growing and preparing food
- making clothing
- leatherwork and writing
- providing shelter
- creating a fire (including switching electricity on or off)
- work completion
- transporting goods
- muktzeh: these are objects which cannot be used on the Sabbath, for example money should not be touched
- sh'vut: Jews should not ask someone to do something on the Sabbath that they cannot do themselves
- uvdin d'chol: weekday things.

AO1+AO2 skills ACTIVITIES

Look at the list of things Jews are not allowed to do on the Sabbath. In pairs, write down examples for each category of things you do between Friday evening and Saturday evening. How would life change if you followed these rules?

Why is prayer so important in Judaism?

Wherever they are and whatever they are doing, Jews try to stop and pray three times a day:

- Shacharit – at dawn
- Minchah – in the afternoon
- Maariv – in the evening.

The **Shema** is always said on going to bed and getting up in the morning. Services in the synagogue contain prayers and readings, mostly from the Jewish scriptures.

Jews are also encouraged to pray spontaneously: for example, a Jew on arriving at the seaside might say 'Blessed are you, O Lord our G-d, King of the universe, maker of the great sea.'

FOR DEBATE

Do you think having statues or pictures in a place of worship would help people to concentrate more on G-d, or would they be a distraction?

A Jew praying in a synagogue.

For daily prayer, male Jews cover their heads with a kippah, wear a prayer shawl and in the morning have tefillin on their arm and forehead. The tefillin contain scrolls with the Shema written on them.

Leviticus 11:2–3

These are the creatures that you may eat from among all the land animals: any animal that has true hoofs, with clefts through the hoofs, and that chews the cud – such you may eat.

It is important to remember that Jews are not blessing G-d, but are saying how blessed G-d is: only G-d can give blessings, not human beings. Jews do not say the name of G-d but replace it with other words such as Lord. This is because, at the time of the Jerusalem Temple, the High Priest spoke the name just once a year and in private. Jews also believe that if the name or a translation of it is written down the paper it is on cannot be destroyed. This is why G-d is used throughout this book.

Food and fasting in Judaism

Food and fasting play a very important part in Judasim. Every year on the Day of Atonement – Yom Kippur – Jews fast for 25 hours: the Torah tells them to and it helps them concentrate on prayer.

In the story of Creation, G-d tells people that they can eat any plant. Later, Noah is told that he can eat meat provided that there is no blood in it (Genesis 9:3–4). After the Exodus from Egypt, the Israelites were given stricter rules – the food laws Jews still follow today. Food that Jews can eat is called kosher – permitted; food that they cannot eat is terefah – forbidden.

The food laws are found in Leviticus 11:1–10, 13–23, 41–42. This means that Jews can eat beef and lamb because cows and sheep have cleft hooves and chew the cud, but cannot eat pork because pigs do not chew the cud. Another important food law is 'You shall not boil a kid in its mother's milk' (Deuteronomy 14:21b). This means that Jews cannot mix meat and dairy products in the same meal.

Jews say special prayers after eating a meal and on occasions such as the Sabbath meal on Friday evening, when blessings are said over the bread and wine before they eat.

 **AO1+AO2 skills ACTIVITIES**

- Choose one Jewish festival and research the particular foods associated with it.
- 'Food and fasting are important ways of showing belief in G-d.' Give reasons for and against this statement, including your own views.

RESEARCH NOTE

What does 'chewing the cud' mean? Find out.

 **AO1 skills ACTIVITIES**

Think of something that might happen and design a blessing like the one in the example opposite.

Sikhism:
Religious and spiritual experience 1

The next two pages will help you to:

- develop your knowledge and understanding of the concept of worship in Sikhism
- explore the significance and meaning behind symbolism and ritual during Sikh worship.

Sikh women praying in a gurdwara.

ACTIVITIES

Make two columns in your book and, with a partner, discuss and write down:

- the advantages of worshipping at home
- the advantages of worshipping in the gurdwara.

Share your answers with the rest of the class and add any new points to your table.

RESEARCH NOTE

Music in the form of kirtan is very important in Sikh public worship. Classical Indian instruments are used. Search for Sikh religious music on the Internet or through a CD, if you have access to one. How does the music make you feel? Can you recognise the use of any Indian classical instruments?

What is worship for a Sikh?

Worship is often understood as paying respect to a deity. One dictionary definition of worship is 'reverence, adoration – to adore, love and admire.'

Worship for Sikhs does not have to take place in a **gurdwara**; it can take place at home too. Essentially, since God is immanent, worship can take place anywhere that is reasonably clean. Only a building that houses a copy of the Guru Granth Sahib Ji can be called a gurdwara.

There is no special day for worship in Sikhism, although Sunday tends to be more popular in the diaspora (scattering of a religious community to other places) due to work arrangements.

The layout of the worship room in a gurdwara.

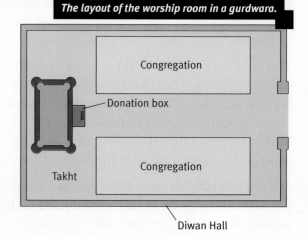

Congregation

Donation box

Congregation

Takht

Diwan Hall

The centrality of the Guru Granth Sahib Ji in the gurdwara

The main worship room in a gurdwara is called the Diwan Hall. This is the room in which a special encasement, the takht, houses the Guru Granth Sahib Ji. There are no seats in this room, everybody sits on the floor – this shows the elevated position of the scripture, which is given royal status. The reader will fan the scripture with a chauri to symbolise its regal position. A donation box will be present for the worshippers. Men and women sit separately on the carpeted floor and there is a walkway leading to the takht, in front of which worshippers will bow in respect to the scripture. The scripture itself is not worshipped and neither are the ten human **Gurus**. It is only **Waheguru** that is worshipped in Sikhism. Before entering the Diwan Hall, shoes are removed and heads are covered.

There are no images of God in Sikhism, but artworks may depict the ten human Gurus and scenes from Sikh history. Musicians will sit alongside the takht since the Guru Granth Sahib Ji is composed in the form of prose that is intended to be sung.

There are two important symbols used in Sikh worship, the Ik Onkar and the Khanda.

Why does a Sikh meditate on the name of God?

Prayer and meditation on the name of God, known as **nam simran**, are central features of Sikh worship. There are three main prayers that devout Sikhs are expected to recite each day. The day begins with the prayer of Japji Sahib in which Sikhs proclaim the Oneness and powerful nature of God. The Rehras is recited in the evening, when Sikhs would thank God for the day that has been. The Kirtan Sohila is recited before retiring to bed.

Both prayer and nam simran help a Sikh to develop a loving and personal relationship with God. The fifth Sikh Guru, Guru Arjan Dev Ji, highlighted the importance attached to nam simran:

> **Guru Granth Sahib Ji, page 1357**
> *Contemplating the Lord's Name and ever uttering the Master's praises in the saint's society, O Nanak, immaculate becomes the mortal.*

Many Sikhs would not eat or drink without reciting the Jap Ji Sahib. Nam simran and prayer help Sikhs feel united with the wider Sikh community. There are many names of God on which Sikhs can meditate, including Waheguru and Satnam – The True Name.

> **Guru Granth Sahib Ji, page 419**
> *Nanak never forgets the Name and his mind is reconciled to the True One.*

The Harmandir Sahib in Amritsar.

REMEMBER THIS

Look back at Topic 1 to remind yourself what **Waheguru** means.

This is the Ik Onkar, which highlights that Sikhs believe in One God who has no form.

This is the Khanda symbol, which shows the eternity and power of God.

AO1+AO2 skills **ACTIVITIES**

Think/pair/share
If you could design your own building where a person from any faith could worship, what features would you include? Explain your choices and what they would symbolise or represent. Discuss your ideas with a partner and compare your architecture with the rest of the class.

Sikhism: Religious and spiritual experience 2

The next two pages will help you to:

- explore the Sikh attitude to food and fasting during worship
- make links between how Sikhs worship, and their attitude to food and fasting, and what you think/believe.

 **ACTIVITIES**

- Search for the dictionary definition of 'fasting'.
- Interview five pupils in your class and ask them whether they think fasting brings people closer to God.

Food had a special significance for Guru Nanak Dev Ji, as shown in the story of Lalo and Malik Bhago (see Topic 1).

The importance of fasting and eating for Sikhs

Fasting

In many religions, fasting is seen as a practice that can bring the devotee closer to God, but there is no insistence on fasting in Sikhism. In fact, the Rehat Maryada (a guide for practical living for initiated Sikhs) strongly denounces the keeping of fasts. Nevertheless, some Sikhs, due to their Hindu heritage, will fast from time to time in order to ask or thank God for good fortune or improvements to their lives.

Sharing food

The distributing and sharing of food is very important in Sikh worship and daily life. Sharing food with people of different **castes** is a practice that initially distinguished Sikhs from Hindus. In the gurdwara, all worshippers are given a sweet, doughy mixture called **karah parshad** – this shows that everyone is equal.

After paying respect to the Guru Granth Sahib Ji, worshippers will have a meal called the langar. Sitting and eating together are concepts that are central to the teachings of the Gurus and emphasise that all human beings are equal. Eating in the langar is an important aspect of all Sikh worship at the gurdwara and special feasts are held for festivals.

 **FOR DEBATE**

Why do you think the food in the langar is always vegetarian?

 **ACTIVITIES**

As a class, think of examples in British society where people from different social backgrounds would not eat together.

Why do Sikhs insist on eating together?

Around the time of Guru Nanak Dev Ji, the founder of Sikhism, Hindus would not eat together with lower caste people for fear of becoming ritually polluted. As a Hindu himself, Guru Nanak Dev Ji would have grown up with these attitudes constantly around him.

In his own mind, he could not understand why, if we are all children of the One God, there are some people referred to as 'untouchables', whose very shadow was considered polluting. Much to the anger of higher caste Hindus, Guru Nanak Dev Ji openly ate with lower caste Hindus in order to show that we are all equal. It is this concept that lies behind the importance of karah parshad and langar in gurdwaras today.

Food for thought

Imagine you are living at the time when Guru Nanak Dev Ji started to teach people about equality and eating with each other. Think carefully about the make-up of Punjabi society in the 15th century, when people would frown upon eating or associating with those of another caste. What might the feelings and emotions of the lower caste Hindus have been, especially those who were at one time regarded as 'untouchables'?

 **ACTIVITIES**

In groups, create a scene from the 15th century. How do you think the higher caste Hindus would have reacted to Guru Nanak Dev Ji's teachings about eating together?

Act out your scene in front of the class. Your teacher will mark you out of ten for your consideration of society at that time.

 ## GradeStudio

AO1

QUESTION

Explain how praying every day might help Sikhs in their daily lives. **[6 marks]**

You could build an answer like this:

Level 1

First, let the examiner know that you know what the question is about. For example, 'Prayer is very important in Sikhism. Sikhs are required to recite three prayers every day at different times of the day.'

Level 2

Next go on to explain in detail how prayer enables a Sikh to develop and enhance a personal and loving relationship with God. You could also develop here the teaching about the immanence of God and hence the importance of prayer over outward rituals.

Level 3

Finally, explain the importance of each of the three Sikh prayers and how the additional practice of nam simran strengthens the concept of worship for Sikhs. You could also mention that many Sikhs will not eat or drink until they have recited the Japji Sahib. Lastly a prayer allows a Sikh to ask for forgiveness.

Welcome to the Grade Studio

Grade Studio is here to help you improve your grades by working through typical questions you might find on an examination paper. For a full explanation of how Grade Studio works, and how the examiners approach the task of marking your paper, please see p. 26.

AO1

Question

Why do some Christians fast?

[6 marks]

Student's answer

Some Christians fast because they believe that this will show them how people feel who do not have enough to eat. Other Christians might choose to give up something special during Lent, such as chocolate. They do this to remember the time when Jesus was in the wilderness.

Examiner's comment

The candidate has given a satisfactory answer to the question. There are two relevant points but they are not explained in any detail. The answer needs to give more information and examples in order to reach Level 3. The candidate could also use more technical terms from the specification to show the breadth of their knowledge and understanding.

Student's improved answer

Some Christians fast because they believe that this will show them how people feel who do not have enough to eat. Other Christians might choose to give up something special during Lent, such as chocolate. They do this to remember the time when Jesus was in the wilderness. This also serves as a preparation for Lent. Lent leads up to Easter and is a period of penitence (being sorry for what you have done). The forty days of Lent remember the time when Jesus was tempted by the devil in the wilderness.

Many Christians fast on certain days of the year and save the money that they would have spent on food to give to charities that support people in other countries who do not have enough to eat. So, as well as helping others, they are also practising self-discipline.

Examiner's comment

This is now a good answer to the question. The candidate has shown a clear understanding of the question. There is good description and explanation of a variety of different reasons why Christians might fast. The candidate has shown some analysis in dealing with the question of fasting. The information is presented clearly and there is good use of technical terms.

AO2

Question

'Everyone should thank God for their food.' *Discuss this statement. You should include different, supported points of view and a personal viewpoint. You must refer to Christianity in your answer.* **[12 marks]**

Student's answer

Christians might say they should always thank God for their food and some people say a prayer after meals. Some Christians have Harvest Festivals when they thank God for food.

Examiner's comment

The candidate has given a limited answer to the question. There are two relevant points but they both address the same point of view and neither is expanded very far. The answer needs to give alternative viewpoints and also include a personal response to reach Level 4.

Student's improved answer

Christians might say they should always thank God for their food and some people say a prayer after meals. Some Christians have Harvest Festivals when they thank God for food.

Some people, on the other hand, might think that, although they should thank God for their food by saying Grace after meals, taking part in the Offertory during the Eucharist or attending a Harvest Festival, it still seems unjust that some people are thanking God when they already have more food than they can eat, while others thank God for a small amount of food that is not really enough to live on.

My personal opinion is that if people do believe in God then they should thank God for the food they have. However, I do think that it is hard for people to thank God for their food when they do not have enough to eat and it makes God seem unjust.

Examiner's comment

This is now a competent answer to the question. The candidate has shown a clear understanding of the question and has presented a range of views supported by evidence and argument. The answer explains Christian views, among others, and includes a personal viewpoint, which is also supported.

These specimen answers provide an outline of how you could construct your response. Space does not allow us to give a full response. The examiner will be looking for more detail in your actual exam responses.

These examples only use Christianity but you could use the Grade Studio to apply to any of the religions you are studying and the structure of the answers would work in the same way.

Topic 3: The end of life

The Big Picture

In this Topic, you will be addressing religious beliefs and teachings about:

- the concept of soul, and the relationship between body and soul
- the concept of life after death, and beliefs about what happens when someone dies
- funeral rites, and how they reflect beliefs and aim to support the bereaved.

You will also think about ways in which these beliefs affect the life and outlook of believers in the world today.

What?

You will:

- develop your knowledge and understanding of key religious beliefs and ideas about life after death
- explain what these beliefs and ideas mean to those who hold them and think about how they might affect how they live
- make links between these beliefs and ideas and what you think/believe.

Why?

Because:

- these beliefs and ideas underpin and are reflected in the ways people live their lives: for example, in helping them to decide how to plan funerals
- understanding people's beliefs can help you understand why they think and act in the way they do
- understanding these beliefs helps you compare and contrast what others believe, including thinking about your own beliefs and ideas.

How?

By:

- recalling and selecting information about beliefs and ideas about what happens when someone dies, explaining their importance for people today
- reflecting on the relevance of these beliefs in 21st-century Britain
- evaluating your own views about these beliefs.

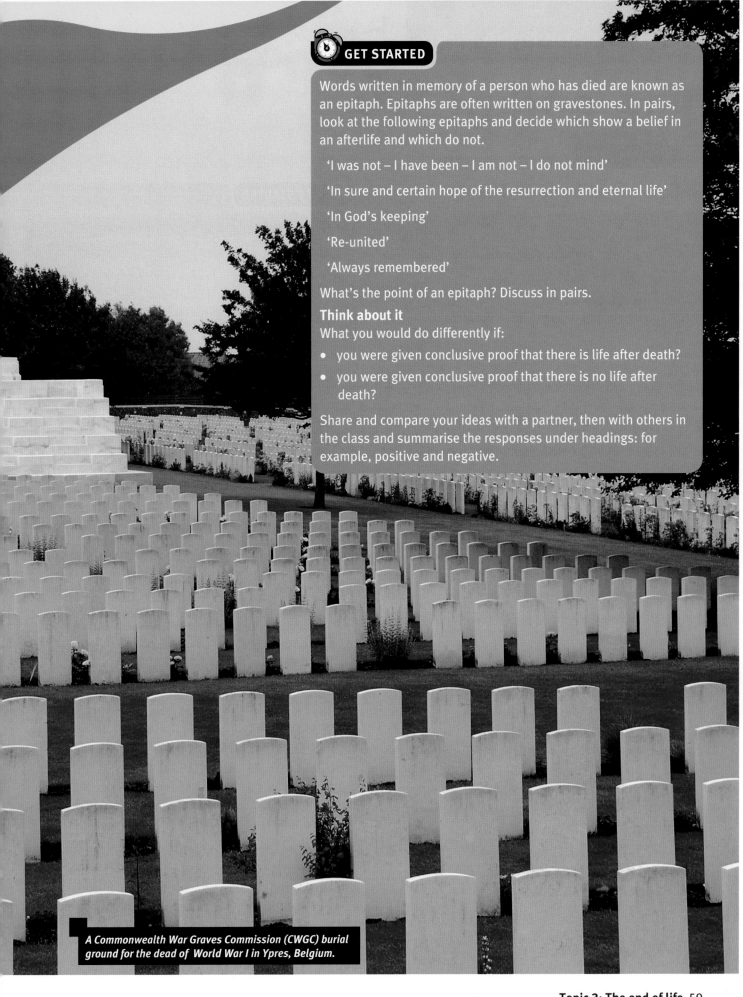

Words written in memory of a person who has died are known as an epitaph. Epitaphs are often written on gravestones. In pairs, look at the following epitaphs and decide which show a belief in an afterlife and which do not.

'I was not – I have been – I am not – I do not mind'

'In sure and certain hope of the resurrection and eternal life'

'In God's keeping'

'Re-united'

'Always remembered'

What's the point of an epitaph? Discuss in pairs.

Think about it

What you would do differently if:

- you were given conclusive proof that there is life after death?
- you were given conclusive proof that there is no life after death?

Share and compare your ideas with a partner, then with others in the class and summarise the responses under headings: for example, positive and negative.

A Commonwealth War Graves Commission (CWGC) burial ground for the dead of World War I in Ypres, Belgium.

The end of life

Beliefs about body and soul

All the major world religions believe that death is not the end, and that an aspect of a person survives in some way after death. Each religion has a different way of describing this.

- Buddhists do not believe in an eternal soul or self but in the concept of **anatta** – no self.

- Christians believe everyone has a soul that is invisible and lives forever, even after the death of the body. They believe Jesus conquered death by rising from the dead.

- Hindus and Sikhs believe in the **atman** or soul.

- Muslims believe that the soul lives on after death.

- Some Jews believe in the idea of a soul that lives on after death.

Beliefs about life after death

Beliefs about the nature of life after death differ between and within the major religions.

- Buddhists believe people are trapped in the wheel of **samsara**, the cycle of birth and rebirth. The aim is to escape this cycle and attain **nibbana**. If you achieve nibbana in this life, when you die you will not be reborn.

- Most Christians believe in some kind of Heaven where those who have died are in the presence of God and are free from suffering and sin. Some Christians believe in Hell, a place of suffering where sinful people will go, and in **purgatory**, where those who die but are not ready to go to heaven spend time.

- Hindus believe people are trapped in the wheel of samsara, the cycle of birth and rebirth. The aim is to escape samsara and reach nirvana.

GET STARTED

"To die would be an awfully big adventure!"
(*Peter Pan*, J.M. Barrie)

"Sometimes, when I think about death, I get some kind of excitement. Instead of fear, I have a feeling of curiosity, and this makes it easier for me to accept death."

(Dalai Lama's *Book of Wisdom*)

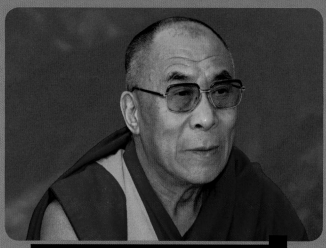

The 14th Dalai Lama: His Holiness Tenzin Gyatso.

What religious beliefs may have influenced the feelings of curiosity and excitement about death described by the Dalai Lama?

KEY QUESTIONS

KNOWLEDGE AND UNDERSTANDING
Compare beliefs and practices relating to death in Christianity and other religions you have studied, identifying some of the similarities and differences.

ANALYSIS AND EVALUATION
What do you believe happens when someone dies? Is death the end? Do you agree with Peter Pan and the Dalai Lama that death is an exciting journey into the unknown?

Akhirah in Islam, everlasting life after death

Anatta in Buddhism, the idea that there is no eternal, unchanging soul or self

Atman the belief in the soul which is part of every living being (used in Hinduism and Sikhism)

Dukkha suffering – the nature of existence according to the first Noble Truth in Buddhism

Gurdwara Sikh place of worship, literally 'the doorway to the **Guru'**

Kaddish a Jewish prayer publicly recited by mourners

Kamma in Buddhism, intentional actions that affect your circumstances in this and future lives

Karma in Hinduism, consequence of actions, in terms of cause and effect

Khandha the five Khandhas of Buddhism together make up the 'person' (form, feeling, perception, mental formation and consciousness)

Moksha in Hinduism, an escape from the cycle of death and rebirth

Nibbana in Buddhism, achieving freedom from greed, hatred and delusion resulting in freedom from rebirth

Omniscient in religion, when God is all knowing

Purgatory for Christians, a place between heaven and hell, where those who die but are not ready to go to heaven spend time

Salah the five daily prayers for a Muslim as required by the Qur'an

Samsara in Buddhism and Hinduism; a continuing cycle of birth, ageing, death and rebirth

Shahadah declaration of faith, in Judaism and Islam

Shema important Jewish prayer that states belief in one G-d

Sheol a shadowy underworld where souls are prepared for the coming of the Messiah

Torah Jewish law, or teaching, made up of the Five Books of Moses

Waheguru a Sikh name for God

Wudu washing before prayer

- Muslims believe in a spiritual and physical resurrection, when all good souls will be awakened from their graves to live eternal life, called **akhirah**, in Paradise. Those who have done wrong will be judged and punished in Hell.

- Some Jews believe in an afterlife where those who have lived a good life will be rewarded and the evil punished.

- Sikhs believe that living life according to God's plan can end the cycle of rebirth in the present life, so that when you die you will not be reborn.

Funeral rites

Religions have different ways of conducting funeral rites and mourning, reflecting the different beliefs. Funerals help those left behind to cope with their bereavement, by providing comfort, reassurance and an opportunity for relatives and friends to celebrate the life and say 'goodbye' to the person who has died.

- Buddhists and Hindus are cremated. Hindus hope that their ashes will be scattered on the sacred River Ganga (Ganges).

- Christians may choose to be buried or cremated.

- Muslims are usually buried on the day of death, with their heads turned to face Makkah.

- Jews believe the funeral and burial should take place within 24 hours of death. Cremation is not allowed by Orthodox Jews because they believe that to burn the body would be to destroy something precious made by God.

- Sikhs are always cremated. The five symbols of their religion – The Five Ks – are placed in the coffin with the body.

 FOR INTEREST

Who wants to live forever? What are the arguments for and against living forever? Take a class vote on the question or hold a class debate.

Buddhism:
The end of life 1

A cremation funeral pyre for a Buddhist monk in Seoul, South Korea.

No soul! Then what am I?

Buddhists do not believe in an eternal soul or Self. Instead, they teach the concept of **anatta** – no-self. Buddhists believe that you can find nothing in a person that remains the same throughout life. They believe that assigning the concept of a Self or soul to a changing aspect of oneself does not make sense. This is explained in an important Buddhist text called *The Questions of King Milinda*.

FOR DEBATE

Consider carefully the Buddhist concept of anatta. Do you think this view would lead to a belief in life after death or not? If so, what form might life after death take?

If we have been good in life, then God will welcome us into heaven.

When we die, that's that. It's all over.

Life is a circle. When one dies, another is born.

Good rewards the good and punishes the bad.

Our behaviour in this life will determine our next life.

Our kamma will affect whether we are reborn, and if we are, what we become.

People have different views about what happens when we die.

 **ACTIVITIES**

Look at these views about what happens when someone dies. Which do you find most convincing? Why? Do you think everyone would agree with you? Why/why not?

The Questions of King Milinda

King Milinda is introduced to the Buddhist monk Nagasena. Nagasena says that although he is known as Nagasena, there is no permanent Self or soul relating to that identity. King Milinda asks for an explanation. Nagasena describes the parts of a chariot. After naming each, he asks if that part *is* the chariot; the King says no. Finally Nagasena says he has not found the essence of a chariot, because the term 'chariot' is just a name for a particular collection of parts, put together in a particular way.

Nagasena then claims that humans are the same. The 'I' that King Milinda is looking for cannot be the body, or the feelings a being has, which constantly change; nor can it be the perceptions (ideas), which develop with new sensations, nor the impulses or consciousness, which are always changing. There is no essence (soul/Self) to a human – just a collection of changing parts dependent on each other, called the five khandhas.

The five khandhas

The five khandhas have a special place in Buddhist belief.

- Body/form – the body, and the five sense organs (eyes, ears, nose, tongue and body).
- Feelings/sensations – the sensations we experience as a result of our contact with the external world.
- Perceptions – the ability to identify, recognise and classify the sensations we experience.
- Impulses/volitions – the attitudes or intentions that determine our patterns of behaviour, conditioned by **kamma**.
- Consciousness – the conscious and unconscious mental responses to sensations, the coordinating part of us, which 'makes sense' of the experiences we have.

Milinda and Nagasena talk about anatta

66 *Nagasena:* *What do you think, great king: when you were a tiny infant, newly born and quite soft, were you then the same as the one who is now grown up?*

Milinda: *No, that infant was one, I, now grown up, am another.*

Nagasena: *If that is so, then great king, you have had no father, no mother, no teaching and no schooling! ... Is the schoolboy one person, and the one who has finished school another? Does one commit a crime, but the hands and feet of another are cut off?*

Milinda: *Certainly not! But what would you say...*

Nagasena: *I was neither the tiny infant, newly born and quite soft, nor am I now the grown up man, but all these are comprised in one unit depending on this very body.* 99

(Source: *King Milinda's Questions* in *Buddhist Scriptures*, Edward Conze)

Buddhism:
The end of life 2

Rebirth in the wheel of samsara

Buddhists believe that people are trapped in the wheel of samsara, experiencing rebirth after rebirth. This is because they do not accept the world as it really is, and crave life and the experiences of life. This craving leads to attachment and when they die they are reborn. The realm into which they are reborn will be determined by their attitudes and by their type of behaviour.

It is often asked what exactly continues to the next life, if there is no Self. Buddhists often respond that body/form is left behind, but the changing collection of the four other khandhas continues, providing the link between one life and the next. The khandhas are always changing, but are connected to each other through a process of cause and effect. This does not stop at death but continues through each life.

Nibbana – escape?

The Buddhist aim is to escape the cycle of samsara, and attain nibbana. Nibbana is freedom from greed, hatred and delusion (the three poisons). The Buddha achieved nibbana and carried on living and teaching for many years. Achieving nibbana in this life means that people can see and accept the world as it is; they no longer crave things, and are not attached to this world; and they do not build up kamma any more, though they can still experience the results of past kamma.

If someone has achieved nibbana in this life, when they die they will not be reborn. Buddhists do not specify exactly what this parinibbana or final nibbana is like: many believe it is impossible to describe an experience so far beyond our understanding. However, Buddhists do agree that form/body will not continue into this experience, and it will be free from dukkha.

Nibbana is not...	Nibbana is...
a place somewhere you go when you die Heaven	an attitude freedom from greed, hatred and delusion seeing the world as it really is freedom from rebirth

Some lay Buddhists believe that nibbana is too hard to achieve in this lifetime, aiming instead for a better rebirth, achieving nibbana in their next life, when circumstances are more favourable.

The next two pages will help you to:

- examine the relationship between kamma, **samsara** and **nibbana**
- evaluate whether Buddhist beliefs about life after death make sense.

Behaviour and attitudes in one life determine the realm people will be reborn into in the next life.

AO2 skills **ACTIVITIES**

Think/Pair/Share

- Does the Buddhist idea of rebirth make sense, given their belief in the concept of anatta? Share your conclusions with two other people. Do they agree with you? Why/why not? Share your views with the class.

- Having listened to other views, have you changed your mind? Why/why not?

Kamma – action and consequence

Buddhists believe that every intentional action has a consequence. This process is referred to as kamma. The word kamma is sometimes used for both the action and the consequence, as well as the whole system.

Many people assume that kamma works as a kind of moral bank account: doing good actions builds up the account, and doing bad actions lowers it. Kamma does not work like this. As far as Buddhists are concerned, every action they choose and have control over will have a consequence: if they do both good and bad things, they will experience both positive and negative consequences.

The kamma that people build up through their actions may help determine the realm they are reborn into when they die and therefore many Buddhists try to act in a way that results in good kamma, to get a good rebirth. Those aiming for nibbana should be acting without attachment to the consequences of their actions. This does not mean they should not act morally, but that they should do so automatically, without thinking about any positive consequence they may get.

You cannot make up for bad actions by doing good ones, since every intentional action has a reaction.

GradeStudio

AO1

QUESTION

Explain what Buddhists mean by 'soul'? **[6 marks]**

Level 1
This might seem confusing given that Buddhists do not believe in a soul. It might seem easy to simply respond that there is no 'soul' in Buddhism. However, what the examiner will expect you to do is to outline the concept of the 'soul' or 'self' that Buddhism is rejecting.

Level 2
You might therefore explain that the 'soul' or 'self' is seen as an eternal and unchanging part of a human being, and as the essential identity of that person.

Level 3
To build on this answer, you might explain that Buddhists believe that a 'soul' cannot be part of the physical body, or that it has no substance separate from the body, and that Buddhists believe they cannot find anything within the body that does not change.

 ACTIVITIES

- Design a leaflet explaining the relationship between kamma, samsara and nibbana.

- Imagine you are an agony aunt writing a response to the problem below for a Buddhist magazine.

  'I found a wallet with £100 in it. No one knows. Should I keep it?'

Christianity:
The end of life 1

The next two pages will help you to:

- examine what Christians believe about the **soul** and the body
- identify key points about Christian beliefs about life after death.

The funeral of Archbishop Paulos Faraj Rahho in northern Iraq.

What do Christians believe about the body and soul?

Christians believe that you have a mind and a body, but they would also say that there is something more that makes us uniquely human – the soul. According to the book of Genesis, God 'created man in his own image', and this gives Christians a belief that they have a divine spark or soul, setting them apart from other living things. All other animals were formed 'out of the ground', but with Adam – the first man – God 'breathed into his nostrils the breath *of life*'.

St Paul suggested that often the body and the soul are in conflict and want different things: the body wishes for its natural desires to be satisfied, while the soul wants spiritual satisfaction. This could lead a human to sin against God. His advice was clear – a Christian should follow his spiritual nature in order to be reunited with God after death: 'if you are led by the Spirit, you are not under law' (Galatians 5:16–18).

Christians believe that, although the body dies, the soul does not, and it is this that is reunited with God. The proof of this, said St Paul, was in the resurrection of Jesus. God raised him from the dead and those who believe this will also be raised back to life to be with God.

> ### 1 Corinthians 15:42–44
>
> *So will it be with the resurrection of the dead. The body that is sown is perishable, it is raised imperishable; it is sown in dishonour, it is raised in glory; it is sown in weakness, it is raised in power; it is sown a natural body, it is raised a spiritual body.*

Christians cannot explain exactly what life after death will be like – it is beyond what they can imagine. However, it is thought that somehow when people die they are reunited with loved ones. Jesus promised that there would be a place for all who believed in him.

> ### John 14:1–3
>
> *In my Father's house are many rooms; if it were not so, I would have told you. I am going there to prepare a place for you. And if I go and prepare a place for you, I will come back and take you to be with me that you also may be where I am.*

Christians do not believe in reincarnation: they believe that there is only one life on this earth, and that life after death is not physical, as we know it. However, they do believe that there will be a resurrection of the body on the Day of Judgement. It is a Christian teaching that there will be an actual day at the end of time when everyone will be made to account for their actions. This is linked to the idea that humans have free will and this means that they must stand by their actions at the Day of Judgement.

This idea is a confusing one when we remember that God is **omniscient**, and some Christians would disagree with the idea of free will, preferring to think that our actions are predestined (controlled by God). Many Christians would say that God does have the power to know everything, but has created humans in a caring manner, enabling them to choose to follow the path to heaven if they wish to do so.

God as a Judge

According to the Apostles' Creed, God will judge the 'living and the dead' at the end of time. It is said in the Book of Revelation that there are two books – one containing all that people have done in their lives, and another containing the names of all who have shown belief in the death and resurrection of Jesus. Christians believe that those who have responded to Jesus will be rewarded, but those who have not will be punished. This is described in the parable (a story told by Jesus to explain a spiritual truth) of the Sheep and the Goats.

 **ACTIVITIES**

- Explain the concepts of body and soul
- Examine the relationship between moral behaviour and life after death.

Make an outline drawing of a person. Write around the outside what makes us a human being. Think about chemicals and water, but don't forget all the things that make us individuals, such as personality and skills.

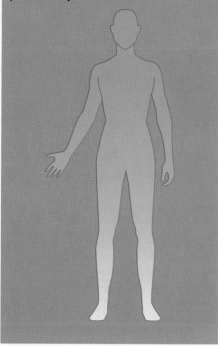

AO1 skills **ACTIVITIES**

Write a summary, in the style of a magazine article, of Christian beliefs about life after death. (See Matthew 25:31–46.)

Christianity: The end of life 2

The next two pages will help you to:

- evaluate Christian beliefs about heaven, hell and **purgatory**, and salvation and redemption
- evaluate how funeral rites reflect beliefs and help the bereaved to grieve.

The Last Judgement by Michelangelo in the Sistine Chapel, Vatican Ciy, Italy.

 ACTIVITIES

AO1+AO2 skills

Complete the following statements:

If heaven were:

a building it would be…
an animal it would be…
a colour it would be…
a season it would be…
a flower it would be…

Now do the same for hell. Compare your ideas with those of others in the class.

What do Christians believe about heaven and hell?

Those who follow God's will faithfully expect to go to heaven, a place free from suffering, where a believer can spend an eternity with God. However, those who refuse to follow Jesus' teaching will not go to heaven. A sinner can repent and turn away from former bad deeds, and will then be able to enter the Kingdom of Heaven.

Nowadays, hell is seen as an absence of God: those who reject Jesus' teachings can expect to spend an eternity away from God. In the past, Christians had a more visual image of hell. Medieval art depicted hell as a place of torment and suffering, where there would be 'wailing and gnashing of teeth'.

Roman Catholics believe in purgatory, where those who die but are not ready to go to heaven spend time. In the Middle Ages, it was common for rich people to leave money for prayers to be said to decrease their stay in purgatory.

FOR DEBATE

'Life does not finish when we die. Death is not the end, but a new beginning.' Prepare a speech for or against this statement.

 REMEMBER THIS

Check the account of the trial, death and resurrection of Jesus to remind you of the events referred to in this Topic.

Christian ideas about salvation and redemption

Jesus is described as 'the Saviour of the world' in the New Testament. Christians believe that he came to earth to save people from their sins. Another title given to Jesus is Redeemer, meaning someone who saves a person from sin and damnation. It is thought that Jesus sacrificed his life on the cross to redeem believers from the original sin of Adam and Eve. By suffering on the cross, Jesus has allowed all those who believe in him to be forgiven and to enter heaven after death.

The parable of the sheep and the goats

Matthew 25:31–33; 41–43; 46

When the Son of Man comes in his glory, and all the angels with him, he will sit on his throne in heavenly glory. All the nations will be gathered before him, and he will separate the people one from another as a shepherd separates the sheep from the goats. He will put the sheep on his right and the goats on his left. Then the King will say to those on his right, 'Come, you who are blessed by my Father; take your inheritance, the kingdom prepared for you since the creation of the world…

Then he will say to those on his left, 'Depart from me, you who are cursed, into the eternal fire prepared for the devil and his angels. For I was hungry and you gave me nothing to eat, I was thirsty and you gave me nothing to drink, I was a stranger and you did not invite me in, I needed clothes and you did not clothe me, I was sick and in prison and you did not look after me.'… Then they (the goats) will go away to eternal punishment, but the righteous to eternal life.

Christian funerals

A funeral reminds Christians that they believe they will live forever with God. Most funerals include readings from the Bible, hymns, prayers, and tributes or eulogies from those who knew the deceased well. In Roman Catholic Churches, a requiem mass may be held, where prayers for the soul of the dead are offered.

Traditionally, a Christian was buried in a cemetery. However, some Christians feel that it is the soul that is important after death, so cremation is now more common. Some Christian denominations, such as the Orthodox, do not accept anything other than the burial of a coffin in the ground.

The final part of a funeral is the committal, when the coffin is lowered into the ground, or curtains cover the coffin during a cremation, with these words:

> 66 *We now commit his/her body to the ground: earth to earth, ashes to ashes, dust to dust: in sure and certain hope of the resurrection to eternal life through our Lord Jesus Christ.* 99

(Common Worship)

In the past, black was the colour of death and funerals. Today, many people use brighter colours or white, to symbolise the hope associated with eternal life in heaven.

ACTIVITIES

Look at the Parable of the sheep and the goats. Make a cartoon strip to show what Jesus said and to explain how it relates to the idea of Judgement for Christians.

Grade Studio

AO1

QUESTION

Explain what Christians believe about life after death. **[6 marks]**

Level 1
First, let the examiner know that you understand the question. For example, Christians believe that when they die they will be judged and go to heaven or hell.

Level 2
Next, go on to explain the ideas of heaven and hell in more detail and also explain that some Christians, Roman Catholics in particular, believe that most people will go to purgatory where their souls will be cleansed from sin until they are in a state where they can go to heaven.

Level 3
Finally, explain that beliefs about heaven, hell and purgatory have changed over the centuries. In the past, most Christians believed very literally in these places. They thought that hell was ruled by Satan and was a place of fire and suffering. They also believed that heaven was a perfect place somewhere in the sky. Today, many Christians believe that heaven is a state of being together with God while hell is the absence of God.

Hinduism:
The end of life 1

The next two pages will help you to:

- analyse Hindu understanding of the soul
- explain Hindu beliefs about the purpose of existence
- explore the concept of all actions having consequences.

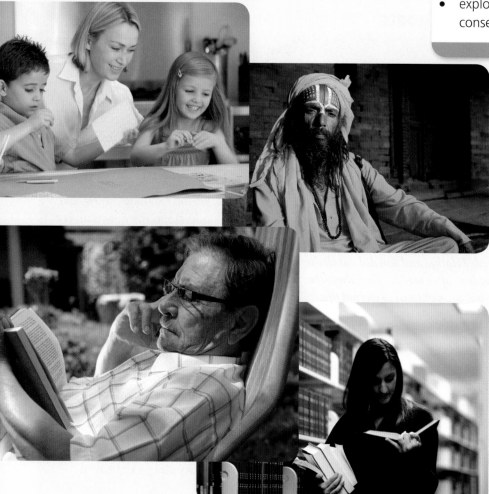

The term *varnashramadharma is used to describe the key roles (varna), stages (ashrama) and duties (dharma) in life.*

AO1 skills ACTIVITIES

Are you:

- a random collection of chemicals?
- a body that requires a brain to make it work?
- something more than the above?
- something different altogether – and if so, what?

AO2 skills ACTIVITIES

- Accounts given by people from a variety of belief systems and age about near-death experiences often include a sense of looking down from above at what is happening, despite the person actually being immobile and unconscious.
- Many people know identical twins who, despite sharing the same DNA and having had the same upbringing, are very different personalities.

Some people believe these situations prove the existence of souls. Evaluate the evidence for and against belief in souls. Explain your own view, giving detailed reasons and examples from your experience or from the media.

What are you?

Most Hindus believe that humans are essentially an **atman** housed in a body. In the Bhagavad Gita, the soul is described as formless and eternal.

> **Bhagavad Gita 2:23**
> *Weapons cut it not, fire burns it not, water wets it not, wind dries it not.*

Most Hindus believe that the soul *is* the person; their body, and to some degree their mind too, is just a means of expression. Think about how some severely physically or academically challenged people are described as 'good souls'.

Many Hindus believe that the ultimate purpose of existence is to attain **moksha** – freedom from the cycle of rebirth and becoming one with the Supreme Spirit. To do this, individuals must:

- seek wisdom
- be detached from material and emotional concerns
- love the Supreme Spirit
- perform good **karma** (actions)
- fulfil dharma (duties).

Many Hindus believe that living well will speed the path to moksha, while creating karmic debt will require the soul to be reborn again. The 'debt' is good actions that must be performed in order to balance bad deeds, and/or lessons that need to be learned.

An example of karmic debt

Some Hindus believe if a person is always greedy, and never learns to share, then in their next life they may experience poverty but also have the opportunity to share whatever they have. If this time, they do share, the soul has learned not to be greedy and is therefore closer to moksha; if they remain greedy, another similar birth may be required.

However, behaving well *just* in order to attain moksha is not desirable. Many Hindus would say the *motive* for deeds is as important as the deed. To attain moksha, a soul must be pure – good karma should come from care for the world and love for God, not the *desire* for moksha.

Those Hindus aiming to be sannyasi may try to go a step further and perform only disinterested or unattached actions, meaning the motive is simply to 'be' – since even acting with love is, in one way, acting for self-interest.

Bhagavad Gita 18:6

... even these actions should be performed leaving aside attachment and the desire for rewards...

Few Hindus believe that God judges or punishes people – each individual soul knows why it does something as well as deciding what to do; and must accept the cosmic consequences, both positive and negative.

Maitri Upanishad, Chapter 6

If men thought of God as much as they think of the (material) world, who would not attain liberation (moksha)?

Examples of Dharma in everyday life.

AO1 skills ACTIVITIES

List at least three things that may be viewed as good karma, and three that may be viewed as bad. (Think about which deeds help the world and which damage it.)

AO2 skills ACTIVITIES

'What goes around comes around.'
'As you sow, so shall you reap.'

The concept of actions having consequences is not unique to Hinduism. Do you agree with the belief that everything eventually balances out, or do you think that people are just good or bad and often do *not* get what they deserve? Try to support your view with examples from your own experience and from the media.

Hinduism:
The end of life 2

The next two pages will help you to:

- explore your own beliefs about the meaning of life and death
- consider the purpose and process of Hindu funerals.

Many Hindus view death as a step to the next stage of existence for the atman.

What is death?

> **Bhagavad Gita 2:22**
>
> *Just as a man casts off worn-out clothes and puts on new ones, so also the embodied soul (or Self) casts off worn-out bodies and enters others that are new.*

> **Bhagavad Gita 2:27**
>
> *For certain is death for the born and certain is birth for the dead; therefore over the inevitable do not grieve.*

This cycle of birth-existence-death-rebirth, is described by some Hindus as the 'stream of existence', and refers to souls being reborn and universes recreated. The word often used to sum up this belief is **samsara**.

 FOR DEBATE

'Death is the end, that's all there is to it!'

'There has to be something after we die, otherwise what is the point?'

Reflect on and discuss these points of view.

What's in a body?

Given the teaching about soul being separate to body, many Hindus choose to be organ donors and some even donate their entire body for medical research. They believe it is good karma to improve or save other lives. If a body is donated for research, there cannot be a funeral, but many Hindus accept that the funeral rites are not essential in order for the soul to be released. Instead, families may celebrate the life of the deceased by holding a memorial service.

Hindu funerals

The beliefs described above mean that, for most Hindus, the main purpose of a funeral is to help to release the soul of the deceased and to help family and friends deal with their own grief. Exact practices vary from family to family, but there are various traditions maintained by many Hindus.

When death is very close, or as soon as possible after death, the person is given a tulsi leaf and water from the River Ganges. Tulsi is believed to be a sacred plant, the Ganges a sacred river, and the aim is to purify the person.

In India, the body is bathed and dressed ready for family and friends who wish to pay their last respects. Many choose to place food or flowers with the deceased as a sign of their love. Cremation takes place as soon as possible, which is good hygiene in a hot country. The body is placed on a pyre of wood, which traditionally is lit by the eldest son.

In the UK, undertakers may oversee the care of the body, although some families prefer to prepare the body themselves, and the cremation will be at a crematorium. The ashes are usually scattered in running water, to purify and release the soul. Many Hindus believe this process is enhanced if the ashes are offered to the River Ganges, which many hold sacred. After the funeral, those who attended may bathe and eat a simple meal.

From the time of death until 12–14 days afterwards, it is customary for family and friends to gather at the home of the deceased to sing religious songs and read from the Bhagavad Gita. They may also share their memories of the deceased and release their grief – which is for the person they knew, not the soul, which has moved on. A portrait or photograph of the deceased, usually adorned with garlands made of fresh flowers or sandalwood, is placed in a prominent position, and a diva is often kept lit.

After this, many Hindus believe the soul of the deceased is free to be reborn. Many Hindu families mark this final farewell by inviting the extended family and friends to a special meal. Pictures of the deceased may be placed in the home shrines of family or friends as a sign that the *person* is now one with God, even though the soul may continue to exist.

AO1+AO2 skills **ACTIVITIES**

- Explain why most Hindus do not believe the body is important.
- Why do you think some families may prefer to prepare the body of a loved one for the funeral themselves rather than leave it to undertakers? Which would you prefer to do? Why?

Islam:
The end of life 1

Body and soul in Islam

What is the soul?

Muslims believe human beings are Allah's highest creation. Allah gives each human an individual soul (nafs) soon after the baby begins to develop in the womb. Allah allows each soul a certain amount of time to inhabit the body. The nafs desires to be perfect, pure and happy through submission to Allah's will. On Judgement Day, both body and soul are resurrected.

Muslims try to keep their soul as pure and clean as possible, in preparation for the Day of Judgement: 'Those who purify their souls will certainly have everlasting happiness and those who corrupt their souls will certainly be deprived (of happiness)' (Surah: 91:5–10).

> **The next two pages will help you to:**
>
> - explain Muslim beliefs about the relationship between the body and the **soul**
> - evaluate Muslim beliefs about life after death and how these beliefs affect the way they live their lives.

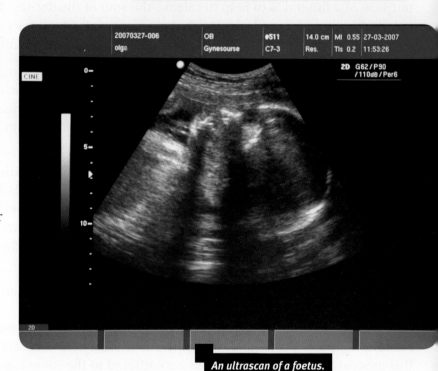

An ultrascan of a foetus.

> **Surah 21:35**
>
> *Every soul shall have a taste of death: and We test you by evil and by good by way of trial. To Us must ye return.*

What is the relationship between the body and soul?

One way of imagining this relationship is that the soul is the master while the body is its obedient servant. The body has physical needs and may try to ignore the spiritual needs of the soul, giving priority to physical appearance and action. In all forms of worship, the intention is that the body and soul are united equally in submission to Allah. To fully understand Islam, body and soul must work together. The act of **wudu** – ritual washing before **salah** – is both a physical act and a spiritual preparation for the prayers ahead.

ACTIVITIES

Draw two circles, one with 'soul' and the other with 'body' in the centre. Around the soul, write what it wants to be according to Islam; around the body, write actions or thoughts that might prevent the soul from being pure: for example, vanity.

FOR DEBATE

Do you have to be religious to believe in the existence of the soul?

What do Muslims believe about life after death?

Here, Sabeel, a Muslim teenager, describes what **akhirah** (life after death) means to him.

> 'I believe life has two parts. First there is a brief stay on earth. This is to test whether we turn towards Allah or turn away from Him. This is followed by eternal life. Eternal life is more important because it lasts forever. On the Day of Judgement, Allah will judge everyone on their deeds and their faith. Believers will be rewarded and will enter Paradise; unbelievers will go to Hell.'

Muslims believe that on Yawmuddin, the Day of Judgement, every body and soul will be resurrected to join the living and be judged by Allah. Before the judgement, the angels Mukar and Nikir will ask three questions:

- 'Who is your Lord?'
- 'What is your way of life?'
- 'Who is your Prophet?'

Allah assesses people according to the good or bad actions they have completed in their lives, referring to the records in a wide-open Book. These will be weighed on a scale, with actions that please Allah on one side and those that do not on the other. Following Judgement Day, akhirah will begin.

Surah 14:48–50
One day the earth will be changed to a different earth, and so will be the heavens, and (men) will be marshalled forth, before Allah, the One, the Irresistible; And thou wilt see the sinners that day bound together in fetters – Their garments of liquid pitch, and their faces covered with Fire.

What do Muslims believe about Paradise and Hell?

The afterlife lasts forever, but is impossible to describe. Muslims whose actions have pleased Allah will enter Al-jannah, Paradise, a place that is far more pleasurable than the current world. The Qur'an refers to a garden where beautiful streams flow, everyone will be reunited with their loved ones and everlasting peace will reign. The most important reward on entering Paradise is that Allah himself welcomes each individual. Muslims whose actions have not pleased Allah are damned and will enter Jahannam or Hell.

Because Allah is merciful, it is possible for a bad person to enter Paradise after they have been punished. Only one crime cannot be forgiven – the crime of shirk, or regarding something as being equal to Allah.

REMEMBER THIS

The information about salah and wudu in Topic 2 will be useful in helping you understand the link between the body and soul in worship.

AO1+AO2 skills ACTIVITIES

- Draw a flow chart to show what happens, in the correct sequence, on the Day of Judgement. Now judge yourself!

- What good or bad actions would you say you have completed in the past week? Draw these out on a chart.

AO1 skills ACTIVITIES

What effect do cigarettes and alcohol have on an individual? Describe how a Muslim would respond to these habits, considering how they might affect the soul.

Islam:
The end of life 2

The next two pages will help you to:

- describe the relationship between obedience and the afterlife
- explain and consider the importance of rituals at death and how it shows the beliefs of a Muslim
- evaluate Muslim attitudes to death.

ACTIVITIES

In what ways might a Muslim change the way they lead their life, knowing that Judgement Day is inevitable?

A Muslim funeral ceremony.

What is the relationship between obedience and the afterlife?

For Muslims, life on earth is their only opportunity to seek submission to Allah and to be rewarded in the afterlife. The way Muslims lead their daily lives and follow the Qur'an has consequences on the Day of Judgement. Following the rules of the Qur'an, showing obedience to Allah's revelation and following the example of Muhammad ﷺ are very important as all good acts will be listed on the Day of Judgement.

What happens at a Muslim funeral?

At death the people gathered around the dying person recite the **Shahadah** – 'There is no God but Allah and Muhammad ﷺ is his messenger' reaffirming they are a Muslim before death and hoping for life in Paradise. The eyes are then closed. The body is washed in a special way – ghusl – by a member of the same sex. The areas normally washed for wudu are washed first, followed by the rest of the body. A responsible and trustworthy adult Muslim is chosen for this important role. The body is then perfumed and traditionally wrapped in three white cloths, five for a female, following the example of Muhammad ﷺ at his death. Often these are ihram – the sheets worn by a Muslim who has completed Hajj.

FOR DEBATE

Mourning and funerals are to comfort the living, and they have no purpose for those who have died.

Muslims do not use a coffin but in Britain burial without a coffin is not permitted.

Cremation is not allowed, as full bodily resurrection is anticipated at Judgement Day. Muslims believe that Allah will put people back together from their bones, not from ashes.

Surah 75:3–4

Does man think that We cannot assemble his bones? Nay, We are able to put together in perfect order the very tips of his fingers.

The burial normally takes place as soon as possible. Burial at night should be avoided. The body must be buried with legs lowered first, laid on its right side, with the face in the direction of the Ka'bah, showing dedication to the house of Allah. As the grave is filled with soil, people say:

Surah 20:55

From the (earth) did We create you, and into it shall We return you, and from it shall We bring you out once again.

Only men attend funerals. They recite the Salat-ul-Janazah, special funeral prayers, which may only be performed in the presence of the body. It is the tradition to stand in an odd number of rows. Included in these prayers is the Dua al Mayyit, a prayer of hope for mercy on the deceased. The grave will normally have a modest stone with no decoration.

In this extract from the funeral prayers forgiveness is asked for both the living and the dead:

❝ Oh Allah! Forgive those of us that are alive and those of us that are dead; those of us that are present and those of us who are absent; those of us who are young and those of us who are adults; our males and our females. Oh Allah! Whomsoever You keep alive, let him live as a follower of Islam and whomsoever You cause to die, let him die a Believer. ❞

How do Muslims support the bereaved?

After a death there is a period of mourning. Traditionally, this is four months and ten days for a husband or wife, and three days and nights for any other relations or friends. Crying is acceptable, but loud wailing is regarded as distracting. It is remembered that Muhammad ﷺ himself wept at the death of his son and it is natural for people to show their sorrow by crying. During the period following the funeral, relatives and friends will gather around the close relatives of the deceased, bringing food and offering emotional support during this difficult time. Relatives will often travel from far away to help families cope.

Muslims regularly visit the graves of relatives to say prayers. They do this to remind themselves:
- that life is short compared with eternal life
- that they must live in submission to Allah to please him and to ensure the rewards of Allah when they die.

AO2 skills **ACTIVITIES**

- What parts of the Muslim funeral service directly show Muslim beliefs?
- Why do you think there are different periods of mourning for direct family and friends?
- Do you think a Muslim would look forward to death? Give your reasons.

 REMEMBER THIS

See Topic 4 for information on how Muslims try to live according to the teachings of the Qur'an and follow the example of Muhammad ﷺ.

Judaism:
The end of life 1

What Jews mean by body and soul

Unlike some other religions, Judaism is not very concerned with explaining the difference between the body and the soul.

Jews believe that G-d breathed Adam's soul into his body:

> **Genesis 2:7**
> *The Lord G-d formed man from the dust of the earth. He blew into his nostrils the breath of life, and man became a living being.*

So Jews believe that it is the soul that gives people life.

According to the Rabbis, the soul leaves the body when people are asleep and is refreshed in heaven. They also say that, during the Sabbath, everyone has two souls to bring them closer to G-d. Jews believe that neither the body nor the soul can survive without each other.

What do Jews believe about life after death?

According to the Jewish scriptures, after death everyone goes to a place called **Sheol.** This was a dark place underground where people stayed for eternity.

Many Jews believe that Adam and Eve were originally immortal, and only became mortal because they ate the fruit from the tree of the knowledge of good and bad. Since then everyone has grown old and died.

The earliest part of the Jewish Scriptures to suggest that there is life after death comes in the book of Daniel:

> **Daniel 12:2**
> *Many of those that sleep in the dust of the earth will awake, some to eternal life, others to reproaches, to everlasting abhorrence.*

This verse seems to suggest that, after Sheol, people will go to either heaven or hell. Later Jewish teaching is that at the end of time G-d will judge people. The soul will judge the body and the body will have to take responsibility for its actions. Good people will go to Gan Eden (Paradise) and bad people to Gehenna (Hell).

> **The next two pages will help you to:**
> - explain the concepts of body and soul
> - examine the relationship between moral behaviour and life after death.

G-d giving Adam his soul as painted by Michelangelo on the ceiling of the Sistine Chapel.

> **Job 7:9**
> *As a cloud fades away,
> So whoever goes down to Sheol does not come up.*

 **ACTIVITIES**

Discuss these questions with a partner.

- Is there any evidence that there is life after death?
- What do people mean by 'soul'?
- What are funeral services for? Try to think of several answers to this question.

 MUST THINK ABOUT!

Although some versions of the Bible translate 'Sheol' as '**Hell**' or 'Hades', there is no suggestion that people are punished in Sheol.

Gan Eden.

Gehenna.

'L'Chaim' – 'to life' – the traditional Jewish toast.

Sheol.

What Jews believe about how they behave and what will happen when they die

According to the **Torah**, Jews will be punished for the sins of their parents and grandparents:

Exodus 20:5b–6

For I the Lord your God am an impassioned God, visiting the guilt of the parents upon the children, upon the third and upon the fourth generations of those who reject Me, but showing kindness to the thousandth generation of those who love Me and keep My commandments.

However, this view changed later and the prophet Ezekiel says that G-d will judge how people live their own lives.

Ezekiel 18:1–4

The word of the Lord came to me: What do you mean by quoting this proverb upon the soil of Israel, 'Parents eat sour grapes and their children's teeth are blunted'? As I live – declares the Lord God – this proverb shall no longer be current among you in Israel. Consider, all lives are Mine; the life of the parent and the life of the child are both Mine. The person who sins, only he shall die.

So, although Jews believe that they may be rewarded or punished after death, there is no clear teaching about the afterlife as in most religions. Therefore, Jews believe that the important thing is how they live their lives on earth, not what might happen after they die. Jews try to live their lives according to the 613 mitzvot (see p. 48) and aim to live an halakhic life – 'walking with G-d'.

ACTIVITIES AO1+AO2 skills

Working in twos or threes, try to work out what people mean by the word 'soul'. Collect all the views together and put them up on a poster.

FOR DEBATE

When Jews give a toast they say 'L'Chaim' – 'to life'. A traditional Jewish birthday card says: 'May you live to be 120.' What does this say about Jewish belief?

ACTIVITIES AO1 skills

- Compare Jewish beliefs about life after death with those of any other religion you have studied. Make a list of similarities and differences.

- Explain why other people might not find Jewish beliefs about life after death very comforting.

Judaism:
The end of life 2

The next two pages will help you to:

- explain the importance of Jewish funeral rites.
- evaluate the way in which mourning rituals may help Jews after a death.

An Orthodox Jewish funeral on the Mount of Olives, Jerusalem.

Jewish funerals

If they can, just before they die, Jews try to say the **Shema** (see p. 20). After the person has died, other people say the **Kaddish**. These are both important statements of faith and belief.

The Kaddish

May His great Name grow exalted and sanctified in the world that He created as He willed. May He give reign to His kingship in your lifetime and in your days, and in the lifetimes of the entire Family of Israel, swiftly and soon. May His great Name be blessed forever and ever. Blessed, praised, glorified, exalted, extolled, mighty, upraised, and lauded be the Name of the Holy One, Blessed is He beyond any blessing and song, praise and consolation that are uttered in the world. May there be abundant peace from Heaven, and life, upon us and upon all Israel. He who makes peace in His heights, may He make peace upon us, and upon all Israel.

 FOR DEBATE

Read the words of the Kaddish. Remember that it is a prayer said when someone has died. What is the prayer actually about?

If possible, Jews are buried within 24 hours of dying. The body is dressed in a plain white shroud and placed in a plain wooden coffin. People sit with the coffin, which is sealed, until the burial. Before the burial takes place, family mourners make a small tear in their clothes called a keriah, to show their grief at the death. Although Progressive Jews allow cremations, Orthodox Jews do not.

The coffin is taken to the Jewish burial grounds and there is a short, simple service. The body is buried and a blessing is said: 'May God comfort you among all the mourners of Zion and Jerusalem.'

There are no flowers at a Jewish funeral and the whole service shows that everyone, rich or poor, famous or not, is equal in death.

The mourning after the funeral is in three parts:

- Shiva – for seven days the family stay at home with the mirrors in the house covered. They say Kaddish three times a day. However, they must break Shiva for the Sabbath or a Jewish festival.
- Sheloshim – for the thirty days after the burial, the mourners return to normal life but do not go to parties or to any place of entertainment, such as a cinema.
- Shana – this is the period until the end of the year. Kaddish is said every day.

After Shana, all mourning must stop. At the end of the year, the tombstone is placed on the grave. The dead are remembered on the anniversary of the death by lighting a yahrzeit candle and saying Kaddish.

RESEARCH NOTE

What is a shroud?

RESEARCH NOTE

Why do Orthodox Jews not allow cremation?

AO1+AO2 skills ACTIVITIES

- Watch the final scene of the film *Schindler's List*. What are people putting on the gravestone? Try to explain why they are doing this.
- 'Funerals are important for the living, not for the dead.' Give views for and against this statement and include your own opinion.

Sikhism:
The end of life 1

The next two pages will help you to:

- develop your knowledge and understanding of the concept of death and the afterlife from Sikh teachings
- analyse the Sikh belief in an immortal **soul** and its journey from one life to the next.

An outdoor Sikh funeral pyre in Northumberland.

The soul in Sikhism

Sikhs believe that everybody has an eternal soul, which will be reborn into either a human or animal body, depending on the actions of the previous life (**karma** or karam). The conditions or body into which a soul is born do not just happen by chance, but because of the accumulative karma of the previous life.

Good karma will result in reincarnation into a human life where the individual will seem to be blessed with good luck. Bad karma may either result in birth into an animal body or, if born into a human body, the individual's circumstances will seem to be cursed with bad luck.

> **Guru Granth Sahib Ji, page 1303**
>
> *I am inebriated with ego, am imbued with other relishes and love evil friends. My Beloved see-est me wandering from lifetimes into further lifetimes.*

> **Guru Granth Sahib Ji, page 658**
>
> *They who, by Good Fortune, are Attuned to the Lord, wrapt in the seedless Trance of Equipoise, They are Illumined from within: and no more is the fear of births and deaths for them.*

 **ACTIVITIES**

- Why do you think death rites are very important for all religions?
- Is it necessary for non-religious people to have a funeral?
- Do you believe in an afterlife? Give reasons for your answer.

Compare your results to those of other pupils in the class.

AO1+AO2 skills **ACTIVITIES**

In pairs, read the quotations from Sikh teachings about the soul's journey.

Discuss what each quote teaches Sikhs about the afterlife. Compare your answers to those of another pair in the class.

Being entangled in the cycle of reincarnation is not the goal

Although the cycle of reincarnation offers many chances to be reborn, it is not the goal for Sikhs to be entangled in the cycle of reincarnation, known as **samsara**. The goal is to escape samsara and attain mukti – no more rebirth. However the soul, due to its eternal nature, will still exist, but in complete bliss with **Waheguru**.

The analogy in Sikhism is often used of a fish and water. The fish (individual soul) cannot survive without water (Waheguru), however it never actually becomes the water.

Fundamental in Sikh teachings is the idea that ultimate union with God is the responsibility of God, rather than that of us, the individual.

> **Guru Granth Sahib Ji, page 1**
> *His Will (forsooth) Inborn in us, ingrained, Thou follow.*
> *(Thus is Truth attained)*

Karma or the Will of God?

At times, there appears to be an anomaly in Sikh teachings as to whether the soul attains mukti through the individual's karma or whether it is in accordance with the Will (hukam) of God. Another important concept here is the idea of the overriding nadar (Grace) of God. Guru Nanak Dev Ji's teachings emphasise the complete supremacy of God. Hence, Sikhism is very much a bhakti faith, in which the individual relies totally on the Grace and Will of God.

However, this does not mean that individuals need not work toward their own liberation.

This is where the very important concept of karma as determining future births comes in. One has been given the golden opportunity of being born into the human life in accordance with the Will of God. The individual now has to work towards being a gurmukh (a god-orientated person) then await God's Grace for the final liberation out from samsara. Karma is important since it is the human mind that can distinguish between right and wrong.

Guru Nanak Dev Ji's teaching

The role of karma and the Will of God is clearly summarised by Guru Nanak Dev Ji in this teaching:

> **Guru Granth Sahib Ji, page 662**
> *As one does, so is one rewarded:*
> *As one sows, so also one reaps.*

RESEARCH NOTE

Sikh beliefs about reincarnation are influenced by Hindu teachings about reincarnation and the path of bhakti. Find out more about the concept of bhakti.

REMEMBER THIS

Look back at Topic 1 for more on the concept of bhakti.

FOR DEBATE

Do you think it is possible for individuals to work toward their own liberation from samsara while also being 'predestined'? In pairs, suggest how a Sikh would answer this question. Remember to answer by fully explaining your point of view.

ACTIVITIES

The saint Ravidas writes the following about reincarnation in the Guru Granth Sahib Ji:

Thou Knowest all and I am so Ignorant: Thou art the Destroyer of 'coming-and-going'. So all life seeks Thy Refuge and Thou Fulfillest all.
  (*Guru Granth Sahib Ji*, page 858)

After reading this, do you think that Sikhism teaches that it is just the responsibility of each individual to attain their liberation from samsara? Is it dependent on something greater? What do you think the 'coming-and-going' is a reference to?

Sikhism:
The end of life 2

The Sikh view of funerals

People often find the final farewell during a funeral comforting, in that it gives them the chance to come to terms with their loss. The service during a Sikh funeral highlights the soul's future journey and wishes it well in the next life.

Rites during a Sikh funeral

Death for Sikhs is not seen as the end: it is the next step on the soul's journey in the cycle of reincarnation. Mourners and the deceased's family will wear white clothes to symbolise the purity of the soul.

The next two pages will help you to:

- explore the significance behind Sikh funeral rites
- make links between the concept of life after death in Sikhism with what you think/believe.

ACTIVITIES

Read the words of the Sohila. How do you think they comfort the family and friends of the deceased? What phrases, if any, do you find particularly poignant?

Sikhs gathered around a coffin at a funeral.

Sikh bodies are cremated, not buried. This is due to the belief that the soul has made use of its physical encasement – the body – in this life: it will have a new body to house its soul in the next life. Although death is not supposed to be a sad time, people will feel sad at the loss of a loved one and there is no overt objection to showing one's sorrow.

Before being buried, the body of the deceased is washed and dressed, complete with the five K's. It is then placed in a coffin or, in India, on a funeral pyre. In the diaspora, the body is taken to the crematorium. The Sohila prayer is recited to comfort both the dead's soul and the living. After the funeral, mourners will go to the **gurdwara** to hear final prayers and there will be a special reading from the Guru Granth Sahib Ji. The ashes of the deceased are taken to India so that they can be scattered in a river, or are taken to a sea or river in Britain.

Mourners sitting in the gurdwara after a funeral.

From the Sohila prayer

Lovers of mammon do not enjoy the taste of God's Elixir, as within them there is the thorn of ego.
When they walk forward, that thorn pricks them more and more severely; they suffer greater pain and finally receive on their heads, the blows from death's staff.
True devotees are absorbed in God's Name, and fear of the pain of birth and death leaves them.
They are united with the Everlasting God and gain great honour in the various regions and universes.
O God! the Greatest of the great, save us, we are poor and humble.
Nanak says: the Name is the Sustainer and support of the mortal, and gives Supreme Joy and peace.

 AO1+AO2 skills **ACTIVITIES**

In small groups, suppose you have been commissioned by the local gurdwara to produce comforting guides for the bereaved, aimed at Sikhs who are not familiar with the philosophical concepts in their faith. Write a guide, and include details of the funeral rites using illustrations and symbols (see the sikhnet website). Share your guide with the rest of the class and be prepared to answer any questions they have.

GradeStudio

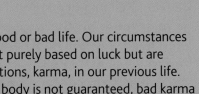

AO1

QUESTION
Explain Sikh views about death and the afterlife. **[6 marks]**

You could build an answer like this:

Level 1
First, let the examiner know that you know what the question is about. For example,

'Sikhs believe in the concept of reincarnation, that is, death is not the end but the soul continues to be housed in a new body in each lifetime.'

Level 2
Next go on to explain that Sikhs do not believe in a heaven or hell but rather our future birth will determine whether we have a good or bad life. Our circumstances in the next life are not purely based on luck but are determined by our actions, karma, in our previous life. Rebirth into a human body is not guaranteed, bad karma may result in the soul taking on an animal's body in the next life.

Level 3
Finally, a developed answer would discuss the concept of liberation, known as mukti. Release from samsara is possible only through the human birth.

GradeStudio

Welcome to the Grade Studio

Grade Studio is here to help you improve your grades by working through typical questions you might find on an examination paper. For a full explanation of how Grade Studio works, and how the examiners approach the task of marking your paper, please see p. 26.

AO1

Question

How many Christian funeral rites reflect beliefs about life after death? **[6 marks]**

Student's answer

Christian funerals take place in a church with a priest to show that people believe in Christianity. Christians believe that when they die they will go to one of three places: heaven, hell or purgatory. They think that which one they go to depends on the way you have lived your life. If you have been good, you will go straight to heaven. If you have been bad, you will go to hell. If you have been in between, then you will go to purgatory where you wait until God thinks that you are good enough to go to heaven.

Examiner's comment

The candidate has given a satisfactory answer to the question. There are a number of relevant points but only the distinction between heaven, hell and purgatory is explained. The answer needs to give more information and examples in order to reach Level 3. Also it needs to focus more clearly on the funeral service and how this reflects these beliefs. The candidate could also use more technical terms from the specification to show the breadth of their knowledge and understanding.

Student's improved answer

Christian funerals take place in a church with a priest to show that people believe in Christianity. Christians believe that when they die they will go to one of three places: heaven, hell or purgatory. They think that which one they go to depends on the way you have lived your life. If you have been good, you will go straight to heaven. If you have been bad, you will go to hell. If you have been in between, then you will go to purgatory where you wait until God thinks that you are good enough to go to heaven.

A Christian funeral service reflects these beliefs by emphasising Jesus' promise that Christians will join him in heaven and continue to live in the hands of God. The service suggests that death is only a stage in life as people go on to eternal life with God. This can comfort the mourners who believe that they will eventually see the person again.

Examiner's comment

This is now a good answer to the question. The candidate has shown a clear understanding of the question. There is good description and explanation of a variety of different aspects of the funeral service. The candidate has shown some analysis in dealing with the question of resurrection in heaven. The information is presented clearly and there is good use of technical terms.

AO2

Question

'When people die that is the end.' Discuss this statement. You should include different, supported points of view and a personal viewpoint. You must refer to Christianity in your answer.　　　　[12 marks]

Student's answer

Christians might say that this statement is not true because they believe that after death people go to heaven or hell. Some Christians might also say that Jesus promised that, for his followers, death would not be the end but the beginning of a new life.

Examiner's comment

The candidate has given a limited answer to the question. There are two relevant points but they both address the same point of view and neither is expanded very far. The answer needs to give alternative viewpoints, and include a personal response to reach Level 4.

Student's improved answer

Christians might say that this statement is not true because they believe that after death people go to heaven or hell. Roman Catholics, in particular, believe that many people will go to purgatory in order to be cleansed from their sins before they can enter heaven. Some Christians might also say that Jesus promised that, for his followers, death would not be the end but the beginning of a new life.

Some non-believers, on the other hand, might say that there is absolutely no evidence that there is any form of life after death and that it is just wishful thinking to believe in it. Others may refer to ghosts and near-death experiences to support the argument.

My personal opinion is that there is not enough evidence either way to decide whether there is any life after death or not. There is no evidence, other than the Bible, to suggest that people go to heaven and no one has ever come back to say whether this is true or not. Events such as ghosts and near-death experiences can all be explained by science.

Examiner's comment

This is now a good answer to the question. The candidate has shown a clear understanding of the question and has presented a range of views supported by evidence and argument. The answer explains Christian views, among others, and includes a personal viewpoint, which is also supported.

These specimen answers provide an outline of how you could construct your response. Space does not allow us to give a full response. The examiner will be looking for more detail in your actual exam responses.

These examples only use Christianity but you could use the Grade Studio to apply to any of the religions you are studying and the structure of the answers would work in the same way.

Topic 4: Good and evil

The Big Picture

In this Topic, you will be addressing religious beliefs and teachings about:

- the nature of good and evil
- the sources and reasons that guide religious people in making moral decisions
- ways of understanding and coping with suffering.

You will also think about ways in which these beliefs affect the life and outlook of believers in the world today.

What?

You will:

- develop your knowledge and understanding of key religious beliefs and ideas about the nature of good and evil
- explain what these beliefs and ideas mean to people of different religions and think about how they might affect how they live
- make links between these beliefs and ideas and what you think/believe.

Why?

Because:

- these beliefs and ideas underpin and are reflected in the ways people live their lives: for example, in helping them to make moral choices
- understanding people's beliefs can help you understand why they think and act in the way they do
- understanding these beliefs helps you compare and contrast what others believe, including thinking about your own beliefs and ideas.

How?

By:

- recalling and selecting information about beliefs and ideas relating to good and evil, explaining their importance for people today
- thinking about the relevance of these beliefs in 21st-century Britain
- evaluating your own views about these beliefs.

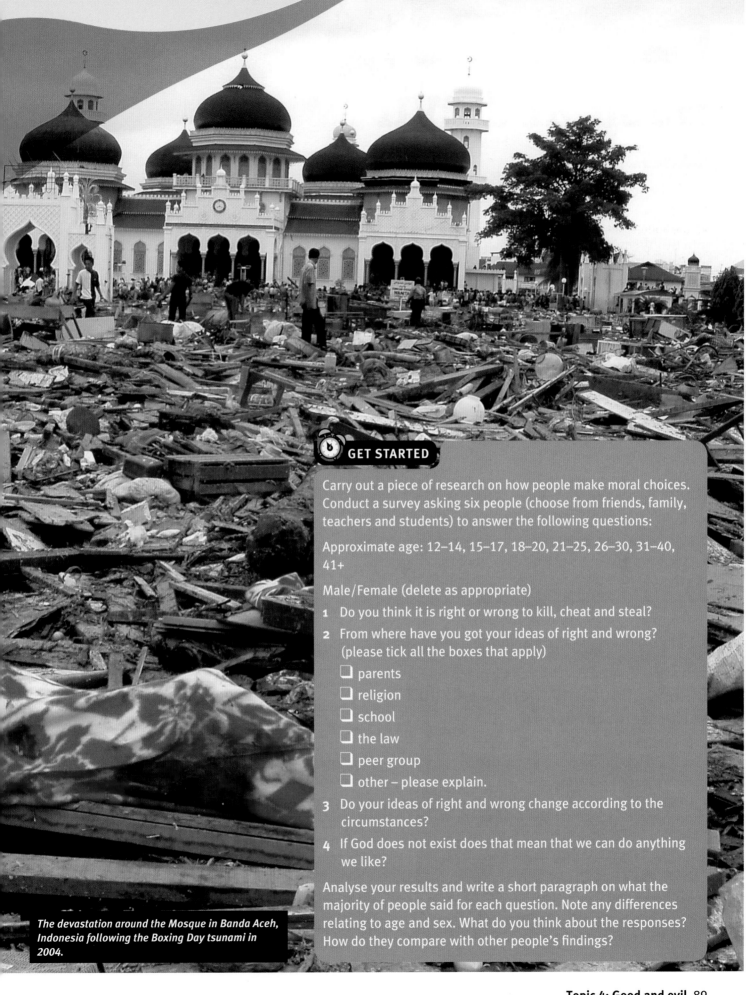

The devastation around the Mosque in Banda Aceh, Indonesia following the Boxing Day tsunami in 2004.

GET STARTED

Carry out a piece of research on how people make moral choices. Conduct a survey asking six people (choose from friends, family, teachers and students) to answer the following questions:

Approximate age: 12–14, 15–17, 18–20, 21–25, 26–30, 31–40, 41+

Male/Female (delete as appropriate)

1 Do you think it is right or wrong to kill, cheat and steal?

2 From where have you got your ideas of right and wrong? (please tick all the boxes that apply)
   ❑ parents
   ❑ religion
   ❑ school
   ❑ the law
   ❑ peer group
   ❑ other – please explain.

3 Do your ideas of right and wrong change according to the circumstances?

4 If God does not exist does that mean that we can do anything we like?

Analyse your results and write a short paragraph on what the majority of people said for each question. Note any differences relating to age and sex. What do you think about the responses? How do they compare with other people's findings?

Good and evil

The existence of evil is a problem that people who believe in a benevolent god have to solve or come to terms with in some way. Evil is often classified into two types: **natural evil**, which is inevitable due to the way the world is, and **moral evil**, which is caused by people choosing to act in an evil manner. Suffering is frequently the result of either natural or moral evil.

Concepts of good and evil

All religions believe evil exists, and often portray it in terms of a devil or demon.

- Buddhists portray evil as the character Mara, who tries to trap beings in the cycle of **samsara** and prevent them from achieving enlightenment.
- Many Christians describe evil in terms of the Devil or Satan, the enemy of God.
- Hindus believe that everything, both good and evil, is contained in God.
- Muslims believe that God allows Iblis (Shaytan) to use evil to tempt them to give up Islam.
- For Jews, the idea of good and evil begins in the **Torah** with story of Adam and Eve.
- Sikhs believe that suffering (**dukkha**) is inevitable and universal.

Beliefs about why there is evil and suffering in the world

- For Buddhists, dukkha is the result of bad actions that lead to rebirth, and keeps them trapped in the cycle of samsara.
- Christians believe that evil and suffering are the result of disobedience to God. This is known as the Fall of Man, and from that time on, all humans have been born in a state of sin (this is known as **original sin**) and have a natural ability to choose evil over good.
- Hindus believe evil and suffering are inevitable, and that people suffer because of their actions in past lives.

GET STARTED

"Not to have known suffering is not to be truly human."
(Midrash)

Rachel weeping for her children (Jeremiah 31:15) – a sculpture at Yad Vashem, Israel.

Do you agree with the statement from Jewish scripture that suffering is an essential part of what it means to be human? Why? Write a caption for the picture using the words 'good' and 'evil'.

- Muslims believe life is a test from God where people can make right or wrong choices.
- The Jewish scriptures teach that G-d gave people free will to choose between good and evil. Suffering can be a punishment or a test from G-d, and also a way of bringing people closer to G-d. Jews try to follow the 613 mitzvot (the 613 commandments by which Jews try to live their lives).
- Sikhs believe that suffering is the result of lust, anger, greed, attachment and pride. If these were eliminated, suffering would be impossible.

KNOWLEDGE AND UNDERSTANDING
Write down the main beliefs about the problem of evil and suffering in Christianity and another religion you have studied. Discuss whether these responses solve the problem or not, and why.

ANALYSIS AND EVALUATION
Can good ever come out of evil? If so, what would this mean for people who believe in a good God?

Beliefs about coping with suffering

- Buddhists believe dukkha is increased if people are unable to accept what happens in the world, and decreased if they can learn to accept the world as it is.
- Christians follow the example of Jesus and help and care for those who suffer.
- Hindus believe it is their dharma (duty) to help people who are suffering and to try and prevent suffering, building up good **karma**. Hindus should also offer sewa (service to others).
- Muslims believe those who stay good Muslims despite evil and suffering will be rewarded in Paradise.
- Jews respond to suffering by praying for those who suffer and providing practical help and support by raising money. The Holocaust or Shoah raised questions for many Jews about evil and suffering.
- Prayer and meditation help Sikhs to endure suffering and its consequences and to find peace. All Sikhs have a responsibility to help people who are suffering. Sikhs should also offer sewa (service to others).

Sources and reasons for moral behaviour

Most religions are guided by the teachings of sacred texts in knowing how to choose between right and wrong and how to behave.

- Buddhists follow the teachings of the Buddha called the Four Noble Truths.
- Christians use the example of Jesus to help them know what to do, and also look at the parables he told as moral guides.
- Hindus follow the teachings in the Bhagavad Gita and other sacred writings to help them follow the right path in life. Swamis or holy men are good examples of how to behave.
- For Muslims, the Qur'an and the teachings of Muhammad ﷺ help them understand how God wants them to behave. Actions that are niyyah are done with the right intention.
- For Jews, the sacred writings of the Torah and the **Talmud** help them make decisions, tell them how to know good from evil and how to live a good life.
- Sikhs follow the writings and lives of the **Gurus** for examples of how to overcome suffering.

KEY WORDS

Ahimsa the Buddhist and Hindu concept of non-killing, non-violence, respect for life

Bhikkhu fully ordained Buddhist monk

Dhamma ultimate truth, universal law

Dukkha suffering – the nature of existence according to the first Noble Truth in Buddhism

Guru teacher; a title reserved for the ten human Gurus and the Guru Granth Sahib Ji

Kamma in Buddhism, intentional actions that affect your circumstances in this and future lives

Karma consequence of actions, in terms of cause and effect

Moksha in Hinduism, an escape from the cycle of death and rebirth

Moral evil evil which is caused by people choosing to act in an evil manner

Natural evil evil which is inevitable due to the way the world is

Nibbana in Buddhism, achieving freedom from greed, hatred and delusion resulting in freedom from rebirth

Omnipotent in religion, when God is all powerful

Omniscient in religion, when God is all knowing

Original sin the Christian idea that, since the Fall, all humans have been born in a state of sin, with a natural ability to choose evil over good

Salah the daily prayers for a Muslim as required by the Qur'an

Samsara in Buddhism and Hinduism; a continuing cycle of birth, ageing, death and rebirth

Talmud collection of teachings and explanations of rabbis, which help Jews understand the written Torah

Tawhid unity; belief in the oneness of Allah; absolute monotheism as practised in Islam

Torah Jewish law, or teaching, made up of the Five Books of Moses

Waheguru a Sikh name for God

FOR INTEREST

“For evil to triumph it is only necessary for good men to do nothing.”

(Edmund Burke, Philosopher)

What does the statement mean? Do you agree?

Give an example of what you think is an evil in the world and what someone might be able to do to change it.

Buddhism:
Good and evil 1

The next two pages will help you to:

- explore Buddhist concepts of good and evil
- explain Buddhist responses to evil and suffering.

Images like this make us all consider why there is evil and suffering in the world.

Natural evil or moral evil – does it make a difference?

Some people classify evil into two types: **natural evil**, which they believe is inevitable due to the way the world is, and **moral evil**, which they believe is caused by human beings choosing to act in an evil manner.

For Buddhists, the classification of evil into natural evil and moral evil is not important. Whether **dukkha** is brought about due to people, or just from the way the world is, does not affect how much dukkha we experience. A person's dukkha is increased if they are unable to accept what happens within the world, and decreased if they can learn to accept the world as it is.

The main focus in Buddhism is therefore to learn to accept what happens, without craving for it to be different. This does not mean that Buddhists do not try to reduce dukkha: for example, by taking medical treatment if they are ill. It simply means that, if dukkha still occurs, it must be accepted.

ACTIVITIES

Look at the picture of the aftermath of the Asian Tsunami in 2004 above, and think about these questions.

- Was it natural evil or moral evil?
- Does it make any difference to those suffering its effects whether it was natural evil or moral evil?

REMEMBER THIS

The information about **samsara** and **kamma** in Topic 3 will be useful to help understand Buddhist beliefs about good and evil, as will the information on the Four Noble Truths in Topic 1.

Good and evil or skilful and unskilful actions

The terms good and evil tend to imply the existence of a judge, determining whether an action is good or bad. Since there is no being to judge people in Buddhism, Buddhists prefer to talk about skilful or unskilful actions.

Skilful actions are those which produce good kamma, or which help a person on the path to achieving **nibbana**. Unskilful actions are those which produce negative kamma, or prevent a person from progressing on the path to nibbana.

Who is Mara?

Mara is sometimes considered to be the Buddhist version of a devil. He appears in the story of the Buddha's life. Just as the Buddha is about to achieve enlightenment, Mara tries to tempt, distract and stop the Buddha.

In Buddhist thinking, Mara represents the three poisons – greed, hatred and delusion – that trap beings in the cycle of samsara, and prevent them from achieving enlightenment (Mara is often depicted holding the wheel of samsara). However, the story of the Buddha shows that Mara (and the three poisons) can be overcome.

Mara is also trapped in the cycle of samsara, and must die and be reborn. When Mara dies, another being is born into Mara's role – there are a series of Maras, rather than one eternal being.

Why is there suffering?

The Four Noble Truths (see Topic 1) are the Buddha's answer to why there is dukkha. Beings suffer because they crave for life, material goods, feelings, and so on. This craving leads to rebirth, and keeps us trapped in the cycle of samsara.

On a more individual level, beings experience dukkha because they are facing the consequences of unskilful actions. In some sense, then, they are responsible for their own suffering – but this does not mean suffering should just be ignored. Buddhists try to reduce suffering on an individual and community level.

At an individual level, Buddhists may try to act more skilfully, to prevent further negative consequences, and might meditate to reduce their craving. On a community level, Buddhist **bhikkhus** and the laity may be involved in projects that aim to reduce dukkha: for example, environmental or drug rehabilitation projects, or projects to help those suffering in the aftermath of the Asian Tsunami.

RESEARCH NOTE

The way in which craving leads to rebirth can be explored more fully if you research the twelve links of dependent origination explained in Topic 6.

FOR DEBATE

- Does the Buddhist explanation for why there is dukkha provide an adequate answer for the suffering experienced throughout the world?
- If dukkha is the result of kamma, should we try and reduce or prevent it?

ACTIVITIES

Which way of coping with dukkha do you think would be most helpful to a Buddhist? Explain your choice.

How do Buddhists cope with dukkha?

Buddhists might meditate. Meditating on the temporary nature of dukkha, or the causes of dukkha, might help them understand why they are suffering. This could then make it easier to cope with dukkha.

Buddhists might seek comfort in the three refuges – the Buddha, the Dhamma and the Sangha. Seeing that the Buddha overcame dukkha might help Buddhists cope themselves. Advice could be sought in the teachings (dhamma) or from others in the Buddhist community (sangha).

How do Buddhists cope with dukkha?

Understanding the concept of kamma might help Buddhists cope with dukkha. If they know that dukkha is caused by previous unskilful actions they might be able to cope with it better. Knowing that if they act more skilfully now they will reduce dukkha can also give a positive attitude.

Buddhists might cope with dukkha by trying to become less attached to things. Most dukkha is caused because we crave things we do not have. If we can become more detached and stop craving things, then dukkha can be reduced.

Buddhists may cope with dukkha in many ways.

Buddhism:
Good and evil 2

How do Buddhists know how to behave?

Buddhists can find out how to behave from a wide variety of sources. These include scriptures, the example of the Buddha, the Three Refuges, and specific moral codes such as the eightfold path and the Five Precepts.

> **The next two pages will help you to:**
> - identify where Buddhists get information about how to behave
> - explore Buddhist scriptures, along with the Three Refuges, the Five Precepts, and the eightfold path.

The Three Refuges

The Three Refuges, where Buddhists may seek comfort and guidance, are the Buddha, the **dhamma** (the Buddha's teachings), and the sangha (the Buddhist community). They could help in the following ways:

- The Buddha – following the example of the Buddha shows Buddhists the best way to behave. Children may be told stories from the Jataka Tales (stories of the Buddha's previous lives), which show the Buddha being compassionate.

- The dhamma – the teachings of the Buddha include guidance on the way Buddhists should behave: for example, the Four Noble Truths, including the eightfold path.

- The sangha – Buddhists can seek guidance from those who have more knowledge of Buddhists teachings, and/or those who have already been through the moral dilemmas they are experiencing.

The Three Refuges help Buddhists know how to behave.

The scriptures

Buddhists have many scriptures (see Topic 5), which contain guidance from the Buddha, or other influential Buddhist leaders, about how they should behave. The eightfold path, and the Five Precepts are moral guidelines found within the scriptures.

The eightfold path

The eightfold path is the fourth in the Buddha's teachings of the Four Noble Truths. It lays out the ways in which Buddhists should behave and think if they wish to gain enlightenment.

The eightfold path is divided into three sections: wisdom, morality and meditation. All three sections of the path work together: wisdom is needed in order to behave morally; only if moral behaviour is followed will the mind be clear enough to meditate; meditation enables you to perceive the world more clearly and increase in wisdom effectively.

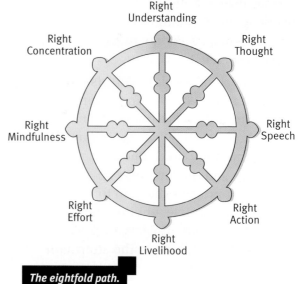

The eightfold path.

The three aspects of the path relating directly to morality are Right Livelihood, Right Action and Right Speech. Right Livelihood indicates that Buddhists should choose a path that corresponds with other Buddhist teachings, such as non-harming. Right Speech indicates that a Buddhist should choose to speak in a way that helps them to think in ways that correspond with other Buddhists teachings: for example, compassion. Right Action indicates that a Buddhist should act in a way that corresponds with other Buddhist teachings: for example, being aware of the world around them. Some consider Right Action to be further explained in the teaching of the Five Precepts.

The Five Precepts

The Five Precepts are perhaps the most widely used moral code for lay Buddhists. They are considered to explain the concept of Right Action within the eightfold path, and can be viewed as having both positive and negative forms.

Negative form	Positive form
Do not harm any living being	Treat all living beings with compassion
Do not take that which is not given to you	Respect other people's belongings, time, etc.
Do not engage in sexual misconduct	Treat sexual partners with respect, and in a way which helps you and them
Do not speak untruthfully or gossip	Speak only in a way which helps others and yourself
Do not take intoxicating substances (e.g. alcohol)	Keep a clear mind, so that you are fully aware of the world around you

GradeStudio

AO1

QUESTION
How might Buddhists explain the problem of evil in the world? [6 marks]

Level 1
A basic answer will refer to kamma, and might say that a person's behaviour in their previous life causes them to suffer in this life.

Level 2
A better response might consider the role of Mara, and whether Mara causes dukkha, or simply the temptations humans face. It could also include reference to skilful and unskilful actions as the cause of positive and negative kammic influences.

Level 3
A very good answer might consider whether all evil is caused by negative kamma, or whether there is such a thing as bad luck. The student might also explain how kamma is passed from one life to another through the processes of samsara.

Christianity:
Good and evil 1

What do Christians believe about God and the Devil (Satan)?

The next two pages will help you to:

- examine Christian ideas about God and the Devil (Satan)
- evaluate the impact of the Fall and **original sin** on Christian behaviour
- explore the Christian concept of evil.

In the Old Testament, God is described as so perfect that Moses cannot look at God: 'Moses hid his face, because he was afraid to look at God' (Exodus 3:6b).

In the New Testament, God is described as loving and forgiving. Christians believe that God is the 'Supreme Being': God is perfect and has qualities that humans simply cannot comprehend. God is seen as Ultimate Good. However, Christians would say that, if there is an Ultimate Good, there has to be an opposite – Ultimate Evil, known as the Devil or Satan.

Traditionally the devil was seen as male, red in colour, with horns and a tail and carrying a pitchfork. The devil has been given many other names, such as Lucifer, the Accuser, the Father of Lies, and the Serpent. There is a suggestion that the devil was a fallen archangel who was cast out of heaven.

Many Christians believe that the snake was the Devil (Satan) in disguise. The devil seems to have had various jobs to perform, for example:

- tempting Adam and Eve in the Garden of Eden
- testing Job, causing him all sorts of suffering to make him lose faith in God
- tempting Jesus, offering him great power and riches.

Nowadays, Christians who interpret the Bible literally believe that Satan is real and rules over hell, but Liberal Christians might suggest that the Devil is the potential we all have to choose evil rather than good: Hell is not a real place, but a place where God is absent.

Eve picking the fruit of the tree of the Knowledge of Good and Evil in the Garden of Eden.

ACTIVITIES

Make a list of your top ten films that are about good versus evil. Does good or evil triumph more often? Why do you think this is the case?

The Fall and original sin

God created Adam and Eve and they lived in the Garden of Eden. Everything was perfect … until Eve was tempted to eat forbidden fruit by the serpent. This is known as the Fall, and shows that, right from the start, humans have rebelled against God. Many Christians believe that God has given humans free will – that is, the ability to make choices for themselves. From this time on, all humans have been born in a state of sin. They have a natural ability to choose evil over good. This is called original sin.

Christians believe that humans have been separated from God since the Fall, and can only return to God through the sacrifice of Jesus on the cross (the crucifixion). This sacrifice redeemed humanity from original sin so that people could go to heaven.

Christians believe that evil exists in the world for a purpose. They believe that God is **omniscient** and **omnipotent** and must be aware of the fact that humans suffer. Some believers think that God chooses to do nothing about suffering; others believe that the free will given to humans at the Creation means that we have to make choices for ourselves, and thus come to appreciate the power and love of God.

Many Christians would turn to the example of Job, who suffered but kept his faith in God. Job eventually realised that God had a plan for him.

Job's first test

> Job 1:13–20
>
> *One day, when Job's sons and daughters were feasting and drinking wine at the oldest brother's house, a messenger came to Job and said, 'The oxen were ploughing and the donkeys were grazing nearby, and the Sabeans attacked and carried them off. They put the servants to the sword, and I am the only one who has escaped to tell you.'*
>
> *While he was still speaking, another messenger came and said, 'The fire of God fell from the sky and burned up the sheep and the servants, and I am the only one who has escaped to tell you!'*
>
> *Another messenger came and said, 'The Chaldeans formed three raiding parties and swept down on your camels and carried them off. They put the servants to the sword, and I am the only one who has escaped to tell you!'*
>
> *Yet another messenger came and said, 'Your sons and daughters were feasting and drinking wine at the oldest brother's house, when suddenly a mighty wind swept in from the desert and struck the four corners of the house. It collapsed on them and they are dead, and I am the only one who has escaped to tell you!'*
>
> *At this, Job got up and tore his robe and shaved his head. Then he fell to the ground in worship.*

REMEMBER THIS

Look back at Topic 1. Remind yourself of the qualities of God.

AO2 skills **ACTIVITIES**

Check out Genesis 3. Decide whether Adam or Eve was to blame for the Fall, or if God was at fault for giving them free will. Share your opinions with the group.

AO1 skills **ACTIVITIES**

Look at the events listed below, and decide whether each is a result of **natural evil** or **moral evil**. Make a chart to show the difference. Some might be caused by both natural and moral evil. Put these in a separate list. Add one event of your own.

terrorism, forest fire, road rage, gas explosion, disease, genocide, tornado, world war, flooding, rape, earthquake

Christianity: Good and evil 2

How might Christians respond to suffering?

There are a variety of possible responses.

- Suffering strengthens a believer's faith. God would not test a Christian with more than they could bear.

- Christians believe that Jesus suffered on their behalf even though he did not deserve to, and this gives them the strength to cope with their own suffering.

- Suffering started with the Fall and all humans have to accept original sin, which leads to suffering.

- If humans have free will, God must have a plan to end suffering in the future.

- Christians have to accept natural suffering as they can do nothing about it.

- Sometimes a Christian may feel that it is hard to believe in the goodness of God, but they would try to accept that there is a purpose to their suffering even though they do not understand what it is.

- For many Christians, prayer is a way of responding to suffering.

The next two pages will help you to:

- identify a variety of ways that Christians may cope with suffering
- explore the sources and reasons Christians have for behaving morally.

 **ACTIVITIES**

Explain in your own words how Christians may choose to deal with suffering. Add any other ways that you think would help people to cope.

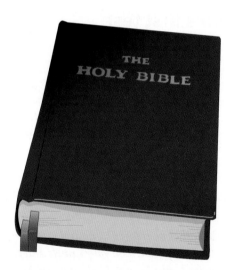

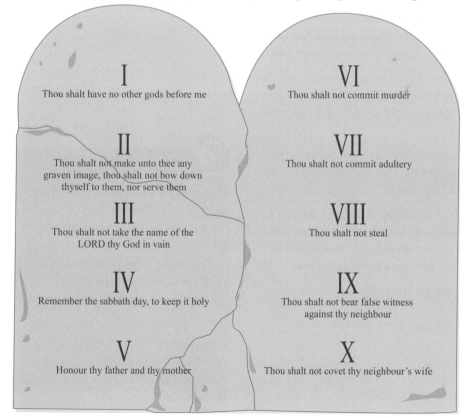

I	VI
Thou shalt have no other gods before me	Thou shalt not commit murder
II	VII
Thou shalt not make unto thee any graven image, thou shalt not bow down thyself to them, nor serve them	Thou shalt not commit adultery
III	VIII
Thou shalt not take the name of the LORD thy God in vain	Thou shalt not steal
IV	IX
Remember the sabbath day, to keep it holy	Thou shalt not bear false witness against thy neighbour
V	X
Honour thy father and thy mother	Thou shalt not covet thy neighbour's wife

 **FOR DEBATE**

'There is no point in trying to act morally.' Prepare an argument for or against this statement, giving reasons to support your opinions.

How do Christians choose to behave morally?

Christians believe that they should make choices, which will enable them to become like God. To do so, they need guidance so that they do the right thing and avoid doing wrong. They look for support from a number of different sources.

Why choose to behave morally?

Christians believe that humans were made 'in the image of God' (Genesis 1:27). To become more like God, they try to follow a code that will help them to behave as they think God wants them to. Christians would say that the moral code and the guidelines written in the Bible are there for a reason and should be followed, as they show the way God wishes them to behave. They believe that, if they do this and try to behave morally, they will be rewarded after death (see Topic 1).

Many believe that their conscience tells them right from wrong. They feel guilty if they do wrong, even if no one else knows about their actions. This could be the way God speaks to a believer. Some people might say that this is not God, but the way we remember what we are told as we grow up.

Rules and laws help people to decide on the right course of action. These may be the laws of the land, but would also include religious laws, such as the Ten Commandments, or 'do to others what you would have them do to you' (Matthew 7:12).

Christians will take advice and support from their faith communities. Often there are support networks in churches, and the priest or minister will help a believer to make decisions on the right way to behave. Sermons during services also act as guidance.

Christians find a lot of guidance in the Bible. They may look in the Gospels to find out what Jesus did. They would also take advice from the teachings of Jesus in the **parables**, as well as the writings of others such as St Paul. They believe that, as Jesus was the son of God, he always acted ther ight way. Today, they would think about what Jesus would have done in their situation.

The teachings of the Church is one way in which Christians learn how to behave morally.

GradeStudio

AO2

QUESTION

'There is no such thing as the Devil, it is people who are evil.' Discuss this statement. You should include different, supported points of view and a personal viewpoint. You must refer to Christianity in your answer. **[12 marks]**

Level 1

First, show the examiner that you understand what the question is about, and then state an opinion.

Level 2

Next, justify this by referring to a religious teaching, such as 1 Peter 5:8b 'Your enemy the devil prowls around like a roaring lion, looking for someone to devour.'

Level 3

Now offer a deeper explanation. Some Christians believe that the Devil is a mythical character, that it is part of human nature to do bad and good things, and that God wants us to make the right decisions. You should also give your own opinion

Level 4

Finally, explain the second viewpoint. There are different Christian views about the Devil. Many people believe that the Devil is just that part of us which is tempted to do the wrong thing and that it is part of being a Christian to resist these temptations and follow God. You should also give your own opinion and support it.

Hinduism:
Good and evil 1

Although many Hindu scriptures describe battles between forces of good and evil (such as that between Prince Rama and Ravana in the story of Divali), most Hindus do not believe in evil as a separate entity. Just as our bodies are capable of producing harmful cancer cells as well as helpful white cells, our souls are capable of committing acts of horror as well as kindness. Evil people are not tempted to do wrong by anything other than their own greed and moral weakness.

It may be argued that if people are created to be capable of evil, it is not really their fault. However, most Hindus believe creation is a fluid process, not one single act by God. The existence of evil is as necessary to the universe as the existence of good, because creation is all about balance. It is up to individual souls to create good **karma** and achieve **moksha**, or build up bad karma and remain part of **samsara** – the cycle of birth, death and rebirth (see Topic 3).

Many Hindus believe an action can only truly be defined as good if a choice has been made to do what is right and something that would be wrong avoided. In addition, many believe that the *motive* determines the morality of an action rather than the action itself.

> **Bhagavad Gita 2:33**
> *'But if thou wilt not fight this righteous war, then having abandoned thine own dharma (duty), thou shalt incur sin.'*

The next two pages will help you to:

- explore and analyse the nature of evil
- consider whether the morality of an action is determined by the action itself; the motive behind the action; or the consequences of the action.

FOR DEBATE

Is evil a separate force that opposes good, or simply the absence of good?

AO1+AO2 skills ACTIVITIES

What makes the characters below good or evil? For each figure, analyse the reasons for their actions and the effects on others.

These figures are famous for being good or evil.

Many Hindus understand this quote to mean that what makes something good or evil is the purpose and context. In the Bhagavad Gita, Prince Arjun, who is of the warrior caste and therefore expected to protect the people of his kingdom, is reluctant to engage in battle against his cousins. God, in the form of Lord Krishna, advises him that, because the purpose of the battle is to protect innocent people and not for material gain, combined with it being Arjun's dharma as a Kshatriya (member of warrior caste) to defend the kingdom (see Topic 6), it would actually be wrong *not* to fight. The sin of not fulfilling one's dharma is worse than taking a life.

Is God both good and evil?

Two common questions are:
- Why is God a god of destruction – isn't God supposed to be good? (see Topic 1)
- Even if humans are responsible for moral evil, because of free will, isn't God to blame for the chaos and despair caused by natural disasters?

Here are two possible answers for a Hindu.
- Many Hindus believe that any violence used by deities is for the greater good and therefore not evil in itself.
- Destruction is necessary for re-creation. For example, it is only after a volcano erupts or a river floods that the nutrients needed for growth are released to create fertile soil; the lessons we learn from heartbreak or illness often make us wiser and stronger people.

Lord Shiva is believed to use his third eye to look into people's souls, just as scripture advises people to themselves search their souls (which many Hindus equate with conscience) to decide if they are creating good or bad karma.

Some Hindus believe those souls that keep building karmic debt may be blind about why they are doing it, and therefore may be unable to pay off the debt by behaving differently: for example, someone who regularly donates to charity, but is also very proud about how generous they are.

FOR DEBATE

If you hold that the motive decides the morality of an action, a drink-driver who has killed someone could say their *intention* was to get home, not to kill, so they haven't committed a sin. These things are either right or wrong; to say 'it depends' is a cop out!
- Debate the 'crime' the drink-driver has committed.
- Evaluate the pros and cons of determining the morality of an action by the motive behind it.

Lord Shiva is the god of destruction and re-creation.

Many Hindus believe that deva (deities) e.g. Rama (left) and asuras or rakshas (demons) e.g. Ravana (right) exemplify good and evil behaviour.

AO1 skills ACTIVITIES

'As long as the charity benefits, it does not matter *why* the donation was given to it.' Explain why some Hindus would disagree with this statement.

Hinduism:
Good and evil 2

Can suffering be overcome?

Many Hindus would answer 'Yes'!

The scriptures advise that one way to overcome suffering is by avoiding the attachments that cause emotional pain and by using the mind to overcome physical pain, by separating the soul from body and emotions.

That is not to say people shouldn't love their families and friends, but that they should be aware that everything, including life, is transient and accept this, rather than grieve when there is loss (see Topic 3). Some people demonstrate how far their minds can be more powerful than their body by walking over hot coals, or even having surgery without an anaesthetic, to prove the power of mind over matter.

Most Hindus believe that helping those in need is part of dharma (see Topic 2). Many believe that, to overcome suffering, individuals must both do their best not to cause any suffering and show compassion towards those who suffer. The latter may be done in any number of ways, such as fundraising, voluntary work, dana (charitable gifts of food, money or goods) and prayer or meditation.

Many Hindus also believe that to experience suffering is to pay off karmic debt (see Topic 3), so the best response is to try to learn from it; suffering is overcome by viewing it as something positive. For example, if during this life someone shows contempt for their parents and treats them badly, despite their always acting with love and kindness towards the child, then in a future life the person may suffer having cruel parents or being an orphan, to show them the value of having good parents.

This belief does not mean that people should view those who suffer as somehow 'deserving' it. Most Hindus would agree that, if this is the position taken, nothing is being learned and is in itself bad karma. The response to all suffering should be compassion.

The next two pages will help you to:

- explain and evaluate some Hindu responses to suffering
- explore the example of correct living set by inspirational Hindus.

Bhagavad Gita 13:8–9

'Indifference to the objects of the senses and also absence of egoism, or reflection on the evils of birth, death, old age, sickness and pain. Non-attachment, non-identification of the Self with child, spouse, home and the rest…'

 **ACTIVITIES**

- Explain the three ways in which some Hindus believe suffering may be overcome.
- Evaluate these views and put forward you own, including reasons and examples.

 **REMEMBER THIS**

Reasons some Hindus may give for why they behave well.

- It's a form of bhakti, meaning a way to show love for God (see Topic 2).
- It's part of their dharma.
- Creating good karma and avoiding bad leads to moksha.
- It's what their conscience tells them to do.
- They follow the teachings of the sacred texts.
- They follow the examples set by gods and goddesses (see above and Topic 1).
- They follow the lead of inspirational Hindus.

CASE STUDY

Sewa International

The word sewa means service to others. Sewa International is a global charity founded by Hindus, which provides emergency support for suffering people (for example, after natural disasters) and ongoing support for disadvantaged people (for example, schools for orphans).

Hindu role models

Swami Vivekananda *(1863–1902) was the founder of the Ramakrishna Mission, which aims to inspire followers to union with God through yoga and bhakti (see below). He was passionate about the need to accept all belief systems – 'I accept all religions of the past and I worship God with them all. I leave my heart open to those of the future.'*

Mahatma Gandhi *(1867–1948) was believed by many to have exemplified how to practise detachment, sewa and good karma (hence the title Maha, meaning great; atman, meaning soul). He believed that all people are equal and was a key figure in introducing equality laws in India. In addition, he followed the principle of* ahimsa *(non-violence in thought, word and deed), and helped achieve independence for India using only peaceful means.*

Pramukh Swami Maharaj *(1921– present) is the spiritual leader of the Swaminarayan Sanstha (a major Hindu organisation within the Swaminarayan faith). He gives sermons based on his interpretation of sacred texts to many thousands of followers, who often base their moral codes and behaviour upon his teachings. In particular he teaches the principles of bhakti yoga and the need for service to society.*

 **ACTIVITIES**

- Try to live for just one day completely following the principle of ahimsa. Reflect on what the experience teaches you about yourself and Mahatma Gandhi.
- Who are the moral role models in your life? Why do you choose to follow their example?

Islam:
Good and evil 1

The problem of evil

Muslims regard the world as a perfect creation by Allah. Any **natural evil** that happens in the world – evil that is not caused by humans, such as death caused by diseases and natural disasters – was created by Allah's will and is Allah's intention for the world. Many Muslims believe that this sort of evil is a test of the faith of Muslims by Allah, and that Allah's actions should not be questioned.

Muslims believe that **moral evil** – suffering caused by humans through their own actions in the world, such as injustice, cruelty, cheating, lying or stealing – exists because of Shaytan, the Devil, who leads them into temptation away from the path of Allah. Shaytan is also called Iblis.

What is the nature of Shaytan/Iblis?

Shaytan/Iblis, the 'enemy', is regarded as the cause of suffering and evil in the world. Islam teaches that, when Allah created Adam, the first man, from clay, Allah also made mala'ikah (angels) from light, and created spirits, called Jinn, out of fire. Allah commanded the angels and the Jinn to bow down to Adam. The angels obeyed but Iblis, one of the Jinn, refused. (Allah) said:

> **Surah 7:12**
> *'What prevented thee from bowing down when I commanded thee?' He said: 'I am better than he: Thou didst create me from fire, and him from clay'.*

In a later passage from the Qu'ran, Allah curses Iblis (Allah) said:

> **Surah 15:34–35**
> *'Then get thee out from here: for thou art rejected, accursed. And the Curse shall be on thee until the Day of Judgement'.*

Iblis's response was to tempt humans to do wrong rather than right, and distract them from dedication and submission to Allah. This temptation can take many forms: for example, ignoring the Five Pillars, especially **Salah**, for something less important. Muhammad warned of Shaytan/Iblis in his final sermon during Hajj: 'Beware of Shaytan, he is desperate to divert you from the worship of Allah, so beware of him in matters of your religion.'

The next two pages will help you to:

- explore the concepts of good and evil in Islam
- investigate the nature of Shaytan/Iblis
- understand and explain the idea of original sin
- investigate the notion of free will in Islam.

RESEARCH NOTE

Read the biblical account of the story of Adam and Eve in Genesis 3 and compare it with the Muslim story in the Qu'ran, Surahs 7 and 15. What are the significant differences in Muslim and Christian beliefs about original sin?

FOR DEBATE

To what extent can humans still have freedom to choose how to act if Allah has already planned their lives? Is this a contradiction?

> **Surah 2:38**
> *Get ye down all from here and if, as is sure, there comes to you guidance from Me, whosoever follows My guidance, on them shall be no fear, nor shall they grieve.*

The **Qur'an** describes how Adam and Hawwa (Eve) were tempted by Shaytan/Iblis and disobeyed Allah by eating the fruit of the forbidden tree in Al-Jannah (Paradise). They begged for Allah's forgiveness and Allah was merciful to them promising to protect all those who followed Allah.

Allah forgave Adam and made him the First Prophet. Therefore humans are born fitrah (without sin), but in a state of ready submission to Allah. A person becomes responsible for their mistakes from puberty. If a person seeks forgiveness, it is the **omnipotent** Allah who grants it.

Free will

Each human is responsible for their actions and has free will. Life is viewed as a series of tests. Each human is able to choose their own path in life and has the chance to prove their faith in Allah. A dedicated Muslim would follow the guidance of the Qur'an, particularly living according to the Five Pillars. Allah allows humans this choice, but is **omniscient** and so knows the path that each human is going to take.

Muslims believe in life after death and that, if they act well in this life, life in Paradise will be better, free from evil, suffering and sin. The Qu'ran suggests that this life is nothing compared with the life to come:

 **ACTIVITIES**

- For each picture above answer the question:
  Is this the result of natural or moral evil?
- Does it make any difference to those who are suffering the effects whether it was natural or moral evil?

REMEMBER THIS

You will find detailed information about Muslim beliefs in life after death in Topic 3.

Surah 29:64
What is the life of this world but amusement and play? But verily the Home in the Hereafter — that is life indeed, if they but knew.

Islam:
Good and evil 2

The next two pages will help you to:

- identify how Muslims cope with suffering
- explore the sources and reasons for moral behaviour in Islam
- explain and consider how Muslims use their conscience in their daily lives
- evaluate the importance of living by a moral code.

Muslims praying in a ruined mosque.

AO2 skills ACTIVITIES

Here are five possible religious explanations for the existence of suffering. Which is closest to the Muslim view of suffering? Which makes most sense to you and why? Which makes least sense to you and why?

- Suffering is God's test to see whether people trust that God cares for them.
- Suffering challenges people and leads them to have a greater understanding of God.
- Suffering allows people a chance to show they care for those who are suffering.
- Suffering is not God's fault; it is humankind's fault.
- Suffering is not caused by evil or the devil and is not God's fault.

How do Muslims cope with suffering?

Muslims believe Allah is good and merciful and will protect them from evil if they follow Islam. Suffering and the existence of evil in the world are tests for Muslims in preparation for the Day of Judgement and their place in the afterlife. Even in adversity, Muslims must remain dedicated to the will of Allah and the teachings of the Qur'an. Through tragic events, dedication to Islam and submission to the will of Allah – for example, through prayer – is seen as an important act of strength.

What are the sources to support moral behaviour?

The Qur'an and the teachings and example of Muhammad ﷺ guide Muslims to make decisions about how they live and act. They provide practical examples for how Allah wants them to behave and to help them distinguish right from wrong. Allah is the one good, supreme God. Followers of Islam must turn away from sin and seek forgiveness by submitting to Allah's will.

Allah is also seen as merciful towards followers of Islam.

Surah 1:1–3

'In the name of Allah, Most Gracious, Most Merciful. Praise be to Allah, the Cherisher and Sustainer of the worlds: most Gracious Most Merciful.'

The Qur'an also gives many rules that are regarded as good for humans to live by, enabling them to show dedication to Allah. Those who do good works receive Allah's favour and will enter Paradise on the Day of Judgement.

The example of Muhammad

Muhammad , as the Final Prophet, led a perfect life, and Muslims are expected to follow his example. Muslims would look at specific stories from his life and would regard him as a role model. He was renowned for his ability to preach that there is only one God, and for the way he could engage people in his speeches, even though he grew up illiterate. His reputation for being trustworthy, honest and a good businessman led many people to respect him.

Conscience

The teachings of the Qur'an, and its authority as a holy book, remain at the forefront of the conscience of a Muslim. In all aspects of the daily and family life of a Muslim, the Qur'an remains the final guide for human judgement on ethical action. Although humans have debated and considered ethical issues among themselves, reference to the Qur'an and its binding authority will always remain the focus. Allah has provided Muslims with this guidance before the Day of Judgement.

Surah 3:115

Of the good that they do, nothing will be rejected of them; for Allah knoweth well those that do right.

Why do Muslims try to follow a moral code?

It is important for Muslims to show their belief in one God, **tawhid**, through following the guidance of Allah in the Qur'an. The Qur'an sets out a clear code of actions that are right and wrong. Muslims will be rewarded for following the Qur'an.

Surah 17:9

Verily this Qur'an doth guide to that which is most right (or stable), and giveth the Glad Tidings to the Believers who work deeds of righteousness, that they shall have a magnificent reward;.

The Five Pillars can be regarded as the foundations of a Muslim's dedication to Allah, but other aspects of teaching, such as food laws and niyyah (having the right intention) also have to be considered.

REMEMBER THIS

The information about the Five Pillars in Topic 2 will be useful in helping you to understand the principles that guide Muslim life.

A Muslim woman reading the Qur'an.

FOR DEBATE

- 'Everyone should have a moral code to live by.' What do you think?
- What moral code guides the choices and decisions you make in your life? Where has it come from?

Judaism:
Good and evil 1

Natural evil and moral evil

Evil is usually divided into two types. **Natural evil** is found in events such as hurricanes and floods; **moral evil** is caused by human beings choosing to act in a certain way.

Jewish beliefs about good and evil

Jews believe that G-d is absolutely good and that, because of the promises in the covenants (see p. 20), G-d will always protect them as G-d did in the past.

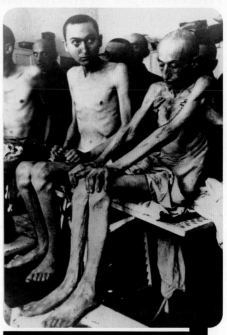

> **Genesis 12:2–3**
>
> *I will make of you a great nation,*
> *And I will bless you;*
> *I will make your name great,*
> *And you shall be a blessing.*
> *I will bless those who bless you*
> *And curse him that curses you;*
> *And all the families of the earth*
> *Shall bless themselves by you.*

Jews believe that all people have free will and can choose for themselves what they do. G-d made people this way so that they can choose to worship G-d and follow G-d's teachings.

Some Rabbis have said that G-d made good and also made evil. These Rabbis believe that people who suffer in this world will be rewarded in Paradise.

> **Isaiah 45:7**
>
> *I form light and create darkness,*
> *I make weal and create woe –*
> *I the Lord do all these things.*

People often say that evil is caused by Satan (or the Devil), who tempts people to go against G-d's teachings. Some people also blame the Devil for events of natural evil. However, this traditional view of the Devil is not found in Jewish teaching.

The idea of the introduction of evil into the world begins in the Garden of Eden, when Adam is told not to eat from the tree of the knowledge of good and evil. Adam's wife, Eve, is tempted by a serpent to eat the fruit.

Prisoners in a Nazi concentration camp. Images like this make us wonder about evil and suffering in the world.

 **ACTIVITIES**

Make two lists of recent events dividing them into incidents of moral evil and natural evil.

 MUST THINK ABOUT!

The Bible does not say anything about an apple; the fruit was more likely to be a fig.

In the Garden of Eden

Genesis 3:1–5

Now the serpent was the shrewdest of all the wild beasts that the Lord God had made. He said to the woman, 'Did God really say: You shall not eat of any tree of the garden?' The woman replied to the serpent, 'We may eat of the fruit of the other trees of the garden. It is only about fruit of the tree in the middle of the garden that God said: "You shall not eat of it or touch it, lest you die."' And the serpent said to the woman, 'You are not going to die, but God knows that as soon as you eat of it your eyes will be opened and you will be like divine beings who know good and bad.

The Garden of Eden.

The text suggests not that the serpent was Satan, but that it was a wild beast. G-d punishes Adam and Eve by throwing them out of the garden and making them truly human and mortal. He also punishes the serpent.

Genesis 3:14–15

Then the Lord God said to the serpent,
'Because you did this,
More cursed shall you be
Than all cattle
And all the wild beasts:
On your belly shall you crawl
And dirt shall you eat
All the days of your life.
I will put enmity
Between you and the woman,
And between your offspring and hers;
They shall strike at your head,
And you shall strike at their heel.'

For Jews, the first time the Devil appears as an evil being is when he tempts King David:

1 Chronicles 21:1

Satan arose against Israel
and incited David to number Israel.

The other occasion when Satan appears is in the book of Job. However, here Satan is seen as a spy working for G-d, who limits what Satan can do.

To learn about punishment for evil deeds, look at p. 79 in Topic 3.

To learn about punishment for evil deeds, look at p. 79 in Topic 3.

FOR DEBATE

If G-d created evil as well as good, does that mean that G-d is not totally good?

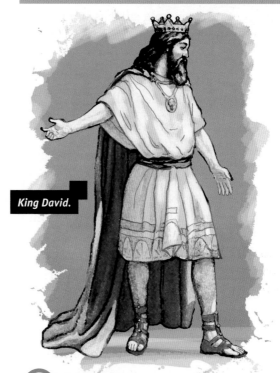

King David.

AO1 skills ACTIVITIES

Read the passage from Genesis 3:14–15 carefully and then explain in your own words what G-d is saying.

Judaism:
Good and evil 2

The Holocaust

From the time when they became slaves in Egypt, Jews have suffered because of their religion.

The Romans drove most of the Jews out of Israel after the destruction of the Temple in 70 CE. Jews then lived all over the world in what is called the Diaspora (scattering), until the State of Israel was established in 1948.

In the mid-20th century, Jews suffered their worst persecution in the Holocaust or Shoah. The German Chancellor, Adolf Hitler, wanted to create a master race of Aryans, which excluded Jews. In the 'Final Solution', he tried to bring all Jews into death camps in Germany and Poland. In all, 6 million Jews were killed by the Nazis. The Germans also killed many millions of other people such as homosexuals, gypsies and communists.

The Final Solution failed, and Hitler was defeated. However, many Jews who survived the camps or whose relatives had been killed began to ask questions about why G-d had let this happen.

Some Jews said that G-d died in Auschwitz (one of the death camps). Others said that, for some reason, G-d had not been in Auschwitz and had let his people suffer. Still others believed that G-d was in Auschwitz and that is why there were survivors from the camps.

How do Jews cope with suffering?

The best example of coping with suffering found in the Jewish Scriptures is the book of Job.

G-d and Satan decided to test Job's faith but whatever happened to him, including losing his whole family, all his property and suffering physically, he never lost his faith.

Because of examples like this, Jews simply aim to accept whatever happens to them as being G-d's will, believing that G-d will always look after them.

The next two pages will help you to:

- explore Jewish responses to the Holocaust
- explain Jewish responses to evil and suffering
- identify where Jews get information about how to behave.

Whatever position people take about the Holocaust, many Jews have had to think carefully about why G-d allowed it to happen.

Job 42:2–6

I know that You can do everything,
That nothing you propose is impossible for You.
Who is this who obscures counsel without knowledge?
Indeed, I spoke without understanding
Of things beyond me, which I did not know.
Hear now, and I will speak;
I will ask, and You will inform me.
I had heard You with my ears,
But now I see You with my eyes;
Therefore, I recant and relent,
Being but dust and ashes.

How do Jews know how to behave?

In deciding how they should behave, Jews try to find out what G-d would want them to do.

The **Torah** and the **Talmud** (see Topic 5) both explain what G-d wants from Jews. The aim of a Jew is to live an halakhic life (walking with G-d) by following the 613 mitzvot or commandments.

Jews believe that these commandments were not designed to make life difficult for them, but to help them to live in such a way that G-d would love them.

For example, after the flood, G-d says to Noah:

Job and his three friends or 'comforters'.

> ### Genesis 9:11
> *I will maintain My covenant with you: never again shall all flesh be cut off by the waters of a flood, and never again shall there be a flood to destroy the earth.*

Jews try to find answers to questions about life in the scriptures and may also discuss with rabbis what the right thing to do is in a particular situation.

When they are suffering, they believe that their conscience is learning how to make the correct decisions in accordance with G-d's will. Rather than the Hebrew word for conscience, the phrase used in the Jewish scriptures means 'fear of G-d' – you can see how Jews feel about the way their conscience works.

An example is seen when Abraham is asked why he pretended that his wife was his sister.

> ### Genesis 20:11
> *'I thought,' said Abraham, 'surely there is no fear of God in this place, and they will kill me because of my wife'.*

According to the book of Genesis G-d made the rainbow as a sign that he would never flood the world again.

FOR DEBATE

Do any of the Jewish responses to the Holocaust provide an adequate answer for what happened to the Jews? Can you suggest any better response?

ACTIVITIES
AO1 skills

Explain what Jews might learn about suffering from the story of Job.

ACTIVITIES
AO1 skills

In twos or threes, make a list of the things which influence how you behave.

RESEARCH NOTE

Find out what happened during the Jewish Exile.

ACTIVITIES
AO2 skills

'A conscience is just you making up your mind and has nothing to do with G-d.' Give reasons why people might agree or disagree with this statement and include your own views.

Sikhism:
Good and evil 1

The next two pages will help you to:

- develop your knowledge and understanding of the concept of good and evil in Sikhism
- analyse how Sikhs address **moral** and **natural evil**, as well as suffering, in the world alongside the essential belief in a loving and caring God.

HURRICANE DESTROYS 300,000 HOMES

EARTHQUAKE HITS CHINA

GIRL MURDERED TWO MEN ARRESTED

WORLD NEWS

TORTURE: WEAPON OF WAR?

How can God and evil co-exist?

Most people agree that there are two types of evil: moral evil, which is human-made, such as rape, torture and murder; and natural evil, which means disasters over which we have no control, such as earthquakes, tsunamis and floods.

One of the main arguments atheists use to deny the existence of a God or Supreme Being is the extent of evil in the world. Many religions describe God as being **omnipotent** and loving. But surely a loving God would have the power to obliterate evil from our lives? Look at the suffering of children in developing countries – can a caring God just look on while it happens?

As an overtly theistic religion, Sikhs cannot deny the overall supremacy and Will of God in all matters (see Topic 3), but Sikh teachings deal with the problem of evil very well.

Free will

Gurbani (Sikh teachings) emphasise the concept of free will. The Guru Granth Sahib Ji has many references to the causes of evil through concepts such as maya (lure of material possessions), haumai (ego), **karma** and rebirth. Sikhs believe that free will has to be taken into account for our own actions. We all have the potential of being good or evil people, depending on how much we let **haumai** and **maya** lure us.

ACTIVITIES

- What do you define 'suffering' as? Give some examples.
- How do you think a theist would address the problem of suffering?
- How do you think an atheist would address why there is evil in the world?

Compare your answers to those of three other pupils in the class.

ACTIVITIES

Think/pair/share
What images come to your mind when the word 'good' is mentioned? What images come to your mind when the word 'evil' is mentioned? Discuss this idea with a partner and then share your answers with the class.

Guru Nanak Dev Ji's teaching on ego

> **Guru Granth Sahib Ji, page 466**
>
> *Yea, (in Ego) do we know not the Essence of Deliverance.*
> *In Ego is (one's involvement with) Maya; in Ego is one shadowed (by Doubt).*
> *Yea, in Ego is our birth upon birth.*

ACTIVITIES

In pairs, discuss why it is the ego that can cause a person to be entangled in the cycle of **samsara** (see Topic 3).

Sikhs will try to follow the teachings of the Guru Granth Sahib Ji in order to both cope with and understand reasons behind human suffering.

There is no concept of a devil in Sikh teachings.

Is the universe an illusion?

Although the teachings of the Sikh **Gurus** constantly remind Sikhs of the binding effects of maya, this does not mean that the universe itself is an illusion and is unreal. To the contrary, the world does, indeed, exist. However, it is the individual's attachment to it that causes the ego to produce feelings of selfishness. It is how we perceive the universe that is important.

Guru Nanak Dev Ji emphasised the stage of the householder (grihasta). He taught that a separation from one's family was unnecessary, and promoted the benefits of hard, honest work. In this sense, the world becomes the karma-bhoomi – the action ground on which one prepares for the afterlife. All this needs to be done without forming attachment to the lures of a physical world that is constantly changing.

RESEARCH NOTE

The concept of free will is one that many religions address in response to the problem of evil. Compare the concept in two different religions. Are there points of agreement and disagreement between the faiths?

Many religious people find that praying, especially in times of need, helps them cope with their suffering.

ACTIVITIES

Think/pair/share
Find a drawing by M. C. Escher. What do you see? Now ask a partner what they can see. Compare your initial responses to the rest of the class. Did you all initially see the same thing in the illusion?

Sikhism:
Good and evil 2

The next two pages will help you to:

- analyse how Sikhs cope with suffering
- explore how and why Sikhs try to follow a moral code.

Guru Angad Dev Ji.

How do Sikhs cope with suffering?

Sikhs address the Will of God in their suffering. The teachings of Sikhism highlight that everything happens for a reason. Also, the law of karma or karam operates in Sikhism. This addresses the problem of evil as our own past actions for which we pay in this life.

Overcoming one's ego will allow the individual to accept the Will of God as supreme. It is the ego that causes one to doubt the supremacy and all-encompassing nature of **Waheguru**.

Teaching of Guru Angad Dev Ji on ego

On this matter, Guru Angad Dev Ji, the second Sikh Guru, stresses that:

> **Guru Granth Sahib Ji, page 466**
>
> *The nature of ego is this: that man goes about his business in pride. The trammel of ego is this that man, again and again, enters into existences.*

 **ACTIVITIES**

Access a variety of teachings from the Guru Granth Sahib Ji in English at the sikhnet website.

Choose one or two teachings you find particularly interesting and copy them onto a poster. Decorate it appropriately and use it as a display in the classroom.

 FOR DEBATE

In small groups, think of examples or scenarios that characterise an individual with ego. How would this individual respond to personal suffering? Now think of another scenario in which an individual suffers. How would an egoless person respond to this?

Why do Sikhs try to follow a moral code?

There are two types of individuals according to the Guru Granth Sahib Ji.

- The first is the **manmukh**, people who are always concerned about themselves and are attracted to maya (illusion). This, in turn, prevents egoless actions and hence results in the **soul**'s entrapment in **samsara**.

- This being is in sharp contrast to the second, the **gurmukh**, who have put their love of God at the centre of their life. One cannot become a gurmukh without having controlled one's ego (haumai).

The Guru Granth Sahib Ji and the lives of the Sikh Gurus provide a Sikh with the moral and philosophical guidance needed to transcend from the level of a manmukh to that of a gurmukh. Reading the scriptures and following the examples of the Sikh Gurus also helps the individual to use their conscience effectively and address the concept of free will with a positive attitude.

The goal of Sikhism is mukti, which is the escape from the cycle of samsara. The gurmukh, due to the loss of ego, will not 'want' nor 'desire' mukti. The gurmukh has now made use of their actions through free will. From this point, the gurmukh goes about daily life until the Nadar (grace) of Waheguru, in accordance with the hukam (Will), enables the soul to escape samsara. The escape from samsara is by no means guaranteed for the gurmukh – mukti is a gift of the nadar of God.

AO1+AO2 skills **ACTIVITIES**

- In small groups, look at the teachings you accessed earlier. Decide what the words are actually trying to say. How will the teaching enable it to be used as either a moral or philosophical guide?

- Present the teachings you have chosen to the rest of the class and start a discussion about your interpretation compared to that of another pupil's interpretation of it. Can we decide upon a uniform interpretation of teachings?

 GradeStudio

AO1

QUESTION
Explain the ways in which a Sikh might try to find out the right answer to a difficult moral problem. **[6 marks]**

You could build an answer like this.

Level 1
Firstly, let the examiner be aware that you know what the question is asking of you, you could begin wording with the following example: 'The Guru Granth Sahib Ji is used as the principal guide for moral and philosophical guidance by Sikhs.'

Level 2
Next go on to explain that because the Guru Granth Sahib Ji is originally written in Gurmukhi, there may be problems in translation for Sikhs who wish to consult the original language of the scripture.

Level 3
Finally, your answer could mention that some Sikhs undertake a special reading of the Guru Granth Sahib Ji, a special 'path' in times of moral dilemmas. The guidance and inspiration from this would enable Sikhs to resolve their moral or philosophical problems.

GradeStudio

Welcome to the Grade Studio

Grade Studio is here to help you improve your grades by working through typical questions you might find on an examination paper. For a full explanation of how Grade Studio works, and how the examiners approach the task of marking your paper, please see p. 26.

AO1

Question

How might Christians explain the problem of evil in the world?

[6 marks]

Student's answer

Christians might say that there are both good and evil in the world. Good things come from God and evil things come from the Devil. Some Christians might say that there is evil in the world because many people are evil and they cause this. Other Christians might say that, although God is good, there is so much evil in the world that God cannot stop all of it.

Examiner's comment

The candidate has given a satisfactory answer to the question. There are three relevant points but none of them is explained in any detail. The answer needs to give more information and examples in order to reach Level 3. The candidate could also use more technical terms from the specification to show the breadth of their knowledge and understanding.

Student's improved answer

Christians might say that there is both good and evil in the world. Good things come from God and evil things come from the Devil. Some Christians might say that there is evil in the world because many people are evil and they cause this. Other Christians might say that although God is good, there is so much evil in the world that God cannot stop all of it.

Some Christians might say that there is a difference between moral evil and natural evil. Moral evil is caused by human beings, and it is part of our life on earth to work against this evil in order to show God our love. There are some people who believe that natural evil, such as volcanic eruptions, is the work of the Devil.

Others may say that there is evil in the world because humans introduced it when Eve took the fruit from the Tree of the Knowledge of Good and Evil. This introduced original sin and it is only because Jesus sacrificed his life that people are not still being punished.

Examiner's comment

This is now a good answer to the question. The candidate has shown a clear understanding of the question. There is good description and explanation of a variety of different ways in which Christians might try to understand the existence of good and evil. The candidate has also shown some analysis in dealing with the question of original sin. The information is presented clearly and there is good use of technical terms.

Question

'It is God who makes people suffer.' Discuss this statement. *You should include different, supported points of view and a personal viewpoint. You must refer to Christianity in your answer.* **[12 marks]**

Student's answer

Christians might disagree with this statement very strongly and say that God is good so God would not let people suffer. Some Christians might say that although God may not always stop suffering, it is not God who causes suffering.

Examiner's comment

The candidate has given a limited answer to the question. It is a good beginning to an answer but does not go far enough. There are two relevant points but the candidate now needs to address an alternative view as well as giving their own opinion.

Student's improved answer

Christians might disagree with this statement very strongly and say that God is good so God would not let people suffer. Some Christians might say that although God may not always stop suffering, it is not God who causes suffering.

Some people, on the other hand, might think that because of the amount of suffering, disease and poverty in the world, there cannot be a God and if there was one then he is not a good God. Other people might say that if there is suffering and God is good, then God is not all-powerful. Some Christians might think that suffering is part of God's plan to make humans stronger and better people.

My personal opinion is that if there is a God and if this God is good then God would not cause suffering. The fact that there is so much suffering in the world makes me think that God probably does not exist.

Examiner's comment

This is now a good answer to the question. The candidate has shown a clear understanding of the question and has presented a range of views supported by evidence and argument. The answer explains Christian views, among others, and includes a personal viewpoint, which is also supported.

These specimen answers provide an outline of how you could construct your response. Space does not allow us to give a full response. The examiner will be looking for more detail in your actual exam responses.

These examples only use Christianity but you could use the Grade Studio to apply to any of the religions you are studying and the structure of the answers would work in the same way.

Topic 5: Religion, reason and revelation

The Big Picture

In this Topic, you will be addressing religious beliefs and teachings about:

- the form and nature of revelation
- the authority and importance of sacred texts.

You will also think about ways in which beliefs in revelation affect the life and outlook of believers in the world today.

What?

You will:

- develop your knowledge and understanding of key beliefs and ideas about revelation and the importance of sacred texts
- explain what these beliefs and ideas mean to believers and think about how they might affect how they live
- make links between these beliefs and ideas and what you think/believe.

Why?

Because:

- these beliefs and ideas underpin and are reflected in the ways many people live their lives: for example, in helping them to decide how to treat others
- understanding people's beliefs can help you understand why they think and act in the way they do
- understanding these beliefs helps you compare and contrast what others believe, including thinking about your own beliefs and ideas.

How?

By:

- recalling and selecting information about beliefs and ideas about revelation and explaining their importance for people today
- reflecting on the relevance of these beliefs in 21st-century Britain
- evaluating your own views about these beliefs.

Sikhs at the Harmandir Sahib in Amritsar.

GET STARTED

SHOCKING REVELATIONS ABOUT BIG BROTHER HOUSEMATES

SEE INSIDE FOR EXCLUSIVE PICS!

When newspapers use the term 'revelation' in this way, what do they mean?

Has anything ever been 'revealed' to you that you had not previously known?

Religion, reason and revelation

The concept of revelation

Revelation describes how religious people come to a deeper understanding of God through personal experience, through ways of seeing and experiencing God in the world, and through sacred writings. People may describe a sense of being **numinous** – in the presence of 'an awesome power'. Such revelations are sometimes described as mystical or **transcendent**, because they are outside normal, everyday experience. These experiences may come through prayer, meditation and reflection.

Revelation through mystical and religious experience

- Buddhists use meditation to bring about change by reducing craving. All meditative practices aim to change attitude of the mind so that enlightenment can be achieved. Zen Buddhists hope to achieve **satori** (awakening).
- Christians have a strong tradition of experiences where they have been drawn into a deeper knowledge and awareness of God.
- Hindus have a tradition of mystical experiences through meditation and the deep concentration of yoga leading to liberation of the self.
- In Islam, religious experience comes through training and meditation. Sufis are Muslim mystics, who practise prayer and meditation, seeking unity with Allah through fanaa, extinction of the self.
- In Judaism, many individuals have had experiences that brought them closer to G-d. Moses experienced G-d through a bush that burned but was not destroyed.
- Sikhs follow **Guru** Nanak Dev Ji's teaching on developing inward spirituality through continuous meditation, **nam simran**.

Imagine yourself in the presence of someone you regard as your idol, hero or heroine. How do you feel? What do you do or say?

Revelation of the divine through the world

- Buddhists believe some truths about **nibbana** have been revealed by the Buddhas and **bodhisattvas** through miraculous experiences.
- Christians believe God cares for each person and is active in the world. The most important way God revealed himself to the world was in

KNOWLEDGE AND UNDERSTANDING
Describe how God has been revealed through a mystical experience in a religion you have studied. What are the key features of the experience?

ANALYSIS AND EVALUATION
Have you ever had an experience where you sensed something outside yourself, perhaps in a beautiful place, or listening to music? How did you feel? How would you describe the experience? What similarities are there between your experience and religious experiences?

the coming of Jesus as 'the Word made flesh' (John 1:14) – the incarnation. The Bible records **covenants** made between God and humans.

- Hindus believe that sometimes a god comes to earth in the form of a person or animal. These **avatars** often appear in times of danger. Hindus believe that avatars of Vishnu sometimes appear in order to fight evil and teach the right way to live.
- In Islam, Allah frequently intervened in the life of Muhammad ﷺ. The revelation of the Qur'an to Muhammad ﷺ, ensuring the future of Islam, is seen as the greatest miracle.
- Jews believe a covenant (agreement) was established between G-d and the chosen people on Mount Sinai.
- Sikhs believe revelation of the divine comes through constant meditation on the nam – the name of God – in the midst of life's responsibilities.

The authority and importance of sacred texts

- For most Buddhists, the teachings revealed by the Buddha, the **dhamma**, are eternal. Theravadan Buddhists use the **Tipitaka** as a guide to their practice. Some Mahayanan Buddhists also use scriptures to guide them but others find scriptures distracting, preferring to use meditation to discover ultimate truths.
- Christians believe the Bible comes from God and that they should respect and obey its teachings.
- Hinduism has many sacred writings, the oldest and most important of which are the **Vedas**. Originally spoken words passed down through generations, the Vedas tell stories of the gods and raise fundamental questions about the meaning of life.
- The holy book of Islam is the Qur'an. Muslims believe that it was revealed by God to the prophet Muhammad ﷺ by the angel Jibril and contains the actual words of Allah.
- The sacred text for Jews is the **Torah** (Law), revealed to Moses by G-d. The Torah is treated with great respect. Jews live according to the 613 mitzvot (commandments) in the Torah.
- The Sikh holy book, the Guru Granth Sahib Ji, contains the teachings of the ten Gurus and is treated with great respect as if it were a living Guru or teacher. It is regarded as the final authority for Sikhs today, providing guidance on how they should live.

KEY WORDS

Avatars Hindu gods who sometimes come to earth in the form of a person or an animal

Bhikkhu fully ordained Buddhist monk

Bodhisattva in Buddhism, a being destined for Enlightenment

Covenant in Judaism and Christianity, a special promise or agreement between God and humans

Dhamma ultimate truth, universal law

Gurdwara Sikh place of worship, literally 'the doorway to the **Guru**'

Guru teacher; a title reserved for the ten human Gurus and the Guru Granth Sahib Ji

Holy Communion Thanksgiving service celebrating the sacrificial death and resurrection of Jesus Christ; also known as **Eucharist** or Mass

Karma consequence of actions, in terms of cause and effect

Nam simran meditation on the divine name, using passages of scripture

Nibbana in Buddhism, achieving freedom from greed, hatred and delusion resulting in freedom from rebirth

Numinous having a sense of being in the presence of a divinity

Samsara in Buddhism and Hinduism; a continuing cycle of birth, ageing, death and rebirth

Satori in Zen Buddhism, an insight into **nibbana** – a brief glimpse of the world as it really is

Talmud collection of teachings and explanations of rabbis, which helps Jews understand the Torah

Tipitaka 'three baskets'; a three-fold collection of Buddhist texts: Vinaya, Sutta and Abhidamma

Torah Jewish law, or teaching, made up of the Five Books of Moses

Transcendent beyond human experience

Vedas 'knowledge'; the oldest and most sacred texts of Hinduism

Waheguru a Sikh name for God

FOR INTEREST

'Angels affect us oft' (John Donne, poet, 1572–1631). There are many references to angels in the religious writings of Judaism, Christianity and Islam, and the idea of angels seems to capture people's imagination. Do they exist? What do they symbolise? What do you think?

Buddhism:
Religion, reason and revelation 1

A Buddhist monk meditating at Sarnath, India.

How are ultimate truths revealed in Buddhism?

As far as most Buddhists are concerned, the **dhamma** – the teachings the Buddha revealed – is eternal. These teachings are always true and in existence. The Buddha merely discovered these teachings, then revealed them to humanity so that we might discover them for ourselves.

In Mahayana Buddhism, the advanced **bodhisattvas** can also reveal ultimate truths. These bodhisattvas have progressed a long way on the path to nibbana, and thus have achieved certain knowledge and understanding beyond that of those still at the beginning of the path. This knowledge may be revealed by the bodhisattvas directly through miraculous experiences, or through scriptures in which they reveal their teachings.

 FOR DEBATE

Think about if you had to learn all the knowledge and understanding you needed for your GCSE without having any textbooks or teachers to help you. Would it be easier or harder? How else could you get the information you needed? How would you know it was reliable?

> 'As the Lotus is unstained by water, so is nibbana unstained by all the defilements.'

> 'As cool water allays feverish heat, so also nibbana is cool and allays the fever of all the passions. Moreover, as water removes the thirst of men and beasts who are exhausted, parched, thirsty and overpowered by heat, so also nibbana removes the craving for sensuous enjoyments, the craving for further becoming, the craving for the cessation of becoming.'

> 'As medicine protects from the torments of poison, so nibbana protects from the torments of the poisonous passions. Moreover as medicine puts an end to sickness, so nibbana to all sufferings.'

> 'And these are the ten qualities which nibbana shares with space. Neither is born, grows old, dies, passes away, or is reborn; both are unconquerable, cannot be stolen, are unsupported, are roads respectively for birds and arhats to journey on, are unobstructed and infinite.'

ACTIVITIES

Read the four quotes about nibbana. What image of nibbana do they present? Does nibbana sound attractive? Which analogy makes most sense to you and why?

How might people know nibbana through scripture?

Most Buddhists would argue nibbana cannot be fully understood by those still trapped in the world of **samsara**: nibbana is far beyond the world of samsara, and thus beyond the ability of those within samsara to describe or explain. Some Buddhists believe that any attempt to explain nibbana will fail and so they should not even try.

However, there is a recognition that, if people do not know at least partially what they are aiming at, they are unlikely to try. Some truths about nibbana have therefore been revealed by the Buddhas and bodhisattvas, and within the scriptures. Most attempts to describe nibbana are negative: they describe what it is not, in reference to the world of samsara.

Knowing nibbana in other ways

How might people know nibbana through the Buddhas and bodhisattvas?

Many Buddhists argue that it is possible to glean what nibbana is like from the observation of the Buddhas and bodhisattvas. Their appearance of serenity indicates that nibbana is peaceful; their equanimity in the face of all situations indicates that strong passions like greed and hatred have been left behind; their wisdom indicates that delusion has been swept away.

How might people know nibbana through meditation?

Many Buddhists would say people can only know nibbana through direct experience of it. For many, the best way to achieve this experience is through meditation. In the Zen tradition, Buddhists are said to be able to experience a moment of **satori** if they meditate correctly. This moment is seen by some to be an insight into nibbana – a brief glimpse of the world as it really is. In other Buddhist traditions, the progress through the stages of meditation is felt to be more gradual, moving closer towards the revelation and experience of nibbana.

ACTIVITIES

- Do you think it is possible to ever understand nibbana fully? Why/why not?
- Which of the different methods is the best way to find out about nibbana? Why?
- 'Without scriptures religion would not exist.' Come up with reasons for and against this statement.

Buddhism: Religion, reason and revelation 2

Buddhist scriptures

There are many Buddhist scriptures, and it would be impossible to list them all in this book, let alone explain their contents and importance. Instead, we will focus on a few of the best-known scriptures.

The Tipitaka or Pali Canon

After the Buddha died, his teachings were initially kept orally by the monastic sangha. Certain **bhikkhus** were probably responsible for remembering certain sayings, and they may have come together to recite them at regular times. Eventually, they were written down in the Indian language Pali. **Tipitaka** means three baskets, and the scriptures are called this because they divide into three sections:

- Sutta Pitaka – the sayings and doings of the Buddha
- Vinaya Pitaka – the rules for bhikkhus and bhikkhunis
- Abhidhamma Pitaka – philosophical speculations and explanations by the early bhikkhus.

For Theravada Buddhists, the Tipitaka is of great importance. It provides them with a clear idea of the Buddha's thoughts and behaviour, to use in their own practice. However, the Buddha always said that his teaching was 'a finger pointing to the moon': it can provide a guide, but cannot make people achieve nibbana. He encouraged his followers to test his teachings and, if they found them useless, to discard them.

The Lotus Sutra

The Lotus Sutra is one of many hundreds of Mahayana Sutras. It was recorded many years after the Buddha's death, and there are two explanations of how it came about. In the first, the Buddha realised his teachings were too hard for people to understand at present. He hid the teachings, and allowed them to be revealed later when people were more able to understand them. The second explanation relies on the Mahayana idea that the Buddha did not die, but removed himself from human view. The Buddha thus could reappear to reveal the teachings at a later date. Some Buddhists are prepared to accept that later Buddhists wrote the teachings.

FOR DEBATE

How can people know that scriptures recorded much later than the death of the founder of the religion are accurate?

The Lotus Sutra is very popular because it uses lots of colourful stories and analogies to explain Buddhist teachings. The main teachings in The Lotus Sutra are that:

- there are lots of Buddhas and advanced bodhisattvas throughout the universe
- all beings can, and will, become Buddhas in the future
- Buddhas can use skilful means to encourage Buddhists along the path to nibbana.

The Lotus Sutra is particularly important in establishing Mahayana teaching, and emphasising the differences between Mahayana and Theravada beliefs.

Skilful means in Mahayana Buddhism

Mahayana Buddhists believe that Buddhas and advanced bodhisattvas can use skilful means to help other Buddhists. This means they can reveal only a partial truth, if the ultimate purpose is to help a person on the path to nibbana. For example, if a nervous swimmer fleeing a sinking ship was told that they had two miles to swim, they might refuse to leave the ship; if they were told that they only had to swim half a mile, they might start out, and then be able to carry on further, until they completed all two miles.

Are scriptures important to all Buddhists?

Within Buddhism, there are many different traditions. Theravada Buddhists tend to place great importance on the Tipitaka, and few would deny that it is an important guide to their practice. Many Mahayana Buddhists would also use scriptures to guide or support their learning and practice. However, some Mahayana Buddhists think scriptures can be distracting, and stop people seeking the path to enlightenment for themselves. These practitioners might well prefer to use meditation techniques to discover ultimate truths, rather than rely on the accounts in the scriptures.

 **ACTIVITIES**

- Draw up a chart comparing the advantages and disadvantages of using scriptures in religion.
- Explain why Theravada Buddhists might claim that Mahayana scriptures are less reliable.
- Explain how Mahayana Buddhists might justify the differences between Theravada scriptures and their own.

GradeStudio

AO1

QUESTION

Explain why Buddhists may have different views about the usefulness of sacred texts. **[6 marks]**

Level 1
You might begin by saying that the scriptures do not have material related to modern ethical issues (e.g. cloning), and so are not very useful.

Level 2
You could continue by saying that it might be more useful for a Buddhist to talk to a bhikkhu, who can apply the teachings of the Buddha to these issues.

Level 3
Finally, you might explain that, since the scriptures (dhamma) are the universal teachings and revelation of Buddha, they can be applied at all times, and to all situations.

Crucially, you must explain which view you hold and why or if you have a different opinion.

Christianity:
Religion, reason and revelation 1

The next two pages will help you to:

- explore how revelation is encountered through mystical and religious experience
- identify how God is revealed in the world and in the person of Jesus.

Revelation in Christianity

Revelation describes how a believer reaches a deeper understanding of God in a personal way, through the world around them and through sacred texts. There are many different ways to experience God and Christians do not all follow the same paths to bring them closer to God. They might claim any of the following forms of religious experience.

Experiencing a conversion

Some people feel that personal contact with God has caused them to change their behaviour or beliefs. One of the best-known accounts of a conversion in the Bible is that of St Paul.

Saul's conversion

Acts 9:1–6

Meanwhile, Saul was still breathing out murderous threats against the Lord's disciples. He went to the high priest and asked him for letters to the synagogues in Damascus, so that if he found any there who belonged to the Way, whether men or women, he might take them as prisoners to Jerusalem. As he neared Damascus on his journey, suddenly a light from heaven flashed around him. He fell to the ground and heard a voice say to him, 'Saul, Saul, why do you persecute me?' 'Who are you, Lord?' Saul asked. 'I am Jesus, whom you are persecuting,' he replied. 'Now get up and go into the city, and you will be told what you must do.'

AO1 skills **ACTIVITIES**

Describe to a partner how you would feel if you could meet and talk to your idol. How would this be different from talking to your friends?

AO1 skills **ACTIVITIES**

Explain why you think this event had such a dramatic effect on Saul/Paul that he stopped persecuting Christians and instead became one of the greatest followers of Jesus.

Communicating with God through prayer or meditation

Prayer is seen as a two-way communication – Christians speak with God and listen for a reply. A believer experiencing this would feel that they have felt the presence of God.

Christians might also meditate to help them to become closer to God. A retreat might also enable a believer to experience the presence of God.

Feeling the presence of God during worship

Any form of worship might help a Christian to experience God. Charismatic services held by groups such as Pentecostalists enable believers to experience God through the gift of the Holy Spirit, which might come upon them during worship. This might cause them to faint, speak in tongues (glossolalia) or to speak the words of God (prophecy). Sometimes they hold faith-healing services and attempt to cure people of illness through faith.

Sacramental services, such as the Roman Catholic Mass, include the celebration of **Holy Communion**. Catholics are taught that, when they take the bread and wine, they are assured of the existence of God in the presence of Jesus.

Feeling God's presence in the world

Many Christians feel that they can experience the presence of God as they walk in the countryside, or look at the beauty in nature. They have feelings of awe and wonder when they see a beautiful sunset and this helps them to believe that God is present in the world of nature.

Experiencing a miraculous event

A Christian who has experienced a miraculous event, such as a cure for a loved one who is suffering a terminal illness, or being saved after an accident, would believe that this is evidence of the presence of God. The evidence of a miracle, or a conversion, might also affect other people, and this might cause them to experience God.

God revealed through Jesus

The incarnation (God in human form) of Jesus is the most important demonstration of God's presence for a Christian. They believe that God cared for humans and wanted them to have the opportunity to find a way back to God's presence, so God sent Jesus into the world. This was explained in John's gospel:

> **John 1:14**
> *The Word became flesh and made his dwelling among us. We have seen his glory, the glory of the One and Only, who came from the Father, full of grace and truth.*

REMEMBER THIS

Retreat – withdrawing from everyday life for a time.

ACTIVITIES

Collect evidence from the media of events that could be described as miraculous. Explain how they might affect the lives of those who experience the events, as well as other people.

Christianity: Religion, reason and revelation 2

The next two pages will help you to:

- examine why the Bible is seen as an authority for Christians
- explore the concept of the Christian **covenant**
- appreciate the significance to Christians of the Ten Commandments.

The Bible

The holy book of Christianity is the Bible. It is divided into two sections.

- The Old Testament – This is the same as the Jewish holy book. It describes Jewish and Christian beliefs about God and how God has been involved in the world over a long period of time. There are 39 books of laws, histories, poems, stories, prophecies and songs.

- The New Testament – The first four books are the Gospels (Matthew, Mark, Luke and John), which give an account of the life, teachings, death and resurrection of Jesus and provide the basis for Christian belief. There are 27 books, including letters to new churches, history and prophecies about the end of the world. Many Christians feel that this part of the Bible is the most important one, as it provides a new and deeper understanding of God.

Christians believe that the Bible is divinely inspired (comes from God). However, there are different ways of understanding the Bible.

- Some Christians believe that the Bible is 'God-breathed': that is, it has come directly from God. Everything in the Bible happened exactly as it is written and nothing should ever be changed or questioned. For example, the accounts in Genesis chapters 1 and 2 about the creation of the world give an accurate description of what happened.

- Other Christians believe that there are different kinds of truth in the Bible. Some sections may be taken literally, while sometimes it is the message in the writing that is important, rather than the actual accounts. Some sections are thought to be myths that do not describe real events.

A late 14th-century illuminated gospel from Ethiopia.

How is the Bible important for Christians?

The Bible has authority for all Christians. They believe that it provides a guide for them to live a Christian life and to behave as they think God wishes. They recognise that the revelation of God through the Bible offers them support and structure in their lives. Christians believe that the Old Testament demonstrates how God gave rules and laws to followers of Christianity, as shown in the covenant made between God and Abraham:

ACTIVITIES

Make a list of all the people who have authority over you. For each one, describe what form the authority takes and how these people affect you.

> **Genesis 17:4–7**
>
> *As for me, this is my covenant with you: You will be the father of many nations. No longer will you be called Abram; your name will be Abraham, for I have made you a father of many nations. I will make you very fruitful; I will make nations of you, and kings will come from you. I will establish my covenant as an everlasting covenant between me and you and your descendants after you for the generations to come, to be your God and the God of your descendants after you.*

The New Testament offers a new covenant made through the blood of Jesus on the cross, which offers believers the opportunity to be forgiven by God and to enter the Kingdom of Heaven.

> **Hebrews 9:15**
>
> *For this reason Christ is the mediator of a new covenant, that those who are called may receive the promised eternal inheritance – now that he has died as a ransom to set them free from the sins committed under the first covenant.*

Christians will use the Bible as a guide. The Ten Commandments are a source of moral guidance, offering a structure to their lives (see Topic 2). They might read a passage each day as a 'bible study', to try to understand what is written. They may use the example of Jesus and his teachings to help them to make decisions. Sometimes, they might have to interpret what is written in the Bible if there is nothing directly relevant to their situation, but in all cases they would feel that they are given strong guidance as to what God wants them to do.

Read during church services, and at special occasions such as weddings, baptisms and funerals, the Bible plays an important part in Christian worship, and is treated with great respect.

AO1 skills ACTIVITIES

Write a 'guide to behaviour' for Christians based on the Ten Commandments and explain how the Bible is important for believers.

Grade Studio

AO1

QUESTION

Explain what Christians mean by revelation. **[6 marks]**

Level 1

First, let the examiner know that you understand what the question is about. For example, Christians believe that the Bible is the revealed word of God and that every word in it was dictated or revealed to humans by God.

Level 2

Next, give an alternative view. Explain in more detail how some Christians regard the Bible in different ways and may not all accept that it is all God's word.

Level 3

Finally, explain both points of view in more detail. Some Christians believe that God revealed the whole of the Bible to people, while others think that the Bible was inspired by God but is actually the work of people. This does not mean that the Bible is not true, but it could mean that people do not have to believe that every word of it is an exact translation.

Hinduism:
Religion, reason and revelation 1

The next two pages will help you to:

- investigate the ways in which some Hindus may experience the divine
- explore the concept of God in nature.

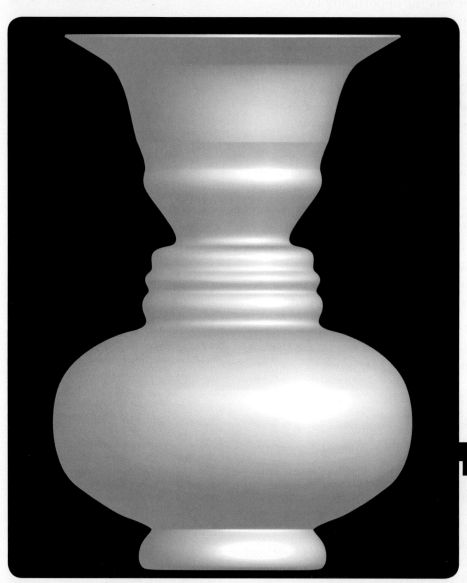

Is this one vase or two faces?

How can I know it's really God?

People say 'seeing is believing'. However, as demonstrated by the image above and by tricks with digital photography, in today's world, that certainly is not the case! Some Hindus believe that the **avatars** of Vishnu (see Topic 1) and other incarnations of God are physical examples of divine revelation – they prove that God exists. For others, it is experiencing the divine that matters, for them, the Universal Spirit is evident in nature, or manifest (revealed) during worship.

AO1 skills ACTIVITIES

- Design a 'two in one' image of your own.
- Explain how your artwork reflects the problem of revelation being 'in the eye of the beholder' – different people see the same thing in different ways.

Evidence of revelation through nature

Some Hindus believe the beauty of the natural world and the complexity of it reflect the incredible complexity and beauty of the Universal Spirit. They may use examples such as the Fibonacci Sequence and the Golden Ratio which can be seen in the natural world and say that these show how amazing the Universal Spirit is. They might say that very few humans are not awestruck and filled with a sense of peace when they experience a glorious sunset.

Some people say that experiencing the Divine during worship is just over-excitement, illusion, or imagination. However, for those Hindus who claim to have had such an experience, their contact with the Universal Spirit or a deity is a clear example of divine revelation.

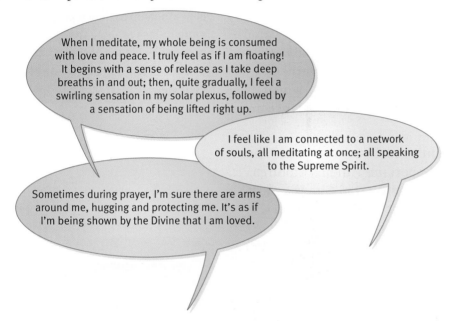

> When I meditate, my whole being is consumed with love and peace. I truly feel as if I am floating! It begins with a sense of release as I take deep breaths in and out; then, quite gradually, I feel a swirling sensation in my solar plexus, followed by a sensation of being lifted right up.

> I feel like I am connected to a network of souls, all meditating at once; all speaking to the Supreme Spirit.

> Sometimes during prayer, I'm sure there are arms around me, hugging and protecting me. It's as if I'm being shown by the Divine that I am loved.

Many Hindus would agree that you can only *know* for yourself, trying to prove it to others is not only impossible, but also misses the point of sanatan dharma (eternal faith) being about each person finding their own path to God.

As Mahatama Gandhi famously said,

❝ If we have listening ears, God speaks to us in our own language, whatever that language be ❞

(Gandhi: In my own words)

meaning that the Divine will reveal differently to individuals in a way that best suits each soul.

Some Hindus would say they believe the Divine is also revealed through the existence of individuals such as Mahatma Gandhi and Martin Luther King Jr. They may give such people the title sant – someone who has lived an exceptional life and helped to make the world a better place. Others follow the teachings of, and worship, wise or miraculous figures whom they also call sant, or sometimes, 'living avatars'.

❝ The Bible is as much a book of religion with me as the Gita and the Qur'an. ❞

(Mahatma Gandhi)

RESEARCH NOTE

Investigate what the Fibonacci Sequence and the Golden Ratio are. Try to find some examples of them in nature for yourself.

AO1+AO2 skills ACTIVITIES

- Do you agree with the concept of God on earth, or do you think this is implausible? Give detailed reasons for your view, including examples if you can.
- Describe some of the ways in which Hindus (and others) may experience the Divine.

FOR DEBATE

'It doesn't matter if a sacred text is the word of God or not, as long the teachings help people to live in a responsible and caring way.' Do you agree? Explain your view using examples from your own experience and from the media.

Hinduism:
Religion, reason and revelation 2

Revelation in Hindu sacred texts

For many Hindus, the existence and wisdom of the many Hindu sacred texts is also a form of Divine Revelation.

Shruti are believed to have been 'heard' by the Holy Men they were revealed to. These are the very oldest – some would say eternal – Hindu scriptures: for example, the **Vedas** and Upanishads, which contain prayers, hymns and rituals as well as providing guidance and wisdom.

Smriti are believed to have been 'remembered' by some **Gurus**. These are the later, but still very ancient and important, Hindu scriptures: for example, the Mahabharata, of which the Bhagavad Gita is a most beloved portion; and the Ramayana, which includes the Laws of Manu.

There are many Hindu sacred texts

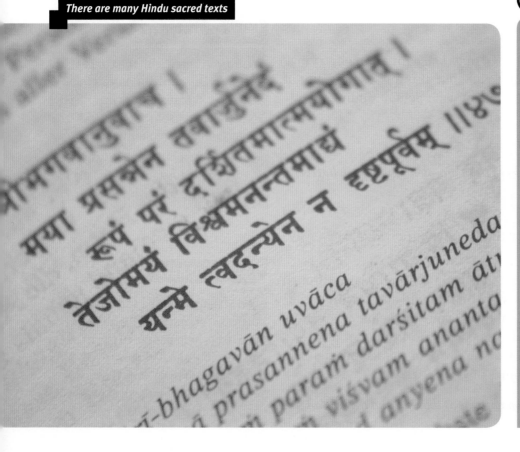

The next two pages will help you to:

- compare Hindu sacred texts
- evaluate the relative value of different types of revelation.

 **ACTIVITIES**

Is personal experience of the Divine more or less reliable than sacred texts, as evidence of the existence of God? Give detailed reasons for your view.

 **FOR DEBATE**

On the one hand:

- the Mahabharata definitely exists and is too old to accurately date
- Vyas is still a fairly common Hindu family name
- portraits and statues of Lord Ganesha as an adult, including some very ancient ones, depict only one full tusk, the other being clearly broken.

On the other:

- A deity acting as scribe for a human?
- A being that has a human body but an elephant's head?
- Can't they use carbon dating?

Discuss these two differing viewpoints regarding the authenticity of Hindu sacred texts.

For many Hindus, the authority of the sacred texts is based on the fact that they are so ancient. However, there are no reliable dates for them; current estimates of their age vary from 2500 to 5500 years old. This lack of provenance (proof of the origins of something) could be viewed as a reason not to accept these sacred books as divine revelation. However, many Hindus believe it is actually proof that their faith really is eternal – sanatan dharma.

Myth, magic or madness? There is a story about how the Mahabharata was written down. During the satya yuga (see Topic 1), the sage Vyas was asked by fellow Gurus to recite his recollection of the Mahabharata, so that it might be written down for the benefit of future generations. It was decided that Lord Ganesha would be the best scribe for this task, since he had the intelligence and wisdom to write down what he heard in a poetic manner, while ensuring that nothing was lost in translation. The account goes on to describe how Lord Ganesha broke his quill during the recitation; but rather than break the flow, broke off a tusk to use instead.

Lord Ganesha is a very popular deity amongst Hindus worldwide. He is believed to bring good luck and deliver wisdom.

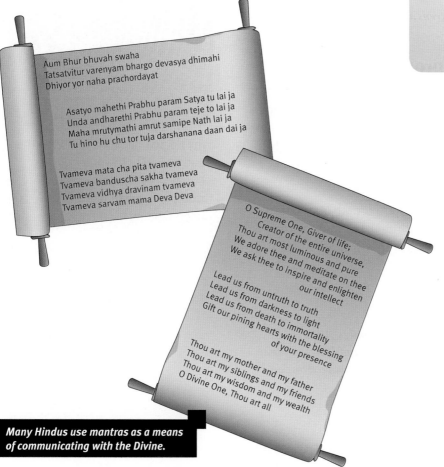

Aum Bhur bhuvah swaha
Tatsatvitur varenyam bhargo devasya dhimahi
Dhiyor yor naha prachordayat

Asatyo mahethi Prabhu param Satya tu lai ja
Unda andharethi Prabhu param teje to lai ja
Maha mrutymathi amrut samipe Nath lai ja
Tu hino hu chu tor tuja darshanana daan dai ja

Tvameva mata cha pita tvameva
Tvameva banduscha sakha tvameva
Tvameva vidhya dravinam tvameva
Tvameva sarvam mama Deva Deva

O Supreme One, Giver of life;
Creator of the entire universe,
Thou art most luminous and pure
We adore thee and meditate on thee
We ask thee to inspire and enlighten
our intellect

Lead us from untruth to truth
Lead us from darkness to light
Lead us from death to immortality
Gift our pining hearts with the blessing
of your presence

Thou art my mother and my father
Thou art my siblings and my friends
Thou art my wisdom and my wealth
O Divine One, Thou art all

Many Hindus use mantras as a means of communicating with the Divine.

NEXT STEP

Explore some of the Hindu sacred texts for yourself – if paper copies are not available, use the Internet to access the texts mentioned and/ or others. Choose a particular story or teaching to present as an example of what may be learned from sacred texts. In addition to writing down and interpreting your chosen text, why not say it aloud, illustrate it, put it to music, dramatise it or choreograph a dance about it?

AO1 skills ACTIVITIES

- Try to say the mantra from the Vedas out loud.
- Analyse the translations. How do you think they help believers feel closer to God?

Islam:
Religion, reason and revelation 1

The concept of revelation

In the study of religion, revelation refers to occasions when something about the nature of God has been shown or revealed to human beings. General revelation happens indirectly and can be perceived by everyone: for example, through understanding truths about Allah through their experiences of awe and wonder at the natural world.

> **From Surah 30:22**
>
> *And among His signs is the creation of the heavens and the earth.*

Allah's revelations through prophets

Special revelation may come to an individual or group, often through powerful spiritual experiences such as dreams, visions or prophecies. In Islam, the Angel Jibril is a channel through which Allah is revealed to the Prophets. Allah may also be revealed to his people through male prophets – 'messengers of God' who give Allah's intention and guidance to His people, which is submission to one God.

Muslims recognise as prophets some people who are also associated with the Christian or Jewish religions. Islam regards them as an important part of the religion's tradition, and records significant stories from their lives.

> **Surah 2:136**
>
> *Say ye: 'We believe in Allah, and the revelation given to us, and to Abraham, Isma'il, Isaac, Jacob, and the Tribes, and that given to Moses and Jesus, and that given to (all) prophets from their Lord: We make no difference between one and another of them: And we bow to Allah (in Islam).'*

All prophets are regarded as totally human and not possessing any divine nature. They were chosen by Allah to reveal a message to all people, and are regarded as role models for Muslim behaviour. All of the previous prophets had their own human characteristics and specific traits. Muhammad ﷺ – the 'Apostle of Allah, and the Seal of the Prophets' (from Surah 33:40) – is regarded as the most important prophet, ending the line and giving a clear message of Allah's intentions through the revelation of the Qur'an.

AO1+AO2 skills ACTIVITIES

Why do you think Muslims see the hand of God in the order of the natural world? Is this view incompatible with a scientific understanding of the natural world?

The Qur'an – a special revelation to Muhammad ﷺ

At the age of about 40, in the year 610 CE, during the month of Ramadan, Muhammad ﷺ made his way to the cave of Hira on Mount Nur, where he would often go for quiet reflection. Here he received his first vision from the angel Jibril who said:

> **Surah 96:3–7**
>
> *Proclaim! And thy Lord is Most Bountiful – He Who taught (the use of) the pen – Taught man that which he knew not – Day, but man doth transgress all bounds – In that he looketh upon himself as self-sufficient.*

The cave of Hira on Mount Nur.

Although he was illiterate, Muhammad ﷺ committed the message to memory. He continued to receive these revelations for about twenty years. He first told his wife, Khadijah, and close family. He later shared it with his friends and family, and began to preach in public. He became a good preacher and the people accepted his message.

The authority of the Qur'an

The Qur'an (meaning *that which is recited*) is the word of Allah directly revealed to Muhammad ﷺ at the cave of Hira on Mount Nur. It is the literal word of God, which is unchangeable and not open to scrutiny. Translations are not even regarded as authentic. To understand the Qur'an fully, Muslims believe it should be read in its original language, Arabic. From a young age, Muslims learn the Qur'an in Arabic and memorise important passages.

The Qur'an.

Muhammad ﷺ wanted to ensure that it was remembered just as it was revealed to him. He would request his followers to recite and remember passages. He was so dedicated to this that he even demanded that his own words were not added, in case these corrupted the direct words of Allah. The definitive written version was agreed after his death.

The significance and importance of the Qur'an

The Qur'an is central to the life of all Muslims. It has one important key theme: the importance of submission to the will of Allah. It is a guide for living that has more significance than any other teachings. Its authority comes from the belief that it is the direct words of Allah himself as revealed to the final Seal of the Prophets, Muhammad ﷺ.

The Hadith refers to it as 'a guide that shows the best path' (al-khafi Hadith).

It is clear in its teaching in a belief in one God, Allah, who although forgiving, requires submission from humans who will be judged on their actions at the Day of Judgement. It is the main source of guidance for the human race and offers a guarantee to Paradise.

RESEARCH NOTE

Look for different versions of the story of the revelation of the Qur'an in the library and on the Internet, including re-tellings for young children. What makes this story so special for Muslims?

Islam:
Religion, reason and revelation 2

How is Allah revealed to Muslims through prayer?

All Muslims try to develop their understanding and relationship with Allah. Through **salah**, the five daily times of prayer, they are communicating directly with Allah. This helps them develop a personal relationship with Allah and increases their consciousness of Allah's presence in their lives.

> **Hadith**
>
> *A man came to the Prophet and said, 'I cannot pray five times a day.' 'Well then, pray three times,' replied the Prophet. We were surprised at him saying this, and asked him to explain. 'If he prays three times, he will soon want to pray five times,' said the Prophet.*

Revelation through mystical and religious experience

Sufism is a movement within Islam of those who believe that Muslims can come closer to Allah through devotion and prayer. Showing belief in Allah in all daily actions is of paramount importance. Sufis try to give up materialistic things in life and devote most of their time to worshipping and trying to please Allah.

Sufism is described as mystical or **transcendent**, because Sufis strive to know Allah beyond the constraints of the physical world. Sufis specifically search for Haqiqa – an inward divine reality. They would seek to achieve this by avoiding a materialistic, worldly life and following a lifelong pathway of spiritual exercise. Constantly seeking Allah in order to be at one with Allah is of great importance. Just as Muhammad was able to experience Allah closely, Sufis believe they too can experience such closeness.

Reading the Qur'an is an important part of Muslim worship.

REMEMBER THIS

The details of what is involved in salah, in Topic 1, will help you to understand why prayer is such an important aspect of the daily life of Muslims and how it develops their close relationship with Allah.

 **ACTIVITIES**

- Do you ever take time out for quiet reflection in the middle of a busy day? How difficult is it for people to make time for this? How might it affect the lives of people who make time for this on a regular basis?
- How might the fact that daily life is punctuated by prayer at regular intervals help develop a Muslim's relationship with God?

I try to immerse myself in prayer and worship. I begin at 4 a.m. with prayers. I have to begin early to complete 13 cycles of prayer. Then I read the Qur'an. I really find guidance there. I read all 114 surahs every two months … on a typical morning I might say Shahaddah 1000 times and 360 blessings for the Prophet. I keep count with a subha. Then I go to work! I'm a trainee teacher. I fast every Monday and Thursday and on the 13th, 14th, and 15th day of every month. Most Sufis go regularly to a Sufi Sheikh for guidance; he is an important part of their life … being a Sufi is about struggle with your inner self to find the true way: Al Haqq – the Truth.

(from an interview with Naphisa Jallo, a British Muslim who was born in the Gambia, West Africa and is a Sufi)

 RESEARCH NOTE

Find out about the experience of the singer Cat Stevens, now Yusuf Islam, who experienced a revelation after nearly drowning in the sea, which led him to convert to Islam. At the Cat Stevens (Yusuf Islam) website, you can listen to music he wrote and performed before and after his conversion to Islam.

 RESEARCH NOTE

Find out more about Sufism on the Haqqani website.

 **ACTIVITIES**

- Write a definition of the word 'mystical'.
- Imagine you are interviewing Naphisa Jallo for a magazine article. Draw up a list of questions you would like to ask her about her life and the impact of her Sufi beliefs and practices.
- What do you devote most time to in your own life?

Judaism:
Religion, reason and revelation 1

The next two pages will help you to:

- evaluate the importance of Jewish scriptures
- understand the origins of the Jewish scriptures.

Jewish scriptures

The Jewish Scriptures are known as the Tenakh, sometimes written as TeNaKh to show that it is in three parts:

- Torah – Law
- Nevi'im – Prophets
- Ketuvim – Writings.

Torah

This contains five books: Genesis, Exodus, Leviticus, Numbers and Deuteronomy. According to Jewish teaching, these five books were all written down by Moses, who received them from G-d – meaning that they are revealed.

Many Jews believe that, because the **Torah** is the word of G-d, everything in it must be literally true. Others think that some of the stories, such as the Creation or Noah's Flood, might be myth – not necessarily true, but containing important teachings.

Some people find it difficult to believe that Moses wrote down the whole of the Torah because, for example, it contains an account of his death. For other Jews, this does not cause a problem, as they believe that there are actions of G-d that humans simply cannot understand.

The Torah has a special status. The scrolls are handwritten by a specially trained scribe and placed on large scrolls, with elaborate covers and bells on. In the synagogue, readings are from the Sefer Torah (see p. 49), which is first carried around in procession. The reader uses a silver pointer (yad) so that they do not touch the scroll itself.

In some places, the text of the Torah does not appear to make sense, but could be understood if one word were changed. Here, the word written is called the k'tiv, while the word read out is the keri.

The other two parts of the Tenakh are seen as inspired by G-d but are not the direct word of G-d.

The Oral Torah

Jews believe that, when Moses was with G-d on Mount Sinai, as well as the Torah (Written Torah) he was also given the Oral Torah.

RESEARCH NOTE

Find out which religions have scriptures that they believe are revealed. Now find out why followers of three of the religions are called 'People of the Book'.

Torah scrolls.

Jews say that G-d gave the Oral Torah as a guide and explanation, to 'fill the gaps' in the Written Torah. For example, in Deuteronomy 12:21, Jews are told to slaughter cattle in the way that G-d has commanded them, but there are no instructions about how to do this. These are found in the Oral Torah.

Mishnah, Gemara and Talmud

Up to the time of the Roman persecution and the destruction of the Temple in 70 CE, the Oral Torah had been passed from teacher to teacher by word of mouth. Afraid that it would be forgotten, Rabbi Judah the Prince wrote the outline of the Oral Torah in the Mishnah. The Mishnah contains 62 sections covering almost every aspect of Jewish life and law.

A scribe writing a scroll by hand.

The persecutions against the Jews continued and the Rabbis in Babylon put together a version of the Oral Torah called the Gemara – a commentary on the Mishnah. Rabbis in Israel started a similar work. Together, the Mishnah and Gemara form the **Talmud** (teachings).

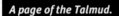
A page of the Talmud.

AO1+AO2 skills **ACTIVITIES**

- Discuss with a partner different ways in which something or someone might be revealed and write them down.

- Draw up a chart comparing the advantages and disadvantages of using scriptures in religion.

RESEARCH NOTE

What is the difference between aural and oral?

AO2 skills **ACTIVITIES**

Your teacher will give you a sentence, which the first person whispers to the next one. When the sentence has been passed all around the class the last person speaks it aloud and then the original sentence is read out. How different are they?

Judaism:
Religion, reason and revelation 2

The revelation of G-d to the Jews

Ideas of what the G-d of the Jews is like are found throughout the Jewish scriptures, where G-d is revealed to followers in different ways.

The Scriptures begin with an account of G-d creating the world. Soon after this, G-d appears in the Garden of Eden speaking to Adam and Eve:

> **Genesis 3:8a**
> *They heard the sound of the Lord God moving about in the garden at the breezy time of day.*

G-d speaks to Noah when he commands him to build the ark and later, after the flood has gone down, but G-d is not seen.

Throughout the story of Abraham, G-d talks to him and makes agreements (**covenants**) with him.

> **Genesis 12:1**
> *The Lord said to Abram, 'Go forth from your native land and from your father's house to the land that I will show you.'*

Later, G-d appears to him too:

> **Genesis 12:7a**
> *The Lord appeared to Abram.*

G-d then speaks to Moses through a burning bush.

> **Exodus 3:1–4**
> *Now Moses, tending the flock of his father-in-law Jethro, the priest of Midian, drove the flock into the wilderness, and came to Horeb, the mountain of God. An angel of the Lord appeared to him in a blazing fire out of a bush. He gazed, and there was a bush all aflame, yet the bush was not consumed. Moses said, 'I must turn aside to look at this marvellous sight; why doesn't the bush burn up?' When the Lord saw that he had turned aside to look, God called to him out of the bush: 'Moses! Moses!' He answered, 'Here I am.'*

The next two pages will help you to:

- explore how G-d revealed himself to the Jews
- understand the importance of revelation in the Jewish scriptures.

Noah's Ark.

 **RESEARCH NOTE**

Find out why Abraham is called Abram in these last two pieces of text.

> **Exodus 33:9–11**
> *And when Moses entered the Tent, the pillar of cloud would descend and stand at the entrance of the Tent, while He spoke with Moses. When all the people saw the pillar of cloud poised at the entrance of the Tent, all the people would rise and bow low, each at the entrance of his tent. The Lord would speak to Moses face to face, as one man speaks to another.*

The scriptures say that Moses spoke to G-d on other occasions. In the following it seems that G-d is a pillar of cloud, but the text suggests that they spoke 'face to face'.

However, when Moses was receiving the Ten Commandments and asks to see G-d:

Exodus 33:18–23

He said, 'Oh, let me behold Your Presence!' And He answered, 'I will make all My goodness pass before you, and I will proclaim before you the name Lord, and the grace that I grant and the compassion that I show. But,' He said, 'you cannot see My face, for man may not see Me and live.' And the Lord said, 'See, there is a place near Me. Station yourself on the rock and, as My Presence passes by, I will put you in a cleft of the rock and shield you with My hand until I have passed by. Then I will take My hand away and you will see My back; but My face must not be seen.'

God speaking to Moses through the burning bush.

Through the rest of the Jewish scriptures, G-d sometimes appears as a pillar of cloud or flame, and sometimes just as a voice, as when G-d spoke to the prophet Elijah:

1 Kings 19:11b–12

And lo, the Lord passed by. There was a great and mighty wind, splitting mountains and shattering rocks by the power of the Lord; but the Lord was not in the wind. After the wind – an earthquake; but the Lord was not in the earthquake. After the earthquake – fire; but the Lord was not in the fire. And after the fire – a soft murmuring sound.

On some occasions, G-d appears in visions as a powerful king. For example:

Silence.

Isaiah 6:1–2

In the year that King Uzziah died, I beheld my Lord seated on a high and lofty throne; and the skirts of His robe filled the Temple. Seraphs stood in attendance on Him. Each of them had six wings: with two he covered his face, with two he covered his legs, and with two he would fly.

As well as the descriptions and ideas about G-d found in the scriptures, Jews would say that they can know G-d through the wonders and majesty of the world around them, all of which G-d created.

This verse by the poet William Blake suggests something of this idea.

> ❝ *To see a world in a grain of sand*
> *And a heaven in a wild flower,*
> *Hold infinity in the palm of your hand*
> *And eternity in an hour.* ❞
> (William Blake, 1757–1827)

(AO2 skills) ACTIVITIES

'It is easier to find out about G-d in silence than through talking about him.' Read this statement carefully and see how many reasons you can find to agree and disagree with it.

(AO1 skills) ACTIVITIES

Find a copy of the hymn 'Immortal, invisible'. Write down each word and phrase used to describe G-d, then explain what each means. Finally, write half a page explaining what this hymn says about G-d.

Sikhism: Religion, reason and revelation 1

The next two pages will help you to:

- develop your knowledge and understanding of the concept of revelation in Sikhism
- make links between the concept of revelation in Sikhism, and what you think/believe.

 **ACTIVITIES**

- Carry out a survey in your class to find out what the class considers to be a revelation.
- Analyse your findings and put them in a table under one of these columns: religious or non-religious.
- In your own words, describe what you consider a 'revelation' to be. How close are you to the dictionary definition of the word?

Guru Nanak Dev Ji.

Revelation through Guru Nanak Dev Ji

Revelation in many religions focuses on a divine being's communication with an individual: for example, God and Moses, God and the Prophet Muhammad ﷺ and God and Guru Nanak Dev Ji.

Transcendent and religious experience is a very important expression of revelation in the Guru Granth Sahib Ji. The significance of Guru Nanak Dev Ji's religious experience, some would argue, begins his religious ministry.

 **ACTIVITIES**

Imagine you are one of Guru Nanak Dev Ji's close friends. He returns from his mystical experience. What are your thoughts and feelings when Guru Nanak Dev Ji tells you where he has been? Do you notice any difference in his personality?

How God's words were revealed to Guru Nanak Dev Ji

Sikhs believe that Guru Nanak Dev Ji vanished under water for three days and was taken to God's court at this time, where the teachings were revealed to him.

On reappearing after three days, Guru Nanak Dev Ji spoke the following words:

> ❝ *There is no Hindu,*
> *There is no Muslim,*
> *So whose path shall I follow?*
> *I shall follow God's path.* ❞

For Sikhs, God is essentially formless or nirguna (see Topic 1). There are no references in Sikh teachings where God actually takes on a form. However, God becomes saguna (manifest) in order for humans to form a relationship with the Divine.

God is particularly immanent in the hearts of human beings. This immanence of the formless God is essential in allowing humans to experience God's immanent revelation.

The concept of Sahaj is often used in the **Gurus'** experience of the divine, highlighted as the feeling of blissful union with the divine through an unconditional loving relationship. The practice of **nam simran** (see Topic 2), enabling one to appreciate the revelations of God, is constantly emphasised in the teachings of the Gurus. The fifth Sikh Guru, Guru Arjan Dev Ji writes:

Guru Granth Sahib Ji, page 1357
Contemplating the Lord's Name and ever uttering the Master's praises in the saint's society, O Nanak, immaculate becomes the mortal.

Those who experience this immanent revelation are referred to as a jivanmukt – essentially an individual who has achieved mukti while still alive. The jivanmukt will not accumulate any further **karma** due to the loss of the ego. Importantly then, the ending of the ego (haumai) is essential in enabling one to experience the Saguna nature of God as immanent.

ACTIVITIES

Think/pair/share
Interview ten different people in the class, asking two questions:

- What do you see around you that makes you think there must be a God or Supreme Being?
- Is there anything in the physical world that would be impossible if there were no God or Supreme Being?

ACTIVITIES

Think/pair/share
In pairs, discuss what implications Guru Nanak Dev Ji's first words have for the nature of Sikhism. Remember that Hinduism and Islam were the two main dominant religions at the time of Guru Nanak Dev Ji. Share your answers with the class.

REMEMBER THIS

Look back at the explanations of immanent, manifest, nirguna and saguna in Topic 1.

Sikhism:
Religion, reason and revelation 2

The next two pages will help you to:

- analyse the importance and authority of the Guru Granth Sahib Ji, and its revelation through the ten human Sikh Gurus
- make links between the importance of sacred texts in Sikhism, and what you think/ believe.

The authority and importance of the Guru Granth Sahib Ji

The Guru Granth Sahib Ji was originally referred to as the Adi Granth (first collection) and was compiled by Guru Arjan Dev Ji in 1604 CE. For over a hundred years, the Sikh community had the scripture alongside a human Guru to guide them. In 1708 CE, prior to his death, the final human Guru, Guru Gobind Singh Ji, proclaimed that the Adi Granth would succeed him as Guru: there were to be no more human Gurus after this. So in 1708, the scripture became the Guru Granth Sahib Ji.

Because of its exalted status as the eternal Guru, the scripture is treated like royalty. It is placed in a special encasement in the **gurdwara** and all worshippers sit on the floor at a level lower than the Guru. It is covered in special cloths (rumulas) and is ritually opened and closed each day. It forms the basis for all religious rites of passage in Sikhism.

Religious tolerance in the Guru Granth Sahib Ji

The Guru Granth Sahib Ji is probably the only religious scripture to contain the writings of more than one religious tradition. Alongside the compositions of the Sikh Gurus, it also contains teachings from both Hindu and Muslim saints. In this respect, Guru Nanak Dev Ji's first words after his mystical experience (see p. 143) have great significance in the universal message of Sikhism.

The Sikh Gurus were extremely tolerant towards the faiths of others. From the composition of the Guru Granth Sahib Ji, they clearly recognised that they alone did not have the monopoly in terms of the revelation of truth.

Guru Arjan Dev Ji.

FOR DEBATE

Do you think that one religion alone can provide the answers to life and contain the unique revelation of Truth? Explain your answer in as much detail as possible.

Share your thoughts with a partner.

Sikh Nanak's teaching

> **Guru Granth Sahib Ji, page 934**
> *They, who are bereft of the Lord's Name, fall like the wall of sand.*
> *O, how are we to be Released without the Name? This wise one falls*
> *into Hell.*

Guru Ravidas' teaching

Guru Ravidas was a Hindu saint.

> **Guru Granth Sahib Ji, page 1106**
> *All epics and Puranas and Shastras are but mere words:*
> *Vyasa, the seer, said the last word, after a great thought, that nothing equals the*
> *Name of God.*

The Guru Granth Sahib Ji uses many names to refer to God, including **Waheguru** (Wonderful Lord), Satnam (The True Name), Rama (a Hindu term) and Allah (a Muslim term).

However, it must be remembered that Sikhism is not just a rehash of Hindu and Muslim thought. Sikhs strongly believe that the message was uttered to Guru Nanak Dev Ji by God during his three-day disappearance. Each succeeding Guru carried on the divine message.

The divine light (jot) that was present in Guru Nanak Dev Ji was vested into each of his succeeding nine Sikh Gurus, and the unified message of Sikhism was revealed to followers of the Gurus. Importantly, the spirit of revelation is now eternally present in the Guru Granth Sahib Ji.

ACTIVITIES

If you could refer to one book as your guide in life, which one would it be? What are your reasons for choosing it as your guide? What is so special about its content and how does it make you feel?

GradeStudio

AO1

QUESTION
Describe Sikh beliefs about the revelation of Sikh teachings. **[6 marks]**

You could build an answer like this:

Level 1
First, let the examiner know that you know what the question is about. For example, 'Guru Nanak Dev Ji's religious experience when he vanished for three days under water forms the basis of revelation in Sikh teachings.'

Level 2
Next, go on to explain Sikh belief that the divine light (jot) that Guru Nanak Dev Ji received from his mystical experience was passed down through each of the nine succeeding Gurus and in 1708 CE eternally in the Guru Granth Sahib Ji.

Level 3
Finally explore the universal and tolerant nature of the Guru Granth Sahib Ji.

GradeStudio

Welcome to the Grade Studio

Grade Studio is here to help you improve your grades by working through typical questions you might find on an examination paper. For a full explanation of how Grade Studio works, and how the examiners approach the task of marking your paper, please see p. 26.

AO1

Question

Explain the importance for Christians of their sacred texts.

[6 marks]

Student's answer

Christians believe that the Bible is the word of God. This means that it is important because every word in it comes direct from God and so must be the truth. Some Christians believe that the Bible was inspired by God but written down by humans and that therefore different parts of the Bible might be truer than others. Some Christians use the Bible as a sort of moral guidebook.

Examiner's comment

The candidate has given a satisfactory answer to the question. There are several relevant points but only the first one is dealt with in any detail. The answer needs to give more information and examples in order to reach Level 3. The candidate could also use more technical terms from the specification to show the breadth of their knowledge and understanding.

Student's improved answer

Christians believe that the Bible is the word of God. This means that it is important because every word in it comes direct from God and so must be the truth. Some Christians believe that the Bible was inspired by God but written down by humans and that therefore different parts of the Bible might be truer than others. Some Christians use the Bible as a sort of moral guidebook.

Other reasons which Christians might give in support of the importance they attach to the scriptures is that they read the Bible on a regular basis and refer to it when they have difficulties in their lives. The Bible can also give people encouragement and hope for the future because they believe it is the word of God and a revealed text, therefore it is more important than other books.

Examiner's comment

This is now a good answer to the question. The candidate has shown a clear understanding of the question. There is good description and explanation of a variety of different reasons why the Bible is so important to Christians. The candidate has shown some analysis in dealing with the interpretation of the Bible. The information is presented clearly and there is good use of technical terms.

Question

'Sacred texts are too old to be useful.' Discuss this statement. You should include different, supported points of view and a personal viewpoint. You must refer to Christianity in your answer. **[12 marks]**

Student's answer

Christians might say that because the Bible is the word of God it does not matter how old it is: it will always be the same. Because the text of the Bible is revealed it means that it will always be useful for all time and that it will always be able to provide an answer to people's questions.

Examiner's comment

The candidate has given a limited answer to the question. There are two relevant points but they both address the same point of view and neither is expanded. The answer needs to give alternative viewpoints, and to include a personal response to reach Level 4.

Student's improved answer

Christians might say that because the Bible is the word of God it does not matter how old it is it will always be the same. Because the text of the Bible is revealed it means that it will always be useful for all time and that it will always be able to provide an answer to people's questions.

Some people, on the other hand, might think that because of the age of the Bible it has very little to say about modern issues and problems such as subjects like euthanasia and fertility treatment. However, other Christians would say that the Bible contains general teachings and the life and example of Jesus, which would all help people to make decisions.

My personal opinion is that the question about whether the Bible is useful depends on whether you believe it is the word of God. If you do, then you will be able to find answers in it to your questions. If, like me, you are an atheist, then the Bible is just an interesting but very old book but it does not help me in my life.

Examiner's comment

This is now a good answer to the question. The candidate has shown a clear understanding of the question and has presented a range of views supported by evidence and argument. The answer explains Christian views, among others, and includes a personal viewpoint, which is also supported.

These specimen answers provide an outline of how you could construct your response. Space does not allow us to give a full response. The examiner will be looking for more detail in your actual exam responses.

These examples only use Christianity but you could use the Grade Studio to apply to any of the religions you are studying and the structure of the answers would work in the same way.

Topic 6: Religion and science

The Big Picture

In this Topic, you will be addressing religious beliefs and teachings about:

- the origins of the world and life, and the relationship between scientific and religious understandings
- attitudes to animals and their treatment
- responses to environmental issues and human obligations towards the environment.

You will also think about ways in which these beliefs affect the life and outlook of religious people in the world today.

What?

You will:

- develop your knowledge and understanding of key religious beliefs and ideas about the relationship between science and religion
- explain what these beliefs and ideas mean to believers and think about how they might affect how they live
- make links between these beliefs and ideas and what you think/believe.

Why?

Because:

- these beliefs and ideas underpin and are reflected in the ways many people live their lives: for example, in helping people to decide what principles should govern their treatment of other people, animals and the environment
- understanding people's beliefs can help you understand why they think and act in the way they do
- understanding these beliefs helps you compare and contrast what others believe, including thinking about your own beliefs and ideas.

How?

By:

- recalling and selecting information about religious beliefs and ideas on the relationship between science and religion, explaining their importance for people today
- thinking about the relevance of these beliefs in 21st-century Britain
- evaluating your own views about these beliefs.

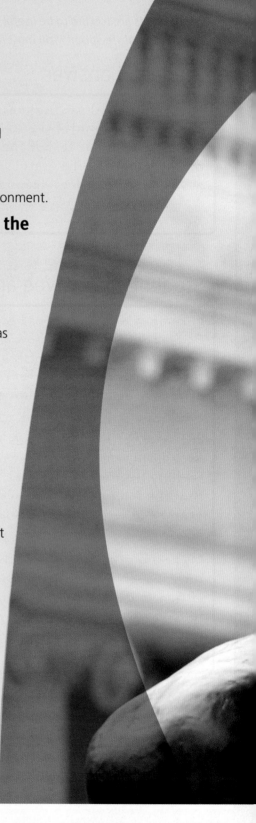

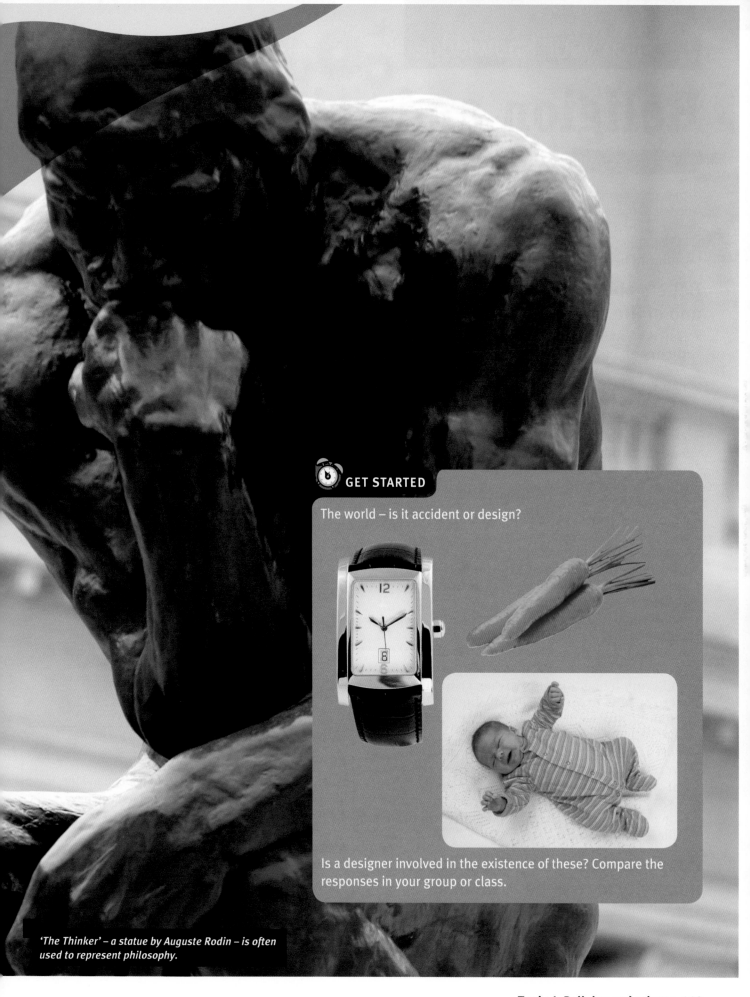

The world – is it accident or design?

Is a designer involved in the existence of these? Compare the responses in your group or class.

'The Thinker' – a statue by Auguste Rodin – is often used to represent philosophy.

Religion and science

KEY INFORMATION

Although there are deep disagreements between scientific and religious views of the world, many people have a religious faith and a career in science. Is it possible for science and religion to work together to help us understand the world?

Beliefs about the origins of the world and of life

- Current scientific views centre on the **Big Bang theory** and the theory of **evolution**.
- For Buddhists, the physical universe is formed naturally by the interaction of five elements: earth, water, fire, air and space. They believe world systems or galaxies pass through cycles of evolution and decline lasting millions of years. Buddhists think that questions like 'How was the world created?' distract them from the main aim of life: removing **dukkha** and achieving **nibbana**, by escaping **samsara**.
- Many Christians believe that God created the universe out of nothing, based on the story in Genesis 1:1. Others accept scientific theories about the origins of the universe and evolution of human beings. Some feel that the theory of **intelligent design** fits well with the idea of God as creator.
- Hinduism does not explain how the world began. Because Hindus believe it is a mystery, their religious beliefs do not clash with scientific theories.
- Muslims believe that Allah created the world and every living thing from water. Humans were created to serve Allah. Muslims welcome scientific discoveries because they help them to understand Allah's creation.
- Most Jews believe that the universe and everything in it was created by G-d and scientific explanations of creation are not acceptable.
- Sikhs believe God created the world and so all life is good. Everything exists through the will of God, called hukam.

People and animals – the place of humanity in relation to animals

- Buddhists do not make a distinction between humans and other life forms and, although human life has special value, they believe all living beings should be respected.

GET STARTED

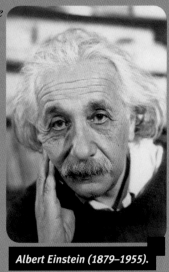

Albert Einstein (1879–1955).

"Religion without science is lame, science without religion is blind."

(Einstein)

What do you think Einstein meant?

- Christians believe people are made 'in the image of God' and that they differ from animals because people have souls.
- Hindus believe all living things are linked because they all come from God and animals are treated with respect.
- Islam teaches that humans have a responsibility to look after animals and treat them well.
- Jews believe that humans are created 'in the image of G-d'. Humans have been given charge of the world and authority over all life on earth.
- Sikhs believe God is in everything, and so treat animals with dignity and respect.

KEY QUESTIONS

KNOWLEDGE AND UNDERSTANDING
What religious ideas can help us to understand the universe? Give examples from religion(s) you have studied.

ANALYSIS AND EVALUATION
Can science and religion agree? Give reasons to support your view.

Attitudes to animals and their treatment

- Buddhist attitudes to animals are governed by belief in **ahimsa**, the sacredness of life. They do not support inhumane treatment of animals.
- Some Christians believe God gave them responsibility to care for animals and that, as animals are part of God's creation, they should be treated with respect and not harmed or exploited.
- The Hindu belief in ahimsa (non-violence) includes not harming animals.
- Muslims follow the teaching of Muhammad ﷺ that animals should be treated well. Animals for slaughter must be treated in a certain way so that the meat is halal.
- Jews follow the teachings of the **Torah** that animals must be respected and causing suffering to animals is to be avoided.
- Sikhs try to live responsibly and without harming or exploiting animals.

Responses to environmental issues and religious teaching relating to environmental issues

- Buddhists believe all beings are interdependent. Humans are not simply the caretakers of the environment but, through their actions, contribute to its creation and destruction. Buddhists believe people should try to live in harmony with their environment.
- Christians believe God created people to be 'stewards' of the earth. This means that they should show responsibility for the planet, care for it and protect it.
- To Hindus, the whole world is part of God, so caring for the world is a way of caring for God. The future of the planet matters because they believe that they will be reborn into this world when they die.
- Muslims believe they do not own the world but are here to look after it for God and for future generations, based on **tawhid**, **khalifah** and **akhirah** (unity, trusteeship and accountability).
- Jews see the work of G-d in everything around them. At the festival of Rosh Hashanah, they thank G-d for the creation of the world. They support projects on the protection of the environment, and respect the notion of tikkun olam – 'repairing the world'.
- Sikhism teaches that humans should be in harmony with the earth and all creation. They believe humans must be concerned to protect the environment to preserve this harmony.

KEY WORDS

Ahimsa the Buddhist and Hindu concept of non-killing, non-violence, respect for life

Akhirah in Islam, everlasting life after death

Avatars the form of a person or animal taken by some Hindu gods when they come to earth

Bhikkhu fully ordained Buddhist monk

Big Bang theory the theory that the earth was created about 18 billion years ago by a massive explosion

Dukkha suffering – the nature of existence according to the first Noble Truth in Buddhism

Evolution theory the theory that groups of organisms change with passage of time, mainly as a result of natural selection, so that descendants differ from their ancestors; ultimately, the theory that all current life forms developed in stages from a single cell millions of years ago

Guru teacher; a title reserved for the ten human Gurus and the Guru Granth Sahib Ji

Intelligent design the theory that certain features of the universe are best explained by the existence of an intelligent cause

Kamma in Buddhism, intentional actions that affect your circumstances in this and future lives

Karma consequence of actions, in terms of cause and effect

Khalifah a key notion in Islam: successor; inheritor; custodian; vice-regent; trusteeship

Mool Mantar a sacred text summarising Sikh beliefs

Nibbana in Buddhism, achieving freedom from greed, hatred and delusion resulting in freedom from rebirth

Omnipotent in religion, when God is all powerful

Omniscient in religion, when God is all knowing

Samsara in Buddhism and Hinduism; a continuing cycle of birth, ageing, death and rebirth

Steward someone who is responsible for resources; a guardian of things that do not directly belong to them

Tawhid unity; belief in the oneness of Allah; absolute monotheism as practised in Islam

Torah Jewish law, or teaching, made up of the Five Books of Moses

FOR INTEREST

Did you know that in the 17th century the Catholic Church imprisoned the astronomer Galileo as a heretic and banned his works? Find out what 'heretic' means, then do some research to find out what Galileo discovered and why it was thought to be so threatening to Christian beliefs. Could this happen to a scientist now?

Buddhism: Religion and science 1

The Buddhist view of the origins of the universe

In essence, Buddhists are not that interested in the origins of the universe or humanity, and there is no widely accepted Buddhist 'creation' story. The Buddha refused to answer questions about the origin of the universe. He believed that knowing the answer to such questions did not help a Buddhist to achieve **nibbana**, and such curiosity was a distraction from the real aim in life: removing **dukkha**.

What Buddhists do generally accept is that the universe is cyclical. Layers of it are created and destroyed in cycles. As beings are reborn into higher realms, lower realms are destroyed, and then recreated for beings to be reborn back into them.

The next two pages will help you to:

- explore Buddhist beliefs about the origins of the world and life
- understand Buddhist teaching about dependent origination.

AO1+AO2 skills ACTIVITIES

- Look at the picture of the world below. Does it make you think about how the world was created? If you were told to put any questions you had about the origin of the world to one side, could you?
- Complete a class survey to find out how many people think the world needs an explanation, and how many are happy to accept it just exists.

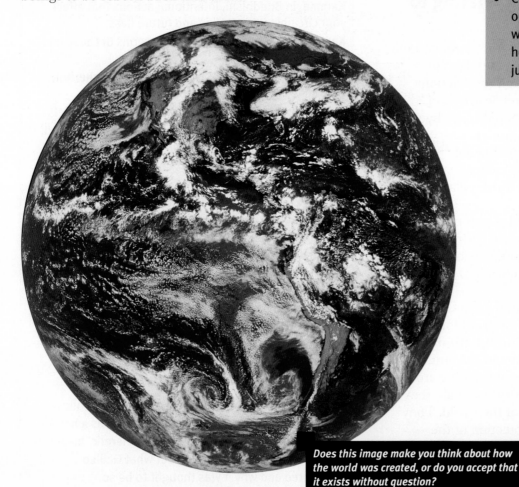

Does this image make you think about how the world was created, or do you accept that it exists without question?

Dependent origination

Buddhists are much more interested in the cycle of cause and effect leading individuals to be reborn within the cycle of **samsara**. The process by which this occurs is called 'dependent origination'. Dependent origination is a series of twelve links showing how the cycle of cause and effect keeps beings trapped within samsara. This cycle is often shown on the outside of the wheel of samsara with twelve small images.

AO1 skills ACTIVITIES

Use the information in the chart to create a diagram demonstrating the process of dependent origination.

	Link	Explanation	Symbol in the Wheel of Life
1	Delusion leads to kammic formations	Ignorance of the basic nature of life explained in the Four Noble Truths leads us to act	Blind man
2	Kammic formations lead to consciousness	Our thoughts and actions lead to impulses and tendencies; these impulses form our consciousness	Potter
3	Consciousness leads to name and form	Consciousness is what passes from one life to the next	Monkey in a tree
4	Name and form leads to the six senses	The five khandhas are reformed based on the continuing consciousness from the previous life	Boat and four passengers
5	The six senses lead to contact	The presence of form allows people to experience the world through the six senses (sight, hearing, touch, smell, taste and mind)	House with six openings
6	Contact leads to feeling	The six senses allow people to make contact with the objects of the senses	Man and woman embracing
7	Feeling leads craving	Making contact allows people to like, dislike or feel neutral about objects	Man with arrow in his eye
8	Craving leads to grasping	Feeling like or dislike allows people to crave for experiences, more life or oblivion	Man taking a drink from a woman
9	Grasping leads to becoming	Craving causes people to grasp at those objects they like, for example, sensual pleasures or more life	Man picking fruit
10	Becoming leads to birth	Grasping at life causes people to become, or join the process of samsara	Pregnant woman
11	Birth leads to suffering, decay and death	Becoming, in the process of samsara leads to rebirth	Childbirth
12	Suffering, decay and death	Birth leads to suffering, decay and death	Corpse

Buddhism:
Religion and science 2

The next two pages will help you to:

- explain Buddhist attitudes to the treatment of animals
- explain Buddhist responses to environmental issues.

How do Buddhists treat animals?

In Buddhism, all beings – both animals and humans – are trapped within the cycle of samsara. Also, because of the Buddhist belief in rebirth, humans will all, at one time, have been reborn as an animal, and any animals may in previous lives have been related to humans. These beliefs tend to blur the distinctions between human and animal lives, and make it less clear that humans are distinctly different to animals than in many other religions.

As a result, Buddhists tend to encourage people to treat animals with respect. This is supported by the Buddhist teaching of **ahimsa** – non-harming – found in the five precepts. Most Buddhists do not see animals as creatures that can be used without regard to their own welfare.

While many Buddhists are vegetarians, this is not universal. The Buddha taught the middle path, and in some Buddhist countries humans would not be able to survive without eating meat or fish. However, Buddhists would not support hunting for sport or the inhumane treatment of animals.

The use of animals for medical research is an area of debate within Buddhism. Some Buddhists feel that such use breaks the first precept of ahimsa, and is treating animals as a means to an end, rather than as valued, sentient beings. Other Buddhists feel that the middle path allows humans to pursue better medical treatment to prevent the suffering of many, through the limited use of animals treated in a humane manner. All Buddhists would welcome suitable alternatives to the use of animals for testing if they were available.

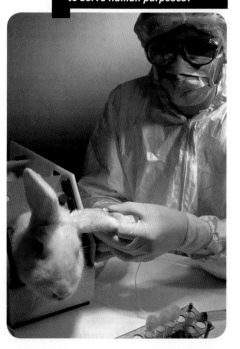

Is it acceptable to use animals to serve human purposes?

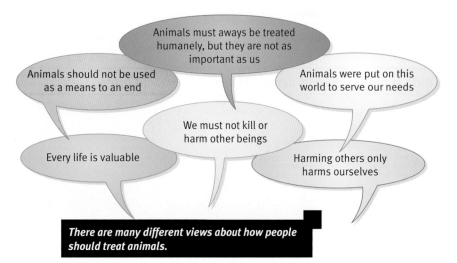

There are many different views about how people should treat animals.

FOR DEBATE

Using the ideas expressed in the illustration, hold a class debate about whether animals can be used by humans for their own purposes or not. Make sure Buddhist views are represented by at least one group.

Caring for the environment

Buddhists believe that all beings are interdependent. This means that if the environment is harmed, all beings living within it are harmed. Some Buddhists believe that the current problems with the environment can be traced to the selfish actions of humans in the past. Such selfishness is in direct contradiction to Buddhist teachings of compassion, and can only result in negative consequences. Buddhists believe that people should attempt to live in harmony with their environment.

Some Buddhists today have started using the term 'engaged Buddhism' to refer to Buddhists' involvement with social problems and issues. This reflects a growing trend for lay and monastic Buddhists to participate in projects that address social concerns.

The **bhikkhus** and bhikkhunis at Chithurst Monastery in Sussex have a long history of environmental work. They are currently engaged in restoring the ecological balance of a woodland called Hammer Wood, which has been donated to them. On their website, they emphasise the importance of the environment for both themselves and others.

Statement from the Buddhists at Chithurst Monastery

66 *The Wood provides a suitable environment for tranquillity and for being with nature – both key features of the* **Forest Tradition of Theravada Buddhism** *... the guiding principle behind the sangha's use and stewardship of the Wood is to maintain it as a place for solitude and an environment where wildlife can live free from threat or disturbance. Therefore it is vital to the welfare of this precious resource that visitors do not bring dogs into the woods, and that they also respect the silence and purity of the environment in every way.* 99

 **ACTIVITIES**

- Think about what you learned about meditation in Topics 2 and 5. Why might preserving the environment be useful for Buddhist practice?
- Design a leaflet for Buddhist children explaining why they should look after the world, and the creatures living within it.

 **ACTIVITIES**

Complete a class survey to see how many people think it is acceptable to use animals to test whether make-up is safe for human use, and how many think it is acceptable to use animals to help research cures for medical conditions like cancer.

Explain why you think people have different views on this issue.

  GradeStudio

AO1

QUESTION
Explain why some Buddhists might not accept scientific theories about the origins of the world. **[6 marks]**

Level 1
It would be acceptable to say that some Buddhists would accept scientific theories. However you should not spend very long on this as your main focus should be on those who may not.

Level 2
You could explain that since the Buddha refused to answer questions on causation some Buddhists would simply be uninterested in scientific views, and thus see

them as irrelevant. You might also consider whether Buddhists views on dependent origination and samsara are in conflict with scientific views of **evolution**.

Level 3
You might continue by saying that if beings are reborn, and can take on any life form dependent upon their **kamma**, this may contradict the scientific view that animals gradually evolve. You could also consider whether the cyclic creation and destruction of the universe is incompatible with the **Big Bang theory**.

Christianity:
Religion and science 1

What theories do scientists have to explain the origins of the world?

In the past, scientists knew very little about how the world was first formed, or how human beings came to be on the earth. Ideas that were put forward were broadly linked to the religious beliefs of the day. However, science has developed a great deal since holy books were written, and now some theories appear to contradict these earlier beliefs.

The study of the origin of the universe is called cosmology. Over the centuries, scientists have come to the conclusion that the world is a lot older than was first thought. Today it is believed that the universe is over 15,000 million years old. There are some theories that suggest that there was actually no real 'beginning', but that the world developed slowly over a long period of time.

The Big Bang

The best-known theory of how the world began is known as the **Big Bang theory**. This states that there was a massive explosion, which caused matter and gases to fly out in all directions. All of the galaxies in the universe were formed from these gases and matter. Slowly the gases cooled, forming first the stars and then the planets, including our world, the Earth.

Evolution

Most scientists would accept Darwin's theory of evolution, described in his groundbreaking book *On the Origin of the Species*. Darwin wrote it after travelling on a ship called the *Beagle* to visit different countries. His theory was that all animals and plants have evolved over millions of years. As conditions change – such as the climate becoming warmer or colder – animals and plants with favourable inheritable traits become more common in successive generations than those with unfavourable inheritable traits. This process is called natural selection.

Darwin thought that humans had evolved over time, rather than having been in existence from the beginning of the world. Many people felt that his ideas were ridiculous and made fun of him, while others were shocked to think he would suggest they had evolved from other species.

The next two pages will help you to:

- examine scientific theories about the origins of the world
- identify Christian beliefs about the origins of the world
- analyse the conflict and similarities between scientific and Christian ideas about the origins of the world.

AO1+AO2 skills **ACTIVITIES**

How do you think the world began? Share your ideas with others in the group, explaining your reasons to them. Make a class list of theories.

The Milky Way.

AO1 skills **ACTIVITIES**

Make a diagram to show the Biblical account of the seven days of creation. Check it out in Genesis 1:1–2:3. Compare this with the scientific theories and make a note of the main differences.

What are Christian beliefs about the origins of the world?

Christian beliefs about the origins of the world come from the book of Genesis in the Old Testament.

> **Genesis 1:1**
> *In the beginning, God created the heavens and the earth.*

There are two stories in Genesis that describe how God planned and made the world over a period of six days, and rested on the seventh day. According to these accounts, all the species of animals and plants were in existence from the beginning of the world. Humans were the most important part of the creation. They were made 'in the image of God' (Genesis 1:26).

The Creation.

Conflict – science versus religion?

Theories about evolution were not new in the 19th century, when Darwin wrote *On the Origin of the Species*. In the 4th century, St Augustine suggested that God only created very simple life forms that then developed over a long time.

Some Christians take the accounts in the Bible literally, exactly as they are written, believing that the creation occurred in seven days and all living things existed from the beginning of the world. These people are known as Creationists and they have a strong following in parts of the United States. In the 19th century, Philip Gosse, a naturalist, even suggested that fossilised remains had been placed in the earth by God as a test of faith.

However, other Christians who are more liberal accept some scientific theories and look on the biblical accounts as myths – stories made up to explain difficult ideas.

One popular theory today is that of **intelligent design**. This is the theory that certain features of the universe are best explained by the existence of an intelligent cause. This theory seems to link the scientific ideas with religious beliefs – that the universe and all that is in it did evolve, but there was a first cause that started it all, which Christians would say was God.

AO1 skills ACTIVITIES

Make a chart or table to show the Creationist views and those of other Christians.

St Augustine of Hippo (354–430).

Christianity: Religion and science 2

What do Christians believe about the treatment of animals?

According to one of the stories of Creation, God created animals before humans and so they are considered to be the responsibility of humans. In the book of Genesis, Adam is allowed to name all the animals and is told to rule over them. It is not clear what this means, but it seems that humans are expected to act as caretakers of the animal kingdom.

> **Genesis 1:27–28**
>
> *So God created man in his own image, in the image of God he created him; male and female he created them. God blessed them and said to them, 'Be fruitful and increase in number; fill the earth and subdue it. Rule over the fish of the sea and the birds of the air and over every living creature that moves on the ground.'*

Most Christians feel that it is acceptable to use animals for food as long as they are slaughtered humanely and are not caused unnecessary pain. One of the apostles, Peter, has a vision where he sees all types of food presented to him. He is told that he can eat any of the food as God gives it all to him. Some Christians, however, feel that their role is to look after and protect animals, so they are vegetarians.

Most Christians believe that the most important difference between animals and humans is that humans have a soul – a divine spark that sets them apart from other living things. Christians believe that it is the soul that is reunited with God when they die.

Many Christians feel that it is the responsibility of humans to protect animals and to prevent the loss of habitat, unnecessary killing and the scientific testing of cosmetics on animals. Some do believe that it is acceptable to undertake medical testing in some cases if the result will be of benefit to humans.

The next two pages will help you to:

- examine what Christians believe about the treatment of animals
- identify how Christians respond to environmental issues.

Environmental pollution is not good stewardship.

 **ACTIVITIES**

Look at the picture and list all the different ways we are polluting our planet.

The Christian approach to environmental issues

In the past, many Christians have not been worried about what has been happening to the planet. However, today there is an awareness that everyone has a responsibility to look after what we have. Christians believe that they have a duty to take care of the world around them, as God told them to be **stewards** (people responsible for resources).

What does being a steward mean?

If Christians believe that they have been appointed as stewards of the world, what should they do? It is difficult to focus on any one aspect of the problems of the planet when there are so many problems. Issues they might be concerned about include:

- global warming
- pollution
- destruction of the ozone layer
- exhausting the world's resources.

Christians generally feel that their responsibility for the planet means that they should take action to preserve the environment, as described in the Bible.

They might:

- recycle things and encourage other people to do the same
- use cars with low emissions and use lead-free fuel to prevent further pollution, or use public transport
- use products that do not contain CFCs to prevent further destruction of the ozone layer
- join an organisation that works for the good of the environment.

AO1 skills ACTIVITIES

Find out how many people in the class have pets. Discuss with them why they keep pets and how they feel about them.

RESEARCH NOTE

Visit the Greenpeace and the Friends of the Earth websites to find out how these groups act to help preserve our environment. Make a poster using the information to promote a Christian response to environmental issues.

GradeStudio

AO2

QUESTION

'The creation stories are fiction, science must be right.' Discuss this statement. You should include different, supported points of view and a personal viewpoint. You must refer to Christianity in your answer. **[12 marks]**

Level 1

First, show the examiner that you understand what the question is about, and then state an opinion.

Level 2

Next, justify this point of view by referring to the Creation stories. If people do not believe these, they are doubting the truth of the whole Bible.

Level 3

Next, offer a deeper explanation. Many Christians would say that science can only produce theories about what happened, while because the Bible is God's word, it must be true. Many other Christians say that it is not necessary to believe every word of the Bible literally. You should also give you own opinion.

Level 4

Finally, offer a deeper explanation of the second viewpoint. Christians who do not believe in the absolute truth of the Creation stories do not dismiss them, but say they are myths that contain an important truth about how God was responsible for the creation of the world. You should also give your own opinion and support your views.

Hinduism:
Religion and science 1

The meaning of life, the universe and everything

Most Hindus have no problem accepting the **Big Bang** and **evolution** theories because of teachings like those below. The numerous creation stories have a common thread of everything originating from, and returning to, the Universal Spirit. Brahma (the creative aspect of God) is himself created *by* God, who is the primal cause – infinite and uncreated.

> **Mundaka Upanishad, part 2, chapter 1**
> *'As from a fire aflame thousands of sparks come forth, so from the Creator, an infinity of beings have life and to the Creator return again.'*

What is the universe?

> **Bhagavad Gita 10:8**
> *'I am the source of all; from Me everything evolves...'*

> **Bhagavad Gita 11:13**
> *'There, in the body of the God of gods, Arjun then saw the whole universe resting in one, with its many groups.'*

AO1 skills
ACTIVITIES

- Analyse the quotes below and explain how many Hindus use them to justify belief in both a creator God *and* scientific theories about creation.
- Compose a diagram that shows the difference between time as linear and time as cyclical.

RESEARCH NOTE

Astrophysicists are currently researching the idea of cyclical universes. Find out more about this theory and compare it to the ancient Hindu belief.

One of many Hindu creation myths. There are as many universes as drops of water in the River Ganges. After one is destroyed, the snake Ananta appears in an ocean of chaos. Lord Vishnu, the preserver, reclines on Ananta and, as they float in the ocean, a lotus flower grows from Lord Vishnu's naval. From the lotus appears Lord Brahma, the creator; from him, everything else is fashioned. For Brahma, one day is longer than four thousand million years to us; each universe is but his daily work. He splits into two – male and female, the source and destiny of all life. Lord Brahma too, is then destroyed by Lord Shiva, who eliminates all, while Lord Brahma sleeps, ready to recreate the next universe ... the great snake Ananta appears in an ocean of chaos ... and so on, eternally.

This account suggests a cyclical understanding of creation, meaning an endless rotation of universes: created – existing – destroyed – recreated – and so on. Many Hindus believe that this universe is just one of an infinite number – a view shared by some astrophysicists.

These ideas are quite different to the traditional understanding of many Western thinkers and those who follow other religions, where creation is placed in time, which is viewed as linear – having a beginning, middle and end. Many Hindus would describe time as a human concept: something to enable us to keep track of things. For the Universal Spirit, time is meaningless, since to be God is to be all that ever was, is and will be, all at once (see Topic 1).

A Hindu text, the Purusha Sukta, describes how many aspects of the universe originate from Purusha. He brings forth both scientific phenomena (for example, the sun; the wind), *and* gods (for example, Agni, the god of fire), from his mind and body; and is depicted holding the four varnas within himself, which, after he was sacrificed (torn apart), had to be upheld by the people that followed.

> **Bhagavad Gita 4:13**
> *'The fourfold caste has been created by Me according to the differentiation of Guna (qualities) and Karma…'*

Many Hindus understand this to mean that the four varnas, correlate not only to a person's role in society, but also to their character or guna (See Topic 2):

- Brahmin should be mostly sattwic (pure)
- Kshatriya, mostly rajasic (passionate)
- Vaishya, a combination of rajasic and tamasic (lethargic)
- Shudra, mostly tamasic.

Over time, what scripture describes as a distinction determined by behaviour (karma + guna = overall behaviour) has become a set of divisions in society which start at birth. Just as people whose families have been in Britain for hundreds of years may have family names linked to the trade, character or role of an ancestor (for example, Baker, Trueman, King), most Hindus have family names associated with a varna and roles within it.

AO1 skills ACTIVITIES

Create a piece of art, model, poem or song that illustrates Purusha being a source of both scientific elements and deities.

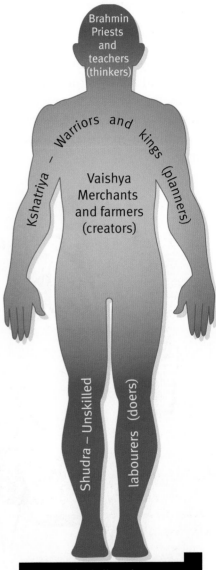

Many Hindus believe that Purusha or Cosmic Man is the origin of the varna system.

AO2 skills ACTIVITIES

'The Hindu varnashramadharma system is at heart no different to the class divide common throughout Europe. In fact, it may be argued that despite many Hindus linking it with birth, at least varnashramadharma is *supposed* to be about how a person lives and behaves, whereas class is only about birth and money.'

Compare the two systems – how different and how similar are they? Do you believe one is any worse or better than the other? Explain your thinking.

Hinduism: Religion and science 2

Many Hindus choose to follow a career in medicine or science, believing it to be good karma to help to relieve or cure the sick and to find out more about how the world works. Many also believe it is their dharma to use and develop the intellect and abilities they are born with. Some however, may be concerned about how far medical intervention may prevent the fulfilment of karmic debt, (see Topic 3); while others may view the use of animals in research to be against **ahimsa** and therefore bad karma.

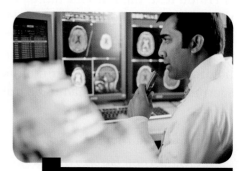

The next two pages will help you to:

- understand why many Hindus believe that science and religion go hand in hand
- research and participate in the vegetarian debate.

Most Hindus believe that scientific research may be a person's dharma.

A01 skills ACTIVITIES

Study the picture opposite and construct a spider diagram detailing at least four uses of a live cow. Add a sentence that explains why many Hindus do not eat beef.

FOR DEBATE

Several eminent scientists have suggested that people in the West in particular have a social and environmental responsibility to eat less meat and fish. Do you agree with their view? Give detailed reasons for your answer.

Many Hindus believe that killing cows for meat is not only against ahimsa, but also ecologically and economically wasteful, given how useful a live cow can be.

The place of science and purpose of existence

There is evidence of ancient Hindu scientists proposing what are viewed as relatively recent ideas, such as the earth revolving around the sun and the Law of Gravity, as much as a thousand years before they were voiced in Europe. Ancient Hindu texts also reveal detailed study of geometry (including the value of π – Pi), astronomy and surgery. All of this points to science being viewed as part of religion in Hindu philosophy.

Most Hindus believe it is part of their dharma and also good karma to care for and protect the environment, because God is believed to be the source of all creation and also present in all creation (see Topic 1).

The place and purpose of humans within creation is viewed by many Hindus to be no different to any other living thing. Again, unlike the traditional understanding of many faiths, humans are not believed, by most Hindus to be the main purpose of creation or to have any more special a relationship with the divine than other life forms. The difference is only that humans are able to create and repay karmic debt, whereas other life forms simply fulfil their dharma without karma having an influence.

The purpose of life, for *all* life, is to become one with the Supreme Spirit. Humans have the option of actively fulfilling their dharma, or preventing fulfilment, while other life forms fulfil dharma just by living according to their nature.

The belief in humans and animals being equal is justified by many Hindus by reference to deities with animal elements (such as Lord Ganesha) and the **avatars** of Vishnu (see Topic 1), which include incarnations such as a fish, tortoise, boar and half lion-half man.

Gandhi on animals and the environment

Many Hindus look to Mahatma Gandhi (See Topic 3) for advice on how to create good karma and avoid bad.

❝ *'To forget how to dig the earth and tend the soil is to forget ourselves.'*
'We should then eat to live, not live to eat. Let anyone who doubts the accuracy of this proposition try to sweat for his bread.'
'I do believe that all God's creatures have the right to live as much as we have.'
'I want to realise brotherhood with or identity not merely with the being called human, but I want to realise identity with all life, even with such beings as crawl on earth.' **❞**

(from *Gandhi: In my own words*)

Varaha (the boar) the second avatar of Vishnu.

ACTIVITIES

Investigate the website for the Vegetarian Society. Use your findings to construct a leaflet or poster that explains why many people choose to not eat meat or fish. Add a section that explains the additional reasons many Hindus would give for why they do not eat meat or fish (see Topic 2).

ACTIVITIES

Reflect on the quotes from Gandhi. In your opinion, are his views sound or misguided? Why?

Islam:
Religion and science 1

Islam teaches that the whole universe is the creation of Allah.

Scientific theories about the origins of the world and humanity

Both science and religion are ways of making sense of the world. Science is the study of the physical, biological and chemical processes of the universe. Religious people often ask similar questions to those asked by scientists: for example, questions about how the world came into existence and why it is the way it is.

Do science and religion give similar or different answers to these questions? Some religious people see science as an attempt to ignore God's revelation or replace it with human answers. Others see science as an approach to understanding the universe in a way that is different, but complementary to religion. Scientists investigate and carry out experiments in order to arrive at the truth. Religious people might say that the only way to the truth is through personal experience, such as through religious practices like prayer and worship.

 **ACTIVITIES**

'At their best, both scientists and people of faith are in a permanent state of awe-struck humility before the wonder and strangeness and messiness of things.'

(Religion vs Science, *The Independent*, Oct 2008)

Explain what you think the writer is saying about the conflict between religion and science. What is meant by 'awestruck humility'? What aspects of the universe might be described as 'wonderful', 'strange' or 'messy'?

Islam and the development of scientific knowledge

Mathematics and astronomy were developed in Islamic cultures in the Middle Ages. They were used to calculate the correct times of prayer and the direction of Makkah, as well as many more non-religious purposes. Between the C9th and C15th CE, Islamic scholars tested and developed ancient Greek medicine, optics, astronomy and astrology. Their motto was: 'Whoever does not know astronomy and anatomy is deficient in the knowledge of God' (al-Ghazali).

Muslim teachings about the origins of the world and humanity

Muslims believe Allah is the Creator and Sustainer. The Qur'an makes it clear that Allah created the world and everything in it from the beginning of time, making humans out of clay and each species separately. Allah has a personal interest in its development and is actively involved in its maintenance.

For Muslims the experience of the natural world – for example, looking at the night sky – is a religious experience that reinforces their belief in the power of God and the complexity of God's creation.

The Qur'an depicts Allah as an **omnipotent** and **omniscient** God, who created the world and is active within it. Allah is involved with creation and all humans who live within it: 'From Allah, verily nothing is hidden on earth or in the heavens' (Surah 3:5).

Where Muslim views meet scientific theories

Some Muslim scientists believe it is possible to put forward a credible scientific view that is compatible with the teachings of the Qur'an. One example of this approach is scientific support for the idea that Allah created everything from water: 'We made from water every living thing' (from Surah 21:30). Links have been made between this quote and the 'primordial soup' theory, which proposes that life on earth originated within a pond or ocean; gradually, it mixed with the atmosphere and through chemical reactions, created the first micro-organisms. These micro-organisms then developed into the first land-based life forms.

Submission

Muslims believe humans were created by Allah and were made for the purpose of submission to Allah: 'I have only created Jinns and men, that they may serve me' (Surah 51:56). Human life is a test, and God will reward humans on the Day of Judgement.

Submission to Allah must take the form of worship, and a person's life on earth is the opportunity to do this. Muslims must show humble submission to the one true God, a total dedication to Allah, Allah's nature and beliefs. Daily prayer and worship, in all its forms, shows a Muslim's dedication to Allah.

REMEMBER THIS

You will have read about the creation of the Jinns in Topic 4.

> **Surah 7:54**
> *Your Guardian-Lord is Allah, Who created the heavens and the earth in six days, and is firmly established on the throne (of authority): He draweth the right as a veil o'er the day, each seeking the other in rapid succession: He created the sun, the moon and the stars, (all) governed by laws under His command. Is it not His to create and to govern? Blessed be Allah, the Cherisher and Sustainer of the worlds!*

FOR DEBATE

'Is it possible to believe in both **evolution** and God?' Organise a class debate on the question from three points of view: that of a scientist, that of a Muslim who does not accept a scientific interpretation of creation, and that of a scientist who is also a Muslim. Note which arguments you find most convincing.

AO1+AO2 skills ACTIVITIES

Can religion and science agree? Do we understand everything about life, the universe and everything or are there still unanswered questions? Create a poster to express your views.

Islam: Religion and science 2

The place of humanity in the world

In 1986, Dr Abdullah Omar Nasseef, the Muslim representative at the World Wide Fund for Nature International, emphasised the commitment of Muslims to care for the environment. He referred to the three central concepts of Islam: **tawhid**, **khalifah**, and **akhirah**, and how they underpin Muslim beliefs about the place of humanity in the world. In particular, he said that tawhid expresses the idea that Allah is Unity and Allah's unity is also reflected in the unity that should exist between people and nature. He said: 'It is these values which led Muhammad ﷺ, the Prophet of Islam, to say: "Whoever plants a tree and diligently looks after it until it matures and bears fruit is rewarded." '

The place of humanity in relation to animals

Islam teaches that humans are given a status above animals, but that they should not take advantage of them. They are equal in sharing praise for the world they live in: 'There is not a thing but celebrates His praise' (from Surah 17:44). People will be made responsible for any cruel act they make towards any of God's creatures. Muhammad ﷺ made it clear that cruelty towards animals is not acceptable, especially mistreating them for any particular reason, such as capturing birds or whipping animals: 'There is no man who kills even a sparrow or anything smaller, without its deserving it, but God will question him about it' (Hadith Al-Nasai).

Eating animals is acceptable, as the Qur'an teaches that livestock has been provided for food. Some Muslims, such as Sufis, practise vegetarianism, as they believe eating meat distracts from a spiritual life. Fair treatment of animals during farming and slaughter is expected.

> **From Surah 40:79**
> *It is Allah Who made cattle for you, that ye may use some for riding and some for food;*

The next two pages will help you to:

- understand and explain Muslim attitudes to animals and their treatment
- explore and evaluate Muslim teaching about environmental issues
- reflect on your own attitudes to the relationship between humans and animals and attitudes to the environment.

 REMEMBER THIS

The concept of tawhid is important in Islam. Make links with the discussion of tawhid in Topic 2 to help you understand its significance for Muslims' understanding of their relationship to Allah and Allah's creation.

Muslim attitudes to animals and their treatment

Everything in Allah's creation should be treated with respect, which includes all animals. They are part of the human community and share in Allah's creation with humans. For this reason, they must be treated with consideration and great value. Animals have an equal right to share in the resources of Allah to live and eat.

> **Surah 79:31–33**
>
> *He draweth out therefrom its moisture and its pasture; And the mountains hath He firmly fixed – For use and convenience to you and your cattle.*

The slaughter of an animal must be done with particular care. The animal is turned towards the Qiblah and the words 'Bismillah Allahu Akbar' ('in the name of God, God is great') are said. The throat is then cut with a sharp knife. All blood must be drained before the meat is eaten. This meat is then halal, meaning approved by Allah.

> **Surah 7:31**
>
> *'Oh Children of Adam! Wear your beautiful apparel at every time and place of prayer: eat and drink: But waste not by excess, for Allah loveth not the wasters.'*

> **Surah 6:165**
>
> *'It is He Who hath made you (His) agents, inheritors of the earth: He hath raised you in ranks, some above others: that He may try you in the gifts He hath given you: for thy Lord is quick in punishment: yet He is indeed Oft-forgiving, Most Merciful.'*

What does Islam teach about environmental issues?

Allah created the world and it belongs to Allah. It is all good and must be respected. The world Allah created must not be abused or mistreated in any way, and its resources must not be wasted.

Stewardship: the concept of khalifah

The term **khalifah** means a '**steward**' or 'representative' of Allah. People are Allah's khalifah on earth. Allah expects people to look after the earth and keep it safe, while still accepting it is not theirs. Muslims should take special care not to waste food or water, as this is instructed in the Qur'an: 'It is He who hath made you (His) agents … that He may try you in the gifts He hath given you' (from Surah 6:165).

Responses to environmental issues

Islamic organisations such as the Islamic Foundation for Ecology and Environmental Science (IFEES) promote the need for ecology and more responsibility for sustainability.

 FOR DEBATE

'Humans are more important than animals.' Do you agree or disagree? Give your reasons.

 RESEARCH NOTE

Find out about the work of Fazlun Khalid the founder of IFEES from the IFEES website. What are the aims of IFEES? How can the work of this organisation help Muslims to carry out their responsibilities as khalifah or stewards of Allah?

Judaism:
Religion and science 1

Darwin changed scientific ideas about the origins of human beings.

The next two pages will help you to:

- look at scientific explanations of the origins of the world and life
- explore Jewish beliefs about the origins of the world and life
- compare these explanations and beliefs with your own beliefs.

AO1+AO2 skills **ACTIVITIES**

Someone from space has just landed on Earth. They know nothing about people's religious beliefs. How might they explain how the Earth and all life on it had come into existence?

Do you think that their explanation would be any different if they had landed in a desert, the middle of the countryside or in a big city? Why?

For Jews, the story of Adam and Eve gives just one version of the story of creation.

Scientific ideas about the origins of the world and humanity

Cosmology

This concerns itself with the origins of the universe. Science suggests that the earth was created about 18 billion years ago by a massive explosion known as the **Big Bang**.

Evolution

Evolution is concerned with the origins of humanity. Developing the work of Charles Bonnet, Charles Darwin's book *On the Origin of Species* proposed that life on earth had begun with a single cell, which eventually developed into the many life forms we have today.

Jewish beliefs about the origins of the world and of humanity

The story of Creation is found at the beginning of Genesis, the first book of the **Torah**.

Satellite view of the earth.

> ### Genesis 1:1–5
>
> *When G-d began to create heaven and earth – the earth being unformed and void, with darkness over the surface of the deep and a wind from G-d sweeping over the water – G-d said, 'Let there be light'; and there was light. G-d saw that the light was good, and G-d separated the light from the darkness. G-d called the light Day, and the darkness He called Night. And there was evening and there was morning, a first day.*

However, from Genesis 2:5–3:24 there is another, different account of Creation, which includes the story of Adam and Eve. Some Jews say that the fact that there are two accounts just means that we are not yet able to understand them properly. Others argue that different people wrote the two accounts at different times – but this causes a problem if all the Torah was written down by Moses and is the word of G-d.

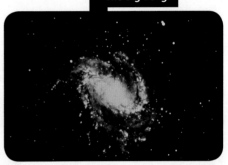

The Big Bang.

One of the differences between the accounts is the creation of human beings. The first account says:

> ### Genesis 1:27
>
> *And G-d created man in His image, in the image of G-d He created him; male and female He created them.*

In the version in Chapter 2, it says:

> ### Genesis 2:21–23
>
> *So the Lord G-d cast a deep sleep upon the man; and, while he slept, He took one of his ribs and closed up the flesh at that spot. And the Lord G-d fashioned the rib that He had taken from the man into a woman; and He brought her to the man. Then the man said,*
> *'This one at last*
> *Is bone of my bones*
> *And flesh of my flesh.*
> *This one shall be called Woman,*
> *For from man was she taken.'*

ACTIVITIES

Has your opinion about the creation stories changed? Explain why your opinion has changed or has not changed.

ACTIVITIES

If you had the chance to ask G-d about creation, what would you ask?

The idea of women being made from men has led many people, for thousands of years, to say that women should be under the authority of men.

If the Torah is, in fact, the word of G-d written down by Moses, this could clash with modern scientific discoveries. However, many Jews have argued that, if a Big Bang kick-started creation, something must have caused the Big Bang, and that could have been G-d. Also, the word translated in Genesis 1 as 'day' actually means a period of time, so this does not necessarily rule out theories of evolution.

Many people would see these two accounts as an attempt to understand the existence of life and to explain G-d's work in creation and G-d's continuing involvement in creation.

> ### Psalm 8:4–9
>
> *When I behold Your heavens, the work of Your fingers,*
> *the moon and stars that You set in place,*
> *what is man that You have been mindful of him,*
> *mortal man that You have taken note of him,*
> *that You have made him little less than divine,*
> *and adorned him with glory and majesty;*
> *You have made him master over Your handiwork,*
> *laying the world at his feet,*
> *sheep and oxen, all of them,*
> *and wild beasts, too;*
> *the birds of the heavens, the fish of the sea,*
> *whatever travels the paths of the seas.*

Judaism:
Religion and science 2

The next two pages will help you to:

- explain Jewish attitudes to the treatment of animals
- explain Jewish responses to environmental issues.

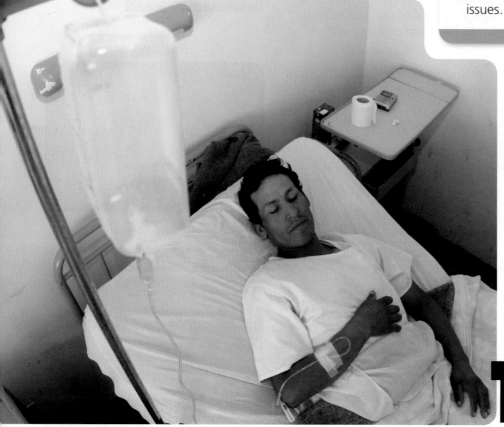

AO1+AO2 skills ACTIVITIES

- Complete a class survey to see how many people think it is acceptable to use animals to test whether make-up is safe for human use, and how many think it is acceptable to use animals to help research cures for medical conditions like cancer.
- Explain why you think people have different views on this issue.

Many life-saving medical treatments have been developed from experiments conducted on animals.

How do Jews treat animals?

Although many animals were sacrificed in the Jerusalem Temple every day, this does not necessarily show that the Jews did not care about animals. Rather, they set great value on them so that they were suitable offerings to make to G-d.

In the first account of creation, G-d gave Adam control over all the animals:

> **Genesis 1:26**
> *And G-d said, 'Let us make man in our image, after our likeness. They shall rule the fish of the sea, the birds of the sky, the cattle, the whole earth, and all the creeping things that creep on earth.'*

In the second account, the man is told by G-d to name all the creatures. Knowing the name of an animal was believed to give the person power over them.

 FOR DEBATE

How far would you agree with this statement: 'For Jews, animals are less important than humans so people can use them in any way they want'?

There are several passages in the Jewish scriptures that talk about caring for animals.

> ## Deuteronomy 5:12:14
> *Observe the sabbath day and keep it holy, as the Lord your G-d has commanded you. Six days you shall labour and do all your work, but the seventh day is a sabbath of the Lord your G-d; you shall not do any work – you, your son or your daughter, your male or female slave, your ox or your ass, or any of your cattle, or the stranger in your settlements, so that your male and female slave may rest as you do. Remember that you were a slave in the land of Egypt and the Lord your G-d freed you from there with a mighty hand and an outstretched arm; therefore the Lord your G-d has commanded you to observe the sabbath day.*

> ## Deuteronomy 25:4
> *You shall not muzzle an ox while it is threshing.*

> ## Proverbs 12:10
> *A righteous man knows the needs of his beast, but the compassion of the wicked is cruelty.*

The use of animals for medical research is an area of debate within Judaism. Some Jews say that the teaching of the Torah that Jews must not cause harm to any living creature means that such research is forbidden. Others argue that humans have a higher status than animals and that if the research helps human life then it is acceptable. However, the minimum of pain must be inflicted on the animal and this research would not include testing cosmetics for example.

Caring for the environment

At the centre of Jewish teaching about caring for the environment is the concept of tikkun olam, usually translated as 'repairing the world'. This repairing can apply to all sorts of social injustices as well as to the environment.

There are several instances in the Jewish scriptures that stress the importance of the world and the thanks that Jews give to G-d for it. At the festival of Rosh Hashanah (New Year), Jews thank G-d for the creation of the world. The responsibility of looking after the world is in the stewardship role G-d gave to humanity, but the earth still belongs to G-d.

Other parts of the scriptures give regulations from G-d about how the world is to be looked after. In Leviticus (25:8–11), there are instructions about resting land every fifty years. In Deuteronomy (20:19a), soldiers are instructed not to cut down trees when they are holding a siege.

Since the establishment of the State of Israel in 1948, particular importance has been given to the festival of Tu B'Shevat – New Year for Trees. Although the scriptures describe the Promised Land as 'flowing with milk and honey' (Exodus 3:8), in fact much of Israel is desert. The work of reclaiming the desert is emphasised by the planting of many trees on this festival and money is collected all over the world for it.

> ## Psalm 24:1
> *The earth is the Lord's and all that it holds, the world and its inhabitants.*

ACTIVITIES

AO1+AO2 skills

Read through these three passages (left) and write an explanation of what they teach about the Jewish approach to animals.

All people, and working animals, should rest on the sabbath.

Planting trees for the festival of Tu B'Shevat.

ACTIVITIES

AO1+AO2 skills

Research Tu B'Shevat in the library or on the Internet. Then look up material on the kibbutz in Israel. Bring this information together to prepare a leaflet explaining Jewish attitudes towards the environment.

Sikhism:
Religion and science 1

The next two pages will help you to:

- develop your knowledge and understanding of Sikh teachings about the origins of the world and life
- evaluate your own views about religious and scientific theories relating to the origins of the world and humanity.

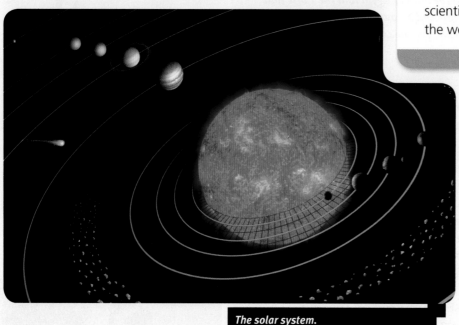

The solar system.

Sikhism and the origins of the world and life

There is no overall passage in Sikh teachings that talks about the process of creation. However, Sikhs refer to God as the Creator of everything. Sikhs also have no issue over accepting that the world (Willed by God) gradually developed over millions of years. Ultimately, however, Sikhs believe in the importance of the human life as the 'golden opportunity' through which one will have the chance to become closer to God. It is highly unlikely, therefore, that a Sikh would accept that humans have simply evolved from apes. Think carefully about how Sikhs can also accept scientific claims of the **Big Bang theory**. In what ways would their beliefs about creation differ from purely scientific claims of the Big Bang and **evolution**?

Guru Granth Sahib Ji, page 52

Imperceptible and Immaculate is the Guru. None else is as great as the Guru. The Guru is the Creator and Guru the Doer ... Nothing is beyond (the jurisdiction of) the Guru.

 **ACTIVITIES**

There are many different arguments and theories as to how the world was created. Question five people in the class about their beliefs as to the origins of the world, and get them to explain their answers. Gather these under two headings: scientific explanations and religious explanations. Do you have any views that do not fit under either?

ACTIVITIES

Think/pair/share
Look at the sacred text. What do you think this verse is saying about the creation of the world? Discuss your thoughts with a partner and share them with the rest of the class.

God the creator – Kurta Purakh

Fundamental to Sikh teachings is that God is the Creator of the world and humanity. The **Mool Mantar** – the basic declaration of the Sikh concept of God – states that God is 'Kurta Purakh', meaning that God is the Creator. Also essential to Sikh thought is the concept of a formless God, nirguna, becoming manifest, saguna, through creation. God is particularly manifest in the hearts of human beings.

Being born as a human is seen as a golden opportunity for one to escape the cycle of reincarnation. Hence, in this respect, it cannot be claimed that humanity simply evolved through a natural process. Although Sikhs are not restricted in believing the Big Bang and evolution theories, they will not deny the role and Will of God behind all creation.

The very concept of God becoming manifest through creation means that the world itself has a purpose, and did not come about by chance or accident. Even if one were to believe in the Big Bang theory, it would be essential to believe that God was the cause behind the Big Bang.

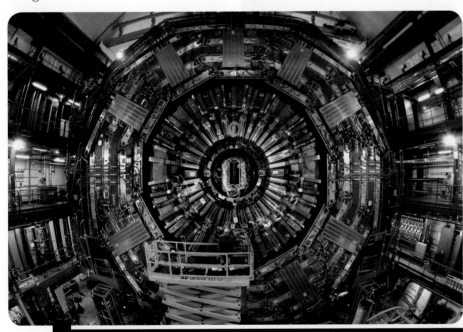

The Large Hadron Collider (LHC) built 175 m below ground on the Franco-Swiss border will be used to test theories such as the Big Bang.

ACTIVITIES

Look around you at the beauty of the natural world. Look at how intricate the human body is and how it functions so amazingly. Do you think this could just be put down to chance, or must there be a designer behind it all? How would the Sikh view of God as Kurta Purakh address this question?

RESEARCH NOTE

Examine the scientific theory of the Big Bang and how evolution fits into it. Also look in detail at how Charles Darwin initially introduced the concept of evolution. Why were his ideas originally rejected by the church?

FOR DEBATE

Split the class into three groups:

- one adopting the opinion of scientific reasoning for the origins of the world and humanity
- one adopting the opinion of religious reasoning for the origins of the world and humanity
- one adopting the opinion of Sikhs who accept scientific explanations of the world.

Each group must argue their opinion as strongly as possible.

Sikhism:
Religion and science 2

The entrance to the Khalsa Wood Project in Nottingham, England.

 **ACTIVITIES**

Think/pair/share

- A significant number of Sikhs are vegetarian. What do you think the Sikh attitude towards animals would be?
- In pairs, discuss whether you think humans are more important than animals and give your reasons why. Share your answers with the rest of the class while one person writes bullet points for the main views in the class.

 MUST THINK ABOUT!
Kosher meat is not the same as halal meat, and there is no mention of kosher meat in Sikh teachings. The only injunction is about halal meat, because of the emphasis of separateness from Muslims.

Sikh attitudes towards animals

Sikhs believe in the reincarnation of the soul. Depending on one's actions, known as **karma**/karam, the soul may take on either the body of a human or animal. For this reason, many Sikhs are vegetarians and believe that consuming animals for food is not what animals were intended for.

Other Sikhs however, have no issue with eating meat, the only exception being to refrain from consuming halal meat. Many Sikhs will not eat beef due to their Hindu heritage.

Some Sikhs believe that an animal should only be killed if absolutely necessary for food and they believe that consuming meat results in negative karma. The use of animals for medical research is generally accepted if the research is genuine and is geared towards eradicating dangerous diseases.

The issue of vegetarianism is much debated among Sikhs. There is no overt teaching that requires a follower of the Sikh Gurus to be a vegetarian. Sikhs are nevertheless taught to respect all forms of life.

Do Sikhs feel people are responsible for the environment?

If humans are regarded as the highest of God's creation, does this mean people are responsible for looking after the environment and everything within it?

Sikhs believe that God is present within all creation, since it is through creation that God becomes manifest. This does not mean that God takes on a form, but rather God lets us know of its nature and enables us to form a loving and personal relationship with it. Therefore, we should treat the environment, which is a manifestation of the Divine, with respect and care. The universe and everything within it is hence to be regarded as sacred since it has been given to us as a gift from God.

Sikhs take part in environmental projects and use initiatives such as recycling and reducing litter. In 1999, Sikhs in Nottingham took part in a green initiative project known as the Khalsa Wood project, marking the 300-year anniversary of the creation of the Khalsa by planting 300 trees in a forest. Sikhs also use examples from the lives of the **Gurus** to illustrate how the Gurus can be used as role models when looking after the environment.

ACTIVITIES

Make a list of all the problems in the environment today, such as pollution and global warming. Do you think humans are responsible for causing these problems or are they inevitable due to natural wear and tear? How can we find solutions to these problems?

ACTIVITIES

Your task is to promote an initiative in your local community to help bring about an awareness of how we all need to do our bit for the environment. In groups, think carefully about who your target audience would be. How are you going to get volunteers to help you? You need to think about what forms of media communication you are going to use.

GradeStudio

AO1

QUESTION

Explain Sikh beliefs about the origins of the world.

[6 marks]

You could build an answer like this:

Level 1
You could begin your answer by referring to the statement of God in the Mool Mantar as being 'Kurta Purakh'.

Level 2
Next go on to explain how ultimately God, according to Sikh teachings, is nirguna – without form. However, in order for humans to form a loving and personal relationship with God, it becomes saguna – manifest in the world.

Level 3
Finally, Sikhs are encouraged to live the life of the householder and use the universe as the action ground on which each individual can work towards mukti.

GradeStudio

Welcome to the Grade Studio

Grade Studio is here to help you improve your grades by working through typical questions you might find on an examination paper. For a full explanation of how Grade Studio works, and how the examiners approach the task of marking your paper, please see p. 26.

AO1

Question

Explain why some Christians might not accept scientific theories about the origins of the world.

[6 marks]

Student's answer

Some Christians do not accept scientific theories about the origins of the world because they agree with the Biblical accounts in the book of Genesis. Some Christians have worked with Christian scientists to disprove scientific theories such as the Big Bang, and to show that the Biblical accounts are true and that God created the world in six days. People say that if you believe in God then you must believe that the Bible is true, so Christians do not have any alternative but to believe in the Genesis creation accounts.

Examiner's comment

The candidate has given a satisfactory answer to the question. There are several relevant points but none of them is explained in any detail. The answer needs to give more information and examples in order to reach Level 3. The candidate could also use more technical terms from the specification to show the breadth of their knowledge and understanding.

Student's improved answer

Some Christians do not accept scientific theories about the origins of the world because they agree with the Biblical accounts in the book of Genesis. Some Christians have worked with Christian scientists to disprove scientific theories such as the Big Bang, and to show that the Biblical accounts are true and that God created the world in six days. People say that if you believe in God then you must believe that the Bible is true, so Christians do not have any alternative but to believe in the Genesis creation accounts.

Some Christians do not see this as a problem. They believe that the stories of creation in Genesis are myth. This means that they are not literally true in themselves, but that they contain essential truth – in this case, that God created the world. If Christians accept this view, then scientific theories do not pose a problem. If there was a Big Bang, it was caused by God.

Examiner's comment

This is now a good answer to the question. The candidate has shown a clear understanding of the question. There is good description and explanation of a variety of different ways in which Christians might respond to scientific theories about the origins of the world. The information is presented clearly and there is good use of technical terms. In addition, the candidate has not written about the origins of humanity and evolution, which are not relevant to the question.

AO2

Question

'The world is ours to treat as we like.' Discuss this statement. You should include different, supported points of view and a personal viewpoint. You must refer to Christianity in your answer.   **[12 marks]**

Student's answer

Christians might say that God put them on the Earth to look after it and that they have to take care of the world. Some Christians might also say that at the creation of human beings God made them stewards, which means they have a duty to take care of creation.

Examiner's comment

The candidate has given a limited answer to the question. There are two relevant points but they both address the same point of view and neither is expanded on. The answer needs to give alternative viewpoints, and also to include a personal response to reach Level 4.

Examiner's comment

Student's improved answer

Christians might say that God put them on the Earth to look after it and that they have to take care of the world. Some Christians might also say that at the creation of human beings God made them stewards, which means they have a duty to take care of creation.

Some people, on the other hand, might think that people were simply placed on the world, or evolved from animals and that therefore they have no more responsibility than any other life form to take care of it. However, even people with no religious belief might think that they owe a duty to generations to come to make sure that the earth is still habitable.

My personal opinion is that all people have a responsibility towards the earth because we all live on it and that, because humans have developed differently from other animals, it is their responsibility to ensure that the Earth and the species on it survive.

This is now a good answer to the question. The candidate has shown a clear understanding of the question and has presented a range of views supported by evidence and argument. The answer explains Christian views, among others, and includes a personal viewpoint, which is also supported.

These specimen answers provide an outline of how you could construct your response. Space does not allow us to give a full response. The examiner will be looking for more detail in your actual exam responses.

These examples only use Christianity but you could use the Grade Studio to apply to any of the religions you are studying and the structure of the answers would work in the same way.

examCafé

Tools and Tips

Now you have finished the course/unit, it is time to revise and prepare for the examination. Before this sends you into a panic, remember that as you have worked through the course you have gained knowledge, understanding and skills. Yes, you will have to refresh your memory and practise your skills but this section of the book is intended to help you to do those things effectively and ensure you do justice to yourself in the exam.

The key to good revision is to **'work smart'**. This section will guide you to know what is needed for success and just as important, what is not. So don't panic! Think positive because the examiner will. GCSE is about what you **can do**, not what you can't.

Key points to note at this stage

1 Your revision needs to focus on what the examiners want in your answers, so you can get the best possible marks.
   - In GCSE Religious Studies there are **two things** that examiners are looking for. These are described in the assessment objectives – AO1 and AO2.
   - Each assessment objective is worth 50 per cent of the marks.

2 You need to understand that the exam questions are designed to measure your performance in each assessment objective. This will ensure you know how respond to the questions so as to reach the highest levels.
   - Each question will have five parts:
     - four questions assessing AO1 – three questions checking on your knowledge, one measuring understanding and analysis. 12 marks in total
     - one question assessing AO2 – assessing your ability to put different points of view on an issue, weigh them up against each other and express your own views backing everything up with evidence and good arguments. 12 marks in total.

If this all sounds rather scary – just hold on. As you work through this section you will see that by knowing what examiners want in each part of the question you can make your revision really count because it will be well focused on success in the assessment objectives.

How to get started

You do need to have a sound knowledge and understanding of all you have studied, so there is some basic factual learning to be done. Techniques for revision are quite personal and depend on how you learn things best. Here are some suggestions:

- Create summary cards to summarise a topic or a part of topic on a small card, using between 5 and 10 bullet points.

- Design memory cards (really good for the visual learner) – use pictures or other visual prompts to recall key facts or, for example, the order of events in a religious story.

- Break your revision time up into **intensive** revision sessions of 5–10 minutes, give yourself a **break** (no more than 5 minutes), and then **test** yourself on what you have revised.

- **Write** your own questions. Write **mark schemes** for them. **Answer** the questions and use the levels of response to **mark** them.

For each Topic, you need to:

- Set everything you learn in the context of the religion you are studying, remembering that it is a living faith, practised by real people in the 21st century.

- Make sure that you cover all parts of each section of the course.

- Know the meaning of all the technical (religious) words in the specification. Learn a short definition for each of them, which you can use in your revision notes and in the exam.

- Make connections in your revision between what you know, and how and why this is important for religious believers. Use spider charts or mind maps for this, if it helps.

Remember that only 25 per cent of the marks are awarded for knowledge – a further 25 per cent depend on you showing you understand what you know. So although knowledge revision is important, it is only the basis for you being able to do well in the understanding questions for AO1 and the evaluation skills questions for AO2.

ExamCafé

Revision
Common errors and mistakes

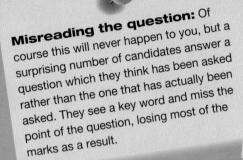

Misreading the question: Of course this will never happen to you, but a surprising number of candidates answer a question which they think has been asked rather than the one that has actually been asked. They see a key word and miss the point of the question, losing most of the marks as a result.

Wasting valuable time: A question worth 1 mark does not need a paragraph response – match the length of responses to the mark allocations and don't waste time.

Disorganised waffle: AO2 responses, in particular, need to be planned otherwise you will waffle and muddle along. In your revision, practise planning responses and then write the plan up, so you get into the habit and feel confident to do this in the exam.

If you feel strongly about an issue in an AO2 response, make sure you take a step back and think calmly about other points of view. A long rant about your view will get few marks.

Poor selection of knowledge: Choose good examples that focus on the religious aspect of the topic. For example – the response to the question, why do Christians hold funerals? – 'because they like to get together when someone dies' is not a good response from a Religious Studies point of view. 'For Christians, a funeral reminds them that they will live forever with God' is much better, and will get more marks.

Using the same information over and over again: Saying in response to different questions, for example, that for some Christians miracles are evidence of the presence of God may be true, but you should not expect the examiner to credit you with many marks unless you link the comment to each of the Topics. Miracles are not the only evidence Christians offer for their belief in God; candidates referring to them over and over again to justify the beliefs or actions of Christians cannot expect to get many marks.

Getting hung up on your view of an issue: This is a real danger when you feel strongly about the issue in the AO2 stimulus. One point of view expressed with lots of personal feeling will get less than 30 per cent of the marks. You must consider various views and have balance, as well as giving your own opinion on the answer.

Revision checklist

This section covers all six Topics in the Philosophy part of the specification, so you need to pick out the ones that you are studying for the examination.

TOPIC 1 BELIEF ABOUT DEITY

This topic has quite a few complicated ideas in it. Make sure that you understand them and can explain them. You need to show the examiner that you really understand them rather than just dropping them into the answer for effect.

TOPIC 2 RELIGIOUS AND SPIRITUAL EXPERIENCE

This topic covers places of worship, the different ways in which people worship and also the way in which people use food and fasting as part of their religion. Focus your responses on the religious aspects of these topics and their possible spiritual effects.

TOPIC 3 THE END OF LIFE

This can be a topic where people have very different opinions. Make sure that you can explain the different ideas in the different sections. For example, for Christianity, you should be able to explain clearly the difference between body and soul, the difference between heaven, hell and purgatory, and also the ideas of judgement and redemption. Make sure that you can explain all of these words clearly. When you are writing about funerals, remember that the examiners are not looking for a detailed account of what happens but an explanation of the **meaning** of what happens.

TOPIC 4 GOOD AND EVIL

Most people probably think that they know what good and evil are. However, you need to be able to explain the difference between ideas of natural evil and moral evil. You should also be able to explain religious ideas of God and the Devil and be able to suggest different ways in which people understand the idea of the Devil. For example, from a Christian perspective, you need to be able to explain the idea of Original Sin. You should know about ways in which people try to cope with suffering and the ways in which they find out how to live.

TOPIC 5 RELIGION, REASON AND REVELATION

In this topic, the most important thing is that you understand what is meant by revelation in relation to sacred texts. You should be able to explain the idea of a revealed text and the issues which can arise when someone believes that a text is revealed.

TOPIC 6 RELIGION AND SCIENCE

This topic covers ground that may be very topical. You may find stories in the news about scientific developments and how these are viewed by different faiths. Reading stories like these may help you with your revision, and give you examples to use. Individuals' views about how to treat animals or the environment can be strongly held. Remember that, while you may have strong views yourself, you will need to show the examiner that you understand other views and how they relate to specific religions.

Exam Café

Revision

The details of the course are known as the specification. It is broken down into the topics listed above. Here is summary of the key areas of each Topic that you need to know about.

Section of the specification	Key topics
Belief about deity	Know the meaning of all the technical terms in the specification, so you could answer factual questions such as, what is meant by the Holy Spirit?
	Know and understand the importance of each topic for Christians and how the beliefs might affect their life style.
	Know and understand how topics connect – for example beliefs about the existence of God, the nature of God and miracles are all linked.
Religious and spiritual experience	Know about how Christians worship in public and at home, and the way in which art and music are used in worship.
	Know and be able to explain the technical terms in the specification such as symbolism, prayer and meditation.
The end of life	You must be able to give clear explanations of religious understandings of body and soul.
	You must be able to explain the technical terms heaven, hell, purgatory, salvation and redemption through the suffering of Christ.
	You need to be able to explain the idea of God as a judge.
	Also you need to have good knowledge of funeral ceremonies, so that you can explain how they reflect belief and support the bereaved.
Good and evil	Here you must be able to show understanding of the concepts of good and evil (including natural and moral evil) and the ideas of God and the Devil.
	You should be able to explain the ideas of the Fall, original sin and redemption.
	Finally, you need to be able to explain how religious people may cope with suffering and the ways in which they decide how to behave morally.
Religion, reason and revelation	Here the most important thing is that you can give a clear explanation of the concept of revelation. You should be able to explain revelation through sacred texts as well as through religious experience.
	Finally, you need to explain the ideas of revelation of God through the world and in the person of Jesus.
Religion and science	You need to be able to explain scientific theories about the origins of the world and of humanity – make sure that you do not confuse them.
	You need to be able to explain religious teachings about the origins of the world and of humanity – again make sure they are not confused.
	You should be able to explain the relationship between humans and animals.
	You need to be able to write about environmental issues and provide religious responses to these.

Spot-check – Christianity

Can you answer these questions?

Question	Response	Mark
What is meant by a miracle?		1
What is the Holy Spirit?		1
State two reasons why Christians believe in God.		2
State three ways in which Christians might worship.		3

Look at the answers in the table below and then work out the question that would generate each response.

Answer	Question	Mark
Where good people go when they die		1
The opposite to the soul		1
Not eating food		1
Natural is the other form		1
A source of moral behaviour		1

Exam preparation

Sample student answer

Now you have done some serious revision it is time to see what sort of response to the questions will get good marks in the exam. Here are some examples of responses with comments from the examiner to show you what is good about them and how they could be improved.

Remember that examiners will use **levels of response** for part **d** which is AO1 and part **e** which is AO2. See pages x and xi of the Introduction for a full explanation of levels. For parts **a**, **b** and **c** responses will be point marked. This means that if there is 1 mark allocated for the question, only one point is expected, if two marks are allocated, then two points are expected and so on. Part **a** is worth 1 mark, **b** 2 marks and **c** 3 marks.

ExamCafé

Exam preparation

What is stewardship? [1 mark]

Looking after something for someone else.

Give two environmental issues [2 marks]

1 Greenhouse gases; 2 Species disappearing; 3 Fuel shortages

How should humans treat animals? [3 marks]

They should treat them with respect. They should not harm them. They should only use them for research if it is absolutely necessary.

Explain how Christians might explain why there is evil in the world. [6 marks]

Response 1 Christians might say that the reason that there is evil in the world is because it is the work of the Devil. They believe that the Devil was Lucifer, a fallen angel, who disobeyed God and was sent to rule in hell. They believe that the Devil causes people to act badly and against God's wishes, and that this is why there is evil in the world.

Response 2 Christians might say that the reason that there is evil in the world is because it is the work of the Devil. They believe that the Devil was Lucifer, a fallen angel, who disobeyed God and was sent to rule in hell. They believe that the Devil causes people to act badly and against God's wishes, and that this is why there is evil in the world.

Other Christians believe that evil is a natural part of human beings, who are tempted to do evil acts. It is the teachings of the Bible and the love of God that persuade them not to do this.

Some Christians might distinguish between moral evil, which is caused by people, and natural evil, which are events such as earthquakes, and which are outside of human control.

And now to part **e** AO2: In this part, each question is worth 12 marks, or 50 per cent of the total. It is really important that you learn how to respond to the statements in a way that will ensure you get the best marks possible and hit the highest level. There are four levels for AO2. Remember that AO2 is about expressing views, including your own, about an issue, and backing those views up with good evidence and argument.

This question and example response are from Topic 3: The end of life.

Examiner says
Students should not equate the length of their answers with how many marks it receives.

People believe in heaven because they are afraid of dying. [12 marks]

Response 1 Lots of people might believe in heaven because they are afraid of dying. Everyone is afraid of dying, and heaven offers a hope that there might be something else after you die. Some people might say that they believe in heaven because it says in the Bible that people will go to heaven.

Response 2 Lots of people might believe in heaven because they are afraid of dying. Everyone is afraid of dying, and heaven offers a hope that there might be something else after you die. However, Christians believe in heaven because it says in the Bible that people who trust in Jesus and follow his teachings will go to heaven.

Response 3 Lots of people might believe in heaven because they are afraid of dying. Everyone is afraid of dying, and heaven offers a hope that there might be something else after you die. However, Christians believe in heaven because it says in the Bible that people who trust in Jesus, follow his teachings and accept him as their saviour will go to heaven. There are many church teachings about heaven as well as about hell and purgatory and it is more likely that people believe in some of these rather than believe in it just because they are afraid. I do not believe in life after death.

Response 4 Lots of people might believe in heaven because they are afraid of dying. Everyone is afraid of dying, and heaven offers a hope that there might be something else after you die. However, Christians believe in heaven because it says in the Bible that people who trust in Jesus, follow his teachings and accept him as their saviour, will go to heaven. There are many church teachings about heaven as well as about hell and purgatory and it is more likely that people believe in some of these rather than believe in it just because they are afraid. My personal opinion is that I do not believe in life after death because there is no evidence for it so I am not worried about dying because I know that will be the end.

Examiner says
This is Level 1. Two relevant viewpoints are stated but there is little support to back them up. This is a simplistic response and shows limited understanding of the question. There is no use of technical terms.

Examiner says
This is Level 2. This is a better answer as it explains to the examiner what the candidate understands the question to be about. However although two viewpoints are stated and slightly developed, the response is still rather limited.

Examiner says
This is a good response and meets the criteria for Level 3. It is reasonably well organised and contains some significant views which are explained well and have evidence to justify them. There is a balance of views. There is good use of technical terms. However, the personal response is not supported and this limits the answer to Level 3.

Examiner says
The personal response presents a new view and comes to a conclusion. The candidate has grasped the significance of the issue. The personal view is backed up by evidence. There is good accurate use of specialist terms and the response is reasonably well organised.

This will take the response to Level 4.

Exam preparation
Understanding exam language

Examiners try to keep questions short, clear and easy to understand. To do this they use words to show what you should do in order to respond to the question. Sometimes a particular word is used to tell you what is required. We call these flag words because they act like flags telling you simply and clearly what is required. Examples of flag words used in Religious Studies exams are:

State:	Usually used in AO1 questions worth 1–3 marks. This means write down a fact about something. For example: 'State one book of the Bible.' – response Genesis.
Give:	This is used instead of 'state' and requires the same sort of response.
Describe:	This is used in AO1 questions and means, tell the examiner factual information about the item, or idea. For example: 'Describe the interior of a church' means, write down factual information about what is to be found inside a church.
Give an account of:	This is asking for the same sort of response as 'describe'.
Explain:	This means show that you understand something. For example: 'Explain why Christians celebrate the Eucharist.' This means the examiner wants you to show you understand the reasons Christians give for celebrating the Eucharist. An 'explain' response will include some knowledge, but the best responses will give reasons and show an awareness of different views on an issue.
Why:	This word is used as shorthand for 'explain'. Put the word explain in front of it and you will know what to do. For example: 'Why do Christians celebrate the Eucharist?' is the same as '**Explain** why Christians celebrate the Eucharist.'
How:	This can be used to ask you for factual information. For example: 'How do Christians celebrate the Eucharist?' It can also be used for questions that are asking for understanding where there is a mixture of fact and understanding required. For example: 'How do Christians react to the death of a loved one?' The response can be factual about what Christians do, or it could be about how Christians will be affected by their beliefs, which is explanation.
Important:	This word is used in AO1 part **d** questions and it indicates that you should say why Christians should or should not do/believe something. For example: 'Explain why the Eucharist is important to Christians' means give reasons to explain why some Christians make the Eucharist the main part of their religious life.
List:	This is used instead of 'give' or 'state' and requires the same sort of response.

Examiner Tips

When answering these questions, ask yourself the question 'why?' as soon as you have written down a reason. There are different levels of explanation and the examiner is looking for depth not for a superficial level.

'What is?' just means describe something.

Check that you know what the word 'environmental' means.

For questions that are awarded 1 mark per point, a one-word answer may be sufficient. You will need to be precise and concise in your response.

Planning and structuring an answer

In some of the grade studios you have seen how to build a response. This is really important for the AO1 responses to part **d** (6 marks) and the AO2 responses to part **e** (12 marks). In each case follow this structure.

- Check you really know what the question is about. In the AO2 questions, work out the key word or words in the statement. For example: 'Worship in church is more important than worship in the home.' The key words are 'more important than'. If the response does not address this, it will not get many marks.
- Make a note of key points to include in AO1 responses and use a spider diagram to note down viewpoints for AO2.
- Begin your response with a brief reference to what the question is asking you to do.
- Write clearly, concisely and in an orderly fashion about the topic or debate. Continually check that you have explained everything and have referred where appropriate to the religion(s) involved.
- Come to a conclusion. In the case of AO1 this may just be – 'so we can see why Christmas is so important'. In the case of AO2, the conclusion should include your personal view and a summing up of the views you have expressed and an evaluation of their significance.
- Write clearly. Manage your time in the exam, so that you can read your responses through to check for sense and accuracy.
- Check spellings and make sure you have used grammar and punctuation correctly. Written communication marks are included in the levels of response.

Glossary

ahimsa: in Buddhism and Hinduism, the concept of non-killing, non-violence, respect for life

akhirah: in Islam, everlasting life after death

anatta: in Buddhism, the idea that there is no eternal, unchanging soul or self

atman: in Hinduism and Sikhism, the belief in the soul which is part of every living being

avatars: the form of a person or animal taken by some Hindu gods when they come to earth

ayah: signs given by God

bhakti: personal loving relationship with God

bhikkhu: fully ordained Buddhist monk

Big Bang theory: the theory that the earth was created about 18 billion years ago by a massive explosion

bodhisattva: in Buddhism, a being destined for Enlightenment

brahman: in Hinduism, the eternal spirit, the source of life in all living things in the universe

covenant: in Christianity and Judaism, a special promise or agreement between God and humans

dhamma: ultimate truth, universal law

dukkha: suffering – the nature of existence according to the first Noble Truth in Buddhism

Eucharist: Thanksgiving service celebrating the sacrificial death and resurrection of Jesus Christ; also known as **Holy Communion** or Mass

evolution theory: the theory that groups of organisms change with passage of time, mainly as a result of natural selection, so that descendants differ from their ancestors; ultimately, the theory that all current life forms developed in stages from a single cell millions of years ago

gurbani: Sikh teachings

gurdwara: Sikh place of worship, literally 'the doorway to the **Guru**'

gurmukh: people who have put the love of God at the centre of their lives

Guru: teacher; a title reserved for the ten human Gurus and the Guru Granth Sahib Ji

haumai: ego

holy: special, pure, set apart

Holy Communion: Thanksgiving service celebrating the sacrificial death and resurrection of Jesus Christ; also known as **Eucharist** or Mass

ibadah: acts of worship in Islam

immanent: within the world and supporting it

intelligent design: the theory that certain features of the universe are best explained by the existence of an intelligent cause

Kaddish: a Jewish prayer publicly recited by mourners

kamma: in Buddhism, intentional actions that affect your circumstances in this and future lives

karah parshad: sweet dough shared after worship in a Sikh **gurdwara**

karma: consequence of actions, in terms of cause and effect

khalifah: a key notion in Islam: successor; inheritor; custodian; vice-regent; trusteeship

manmukh: people characterised by their orientation towards the ego and attachment to the lure of maya

maya: lure of material possessions

moksha: in Hinduism, an escape from the cycle of death and rebirth

Mool Mantar: a sacred text summarising Sikh beliefs

moral evil: evil which is caused by people choosing to act in an evil manner

nam simran: in Sikhism, meditation on the divine name, using passages of scripture

natural evil: evil which is inevitable due to the way the world is

nibbana: in Buddhism, achieving freedom from greed, hatred and delusion resulting in freedom from rebirth

nirguna: without form or gender

numinous: having a sense of being in the presence of a divinity

omnipotent: in religion, when God is all powerful

omniscient: in religion, when God is all knowing

original sin: the Christian idea that, since the Fall, all humans have been born in a state of sin, with a natural ability to choose evil over good

polytheism: belief in many Gods

purgatory: for Christians, a place between heaven and hell, where those who die but are not ready to go to heaven spend time

saguna: manifest through creation

salah: the five daily prayers for a Muslim as required by the Qur'an

samsara: in Buddhism and Hinduism, a continuing cycle of birth, ageing, death and rebirth

satori: in Zen Buddhism, an insight into **nibbana** – a brief glimpse of the world as it really is

Shahadah: in Islam, declaration of faith

Shema: important Jewish prayer that states belief in one G-d

Sheol: a shadowy underworld where souls are prepared for the coming of the Messiah

steward: someone who is responsible for resources; a guardian of things that do not directly belong to them

Talmud: collection of teachings and explanations of rabbis, which helps Jews understand the Torah

tawhid: unity; belief in the oneness of Allah; absolute monotheism as practised in Islam

Tipitaka: 'three baskets'; a three-fold collection of Buddhist texts

Torah: Jewish law, or teaching, made up of the Five Books of Moses

transcendent: beyond human experience

Trimurti: in Hinduism, the three faces of Brahman: Brahma the Creator, Vishnu the Sustainer and Shiva the Destroyer

Trinity: Christian belief that there are three persons within one God – Father, Son and Holy Spirit

Vedas: 'knowledge'; the oldest and most sacred texts of Hinduism

Waheguru: a Sikh name for God

wudu: washing before prayer

Index

Single User Licence Agreement: GCSE OCR B RS Philosophy ActiveBook

Warning:

This is a legally binding agreement between You (the user or purchasing institution) and Pearson Education Limited of Edinburgh Gate, Harlow, Essex, CM20 2JE, United Kingdom ('PEL').

By retaining this Licence, any software media or accompanying written materials or carrying out any of the permitted activities You are agreeing to be bound by the terms and conditions of this Licence. If You do not agree to the terms and conditions of this Licence, do not continue to use the GCSE OCR B RS Philosophy ActiveBook CD-ROM and promptly return the entire publication (this Licence and all software, written materials, packaging and any other component received with it) with Your sales receipt to Your supplier for a full refund.

Intellectual Property Rights:

This GCSE OCR B RS Philosophy ActiveBook CD-ROM consists of copyright software and data. All intellectual property rights, including the copyright is owned by PEL or its licensors and shall remain vested in them at all times. You only own the disk on which the software is supplied. If You do not continue to do only what You are allowed to do as contained in this Licence you will be in breach of the Licence and PEL shall have the right to terminate this Licence by written notice and take action to recover from you any damages suffered by PEL as a result of your breach.

The PEL name, PEL logo and all other trademarks appearing on the software and GCSE OCR B RS Philosophy ActiveBook CD-ROM are trademarks of PEL. You shall not utilise any such trademarks for any purpose whatsoever other than as they appear on the software and GCSE OCR B RS Philosophy ActiveBook CD-ROM.

Yes, You can:

1 use this GCSE OCR B RS Philosophy ActiveBook CD-ROM on Your own personal computer as a single individual user. You may make a copy of the GCSE OCR B RS Philosophy ActiveBook CD-ROM in machine readable form for backup purposes only. The backup copy must include all copyright information contained in the original.

No, You cannot:

1 copy this GCSE OCR B RS Philosophy ActiveBook CD-ROM (other than making one copy for back-up purposes as set out in the Yes, You can table above);

2 alter, disassemble, or modify this GCSE OCR B RS Philosophy ActiveBook CD-ROM, or in any way reverse engineer, decompile or create a derivative product from the contents of the database or any software included in it;

3 include any materials or software data from the GCSE OCR B RS Philosophy ActiveBook CD-ROM in any other product or software materials;

4 rent, hire, lend, sub-licence or sell the GCSE OCR B RS Philosophy ActiveBook CD-ROM;

5 copy any part of the documentation except where specifically indicated otherwise;

6 use the software in any way not specified above without the prior written consent of PEL;

7 subject the software, GCSE OCR B RS Philosophy ActiveBook CD-ROM or any PEL content to any derogatory treatment or use them in such a way that would bring PEL into disrepute or cause PEL to incur liability to any third party.

Grant of Licence:

PEL grants You, provided You only do what is allowed under the 'Yes, You can' table above, and do nothing under the 'No, You cannot' table above, a non-exclusive, non-transferable Licence to use this GCSE OCR B RS Philosophy ActiveBook CD-ROM.

The terms and conditions of this Licence become operative when using this GCSE OCR B RS Philosophy ActiveBook CD-ROM.

Limited Warranty:

PEL warrants that the disk or CD-ROM on which the software is supplied is free from defects in material and workmanship in normal use for ninety (90) days from the date You receive it. This warranty is limited to You and is not transferable.

This limited warranty is void if any damage has resulted from accident, abuse, misapplication, service or modification by someone other than PEL. In no event shall PEL be liable for any damages whatsoever arising out of installation of the software, even if advised of the possibility of such damages. PEL will not be liable for any loss or damage of any nature suffered by any party as a result of reliance upon or reproduction of any errors in the content of the publication.

PEL does not warrant that the functions of the software meet Your requirements or that the media is compatible with any computer system on which it is used or that the operation of the software will be unlimited or error free. You assume responsibility for selecting the software to achieve Your intended results and for the installation of, the use of and the results obtained from the software.

PEL shall not be liable for any loss or damage of any kind (except for personal injury or death) arising from the use of this GCSE OCR B RS Philosophy ActiveBook CD-ROM or from errors, deficiencies or faults therein, whether such loss or damage is caused by negligence or otherwise.

The entire liability of PEL and your only remedy shall be replacement free of charge of the components that do not meet this warranty.

No information or advice (oral, written or otherwise) given by PEL or PEL's agents shall create a warranty or in any way increase the scope of this warranty.

To the extent the law permits, PEL disclaims all other warranties, either express or implied, including by way of example and not limitation, warranties of merchantability and fitness for a particular purpose in respect of this GCSE OCR B RS Philosophy ActiveBook CD-ROM.

Termination:

This Licence shall automatically terminate without notice from PEL if You fail to comply with any of its provisions or the purchasing institution becomes insolvent or subject to receivership, liquidation or similar external administration. PEL may also terminate this Licence by notice in writing. Upon termination for whatever reason You agree to destroy the GCSE OCR B RS Philosophy ActiveBook CD-ROM and any back-up copies and delete any part of the GCSE OCR B RS Philosophy ActiveBook CD-ROM stored on your computer.

Governing Law:

This Licence will be governed by and construed in accordance with English law.